LEISURE ARTS PRESENTS

FOREVER FAVORITES

FIFTY YEARS OF FAMILY CLASSICS

Dear Friends,

It is our tradition to bring you the finest designs and instructions available for your needlework pleasure. We are delighted to have discovered this collection of timeless knit and crochet designs photographed in today's popular colors and styles. Originally produced by Patons, respected for its fine yarns, these stylish garments and afghans are truly "forever favorites." You'll want to stitch them time and again, using your very own favorite yarns and colors. We're very pleased that Patons has worked so graciously with us to reissue this wonderful collection.

— The Leisure Arts Staff

ACKNOWLEDGMENTS
We would like to thank the many talented people who contributed to this book: Jurek Wyszynski for the beautiful modern photography, Mercedes Rothwell for the interior graphic design and Legal Graffiti for the cover graphic design; Carla Scott, Ann Smith and Lisa Allen for pattern checking, and the Patons Design and Marketing team, which includes Sara Arblaster, Svetlana Avrakn, Jackie Brenkel, Gayle Bunn, Kirsten Cowan, Linda Wardlaw, and Joanne Yordanou.

Special thanks to all the knitters who helped: Janet Clark, Shirley Culbert, Olga Dolhan, Margaret Edwards, Queenie Fulcher, Sharron Harling, Beverley Henderson, Freda Karlo, Nellie Madill, Patricia McClymont, Anita McGlade, Louise McLean, Maude Morgan, Mary Phillips, Sandi Prosser, Irene Proudfoot, Joyce Samuel, Kamla Sharma, Marlene Sheehan, Hilda Thompson, Lilas Wonta, Marion Zachary

First Published in Canada in 1999 by Patons, 1 -2700 Dufferin Street Toronto, Ontario, Canada M6B 4J3

Copyright © Patons 1999
Text copyright © Patons 1999
Photographs copyright
© Patons 1999

Canadian Cataloguing in Publication Data
Patons Forever Favorites:
Fifty Years of Family Classics
ISBN 1-894411-04-8
1. Knitting--Patterns. 2. Crocheting-- Patterns I. Bunn, Gayle II. Cowan, Kirsten I. Title: Forever Favorites.
TT825.P36 1999
736.43'0432 C99-901152-9

Editors: Gayle Bunn and Kirsten Cowan
Designers: Legal Graffiti (covers), Mercedes Rothwell (inside pages)
Photography: Jurek Wyszynski

Printed and bound in Canada

AT THE BEGINNING OF A NEW MILLENNIUM we find ourselves looking forward – and looking back, too. Patons Yarns have been part of knitting history since the turn of the century and this retrospective, is a perfect way to celebrate that history. Reviewing our vast archives, we found many styles that evoked memories and shared reminiscences. The Service Cardigan, knit by many loving wives and mothers who sent their men off to fight in the battles of WWII; the baby layettes that many of you will remember from old family photos; the Reindeer Jacket handed down from father to son – all are nostalgic reminders of our own family histories. Many of you have requested that we reissue your favorites – and our only regret is that we don't have room for all of them!

Today's knitters ply their craft for different reasons than knitters of the past, when ready-made sweaters were scarce and expensive. To suit the modern knitter, we've updated many of the designs in this book. Some have been reworked in slightly thicker yarns for faster knitting and many have been given a more contemporary fit. All feature current Patons yarns in modern shades.

This book is really about what knitters and crocheters have always had in common throughout the decades – a love of the creative satisfaction and tactile pleasure of working with yarn, as well as a sense of connection with other crafts people, past and present. With this book, we at Patons take a fond look back – and we also look forward, to being a memorable part of the future of knitting and crochet.

POPPY

The Thirties was a time of elegance in fashion – and this lovely pointelle cardigan is wearable today in Patons Cotton DK. Both designs on this page use a variation of lace once used in stockings for Queen Elizabeth 1 – a testament to the timelessness of knitting. **Intermediate**. *Instructions on pg 26.*

1 9 3 0 ' s

1 9 3 0 ' s

FORSYTHIA

Knitwear in the Thirties was characterized by special dress-maker details, like this feminine lace top with bow at neck, in Patons Cotton DK. **Intermediate**. *Instructions on pg 28.*

BABY SLIPPERS

These tiny slippers with jaunty poms may have been made by your grandmother for her newest arrival. In garter stitch, they're easy to knit in lightweight Patons Kroy 3 Ply yarn or Beehive Baby. **Easy**. *Instructions on pg 30.*

KNIT TRIANGULAR SHAWL

A piece to hand down with love, this shawl mixes two colors of finely-spun Patons Kroy 3 Ply or Beehive Baby with an exquisite lace edging. **Intermediate**. *Instructions on pg 30.*

1930's

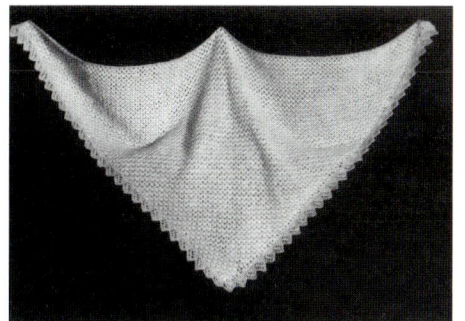

1930's

COBWEB AFGHAN

Crochet medallions, with a unique raised texture pattern that mimics cobwebs, look splendidly rich in deep variegated tones of Patons Decor. **Experienced**. *Instructions on pg 31.*

1930's

WINDBREAKER

The little sportsman shown above had his jacket knit for him almost six decades ago – but today's little boys (or girls) will still love the simple good looks of this windbreaker – and the knitter will love its simplicity, too! In Patons Classic Merino Wool. **Easy**. *Instructions on pg 33.*

1930'S

1930'S

DAHLIA AFGHAN

Another crochet pattern shows the timeless appeal of floral motifs. We worked this afghan in Patons Decor in a tonal mix of blues and greens, to give it a fresh look for today's interiors. **Intermediate**. *Instructions on pg 32.*

ANCASTER

Cables have long been part of the knitter's vocabulary. In the Thirties a vest like this was for gentlemen only, as shown in our archival photo, but today's knitters will love making it for women too in Patons Rustic Wool. **Intermediate**. *Instructions on pg 35.* —

RESTIGOUCHE

The continuing importance of cables is demonstrated here in this handsome turtleneck pullover, worked in Patons Classic Merino Wool. For the modern man (or woman) we've updated this pullover with a more roomy fit. **Intermediate**. *Instructions on pg 36.*

1930'S

CROCHET SHAWL

This airy triangular shawl was originally designed in the Forties. Updated for today in easy-care Patons Kroy 3 Ply or Beehive Baby, this open mesh pattern is simple to crochet. **Intermediate**. *Instructions on pg 38.*

1940's

SLEEPSUIT

A real charmer, this little sleepsuit makes a cherished hand-me-down in soft Patons Beehive Baby yarn or Kroy 3 Ply. **Intermediate**. *Instructions on pg 39.*

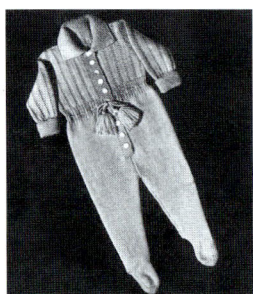

1940's

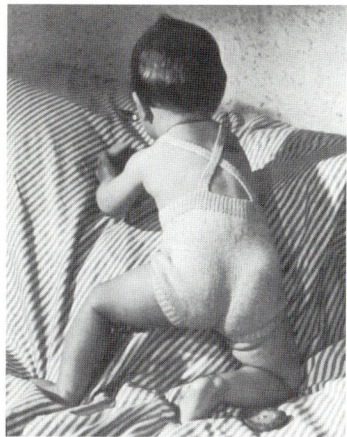

1940's

PLAYING IN THE SUN

Definitely one of our favorites, this adorable sunsuit with crossed back straps is easy to work in basic stocking stitch. Worked in Patons Beehive Baby yarn or Kroy 3 Ply, it's easy to care for too. **Intermediate**. *Instructions on pg 41.*

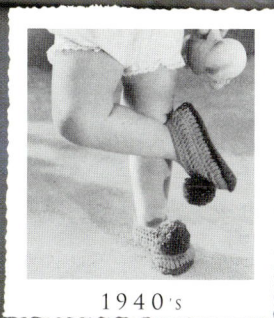

1940's

TWINKLE TOES

With contrast soles and pompom detail, these slippers are fun to wear. They're fun to make too, in an easy double crochet stitch in Patons Look at Me! **Easy**. *Instructions on pg 42.*

PHILLIP'S CABLE PULLOVER

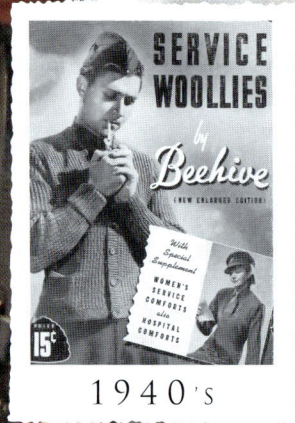

1940's

SERVICE CARDIGAN

1940's

SERVICE WOOLLIES
by Beehive
(NEW ENLARGED EDITION)

With Special Supplement
WOMEN'S SERVICE COMFORTS
also HOSPITAL COMFORTS

15¢

1940's

SNOW TRAIN
AND
ACCESSORIES

A cardigan with staying power – the cropped fit and zipped V-neck look is as fresh today as it was over fifty years ago. In Patons Classic Merino Wool, it will keep its good looks for years to come. The accessories add extra impact: a headband with convertible ear flaps, cozy mitts and scarf – all in lively colors of Patons Kroy 4 Ply. **Experienced.**
Instructions on pg 47 & 48.

CABLE AND POPCORN

Popcorns nestled in lattice cables give this deeply textured cardigan a timeless appeal. It's quick to knit in Patons Shetland Chunky. **Experienced**.
Instructions on pg 50.

1950's

1950's

PERKY POM-POMS HAT

This cute hat evokes the sock-hops and soda fountains of the Fifties – and it's still a fun piece to make and wear today in Patons Shetland Chunky. **Easy**.
Instructions on pg 52.

1950's

MAN'S SWEATER COAT

This rugged, subtly textured cardigan with pockets, is a classic choice from the Fifties. Today it's still a favorite in Patons Shetland Chunky. **Intermediate**. *Instructions on pg 53.*

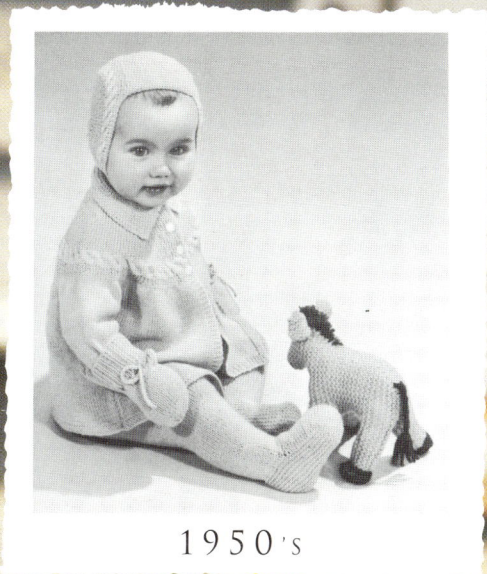

1950's

CARRIAGE SET

A wonderful gift for babies of any generation, this cozy cable-detailed set includes leggings, mitts, a unique hat, even a matching toy. We've given it a modern take in vibrant primary bright shades of Patons Kroy 4 Ply or Beehive Baby. **Experienced**. *Instructions on pg 56.*

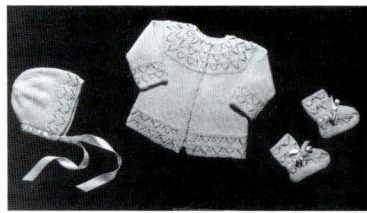

FIRST SIZE KNITTED SET

1 9 5 0 's

No one can resist the timeless charm of a traditional baby layette in soft pastel colors. Worked in Patons Beehive Baby or Kroy 3 Ply, this soft and delicate set includes bonnet, buttoned jacket and booties. **Intermediate**. *Instructions on pg 60.*

1 9 5 0 's

YOUR CLASSIC EYELET

It's the simplest styles that sometimes have the most longevity, as shown here in this Fifties original. The refined pointelle detailing of this lovely top with optional bow, shows to perfection in Patons Kroy 3 Ply. **Intermediate**. *Instructions on pg 62.*

1950's

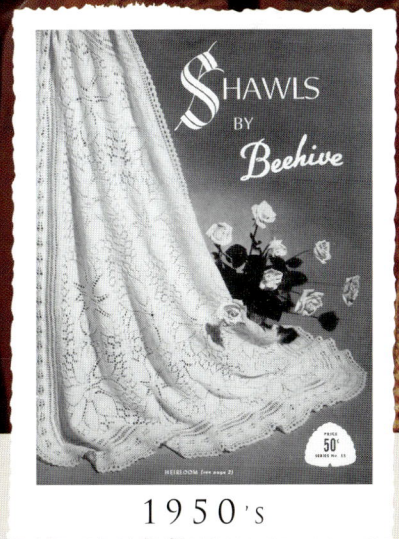

HEIRLOOM SHAWL

Requested by many Patons knitters, this shawl is
truly a masterpiece of the knitter's art. Elegant lace
edging trims floral lace panels, in Patons Kroy 3 Ply.
Experienced. *Instructions on pg 64.*

CUDDLY BEARS

In the Sixties, fashion took a fun and colorful turn – and we still love this cardigan for today's kids, with its sturdy little bears and bright red edgings, in Patons Decor. **Intermediate**. *Instructions on pg 66.*

RAGLANS FOR 2 TO 12
in Chanella or Canadiana
by Beehive

25 CENTS

PATONS-BEEHIVE
2039

1960's

CHILDREN'S RAGLANS

Variations on a classic theme, these three raglans show the long-lasting versatility of simple shapes. Easy to knit in Patons Canadiana, Canadiana Colours, or Canadiana Tweeds. **Easy**. *Instructions on pg 69.*

LEAF AND LACE SET

Leaf-edged pointelle stitch is worked in this pretty design, in Patons Beehive Baby yarn or Kroy 3 Ply. This layette set, has been knit with love for many cherished babies over the last three decades. **Experienced**. *Instructions on pg 72.*

1960's

REINDEER JACKET

A classic of the era, the rugged Reindeer jacket in Patons Shetland Chunky features the kind of outdoorsy good looks that never go out of style. **Intermediate**. *Instructions on pg 74.*

TEEN-AGER'S
Reindeer Sweater *by* **Beehive**

15¢ Chieftain SERIES NO. 5

1960's

HARMONY PULLOVERS

These beautifully cabled pullovers with neckline variations promise generations of great casual style in Patons Classic Merino Wool. **Experienced**. *Instructions on pg 78.*

Canadtana No. 1029

PRICE 25¢

Harmony Pullovers
IN 8 SIZES

by *Beehive*

ALSO INSIDE:
How to knit a smart dress from this design.

1960's

1960's

HOCKEY JACKET

Sport motif sweaters have always been a popular way to show allegiance to a favorite team. We provide charts for the alphabet, so you can stitch the name of your choice on the sleeve! In Patons Shetland Chunky. **Intermediate**. *Instructions on pg 81.*

BALTIC CARDIGAN

This shawl-collared cardigan, borrowed from the Sixties, in turn borrows vintage Fair Isle patterns from the Baltic countries. Our updated version has a zip front and a more relaxed fit. Worked in Patons Classic Merino Wool. **Intermediate**. *Instructions on pg 84.*

Canadiana No. 1026

PRICE 25¢

Baltic Cardigan
SIZES 38, 40, 42, 44

by *Beehive*

ALSO INSIDE:
This raglan Cardigan without the design.

1960's

ARAN PONCHO

Ponchos, so popular in the Seventies, are enjoying a revival. These intricate Aran cables are quick to knit in two strands of Patons Decor. We made our modern version longer and gave it a neater fringe. **Experienced**. *Instructions on pg 87.*

1 9 7 0's

1 9 7 0's

ARAN AFGHAN

While this design dates from the Seventies, Aran patterns have been an important part of knitting for hundreds of years. We made this instant heirloom in double-stranded Patons Decor. **Experienced**. *Instructions on pg 88.*

1970's

HOUNDSTOOTH JACKET

This jacket envelops you in the warmth of Patons Shetland Chunky and Shetland Ragg Chunky. We've given it a modern perspective with neutral tones and a comfy oversized fit, with optional belt. **Intermediate**. *Instructions on pg 89.*

PARTY
PRETTY

Every little girl –
back in the
Seventies and
still today – loves
a pretty dress.
Crochet this one
in breezy Patons
Cotton DK.
Experienced.
Instructions on pg 92.

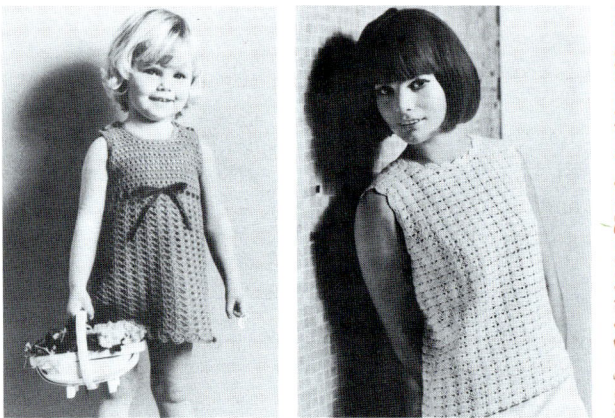

CROCHETED
BEAUTY

A lovely crochet shell with scallop
edges, demonstrates the staying
power of beautiful stitch patterns
worked in simple shapes. We
made ours in season-spanning
Patons Cotton DK. **Experienced**.
Instructions on pg 93.

1 9 7 0's

Patons
FOREVER FAVORITES
TABLE OF CONTENTS

Every effort has been taken to ensure the accuracy of these instructions. Patons, however, cannot accept responsibility for typographical errors or misinterpretation of instructions.

POPPY

1930s

as shown on page 4

as shown on page 4

SIZES

Bust measurement

Small	30–32 ins	[76–81 cm]
Medium	34–36 "	[86–91 "]
Large	38–40 "	[97–102 "]

Finished bust

Small	40	ins [101.5 cm]
Medium	43	" [109 "]
Large	46	" [117 "]

MATERIALS

Patons Cotton DK (50 g)

Size	S	M	L
6309	7	8	10 balls

Sizes 3¼ mm (U.S. 4) and 4 mm (U.S. 6) knitting needles **or size needed to obtain tension**. 14 buttons.

TENSION

22 sts and 30 rows = 4 ins [10 cm] with larger needles in stocking st.

INSTRUCTIONS

The instructions are written for smallest size. If changes are necessary for larger sizes the instructions will be written thus ( ).

Panel Pat (worked over 35 sts).
1st row: (Right side). *K2togtbl. yfwd. K4. yfwd. K3tog. yfwd. K2. K2togtbl. yfwd. K2.* (P1. K1) twice. P1. Rep from * to * once more.
2nd row: *P2tog. yfwd. P9. P2tog. yfwd. P2.* (K1. P1) twice. K1. Rep from * to * once more.
3rd row: *K2togtbl. yfwd. K2. K2tog. yfwd. K3. yfwd. (K2togtbl) twice. yfwd. K2.* (P1. K1) twice. P1. Rep from * to * once more.
4th row: As 2nd row.
5th row: As 1st row.
6th row: As 2nd row.
7th row: *K2togtbl. yfwd. K9. K2togtbl. yfwd. K2.* (P1. K1) twice. P1. Rep from * to * once more.
8th row: As 2nd row.
9th row: As 7th row.
10th row: As 2nd row.
These 1st to 10th rows form Panel Pat.

BACK

With smaller needles, cast on 101 (**109**-117) sts.
1st row: (Right side). K1. *P1. K1. Rep from * to end of row.
2nd row: P1. *K1. P1. Rep from * to end of row.
Rep these 2 rows in (K1. P1) ribbing

for 3½ ins [9 cm] ending on 2nd row and inc 10 sts across last row. 111 (**119**-127) sts.

Change to larger needles and proceed as follows:
1st row: (Right side). K14 (**16**-19). Work 1st row of Panel Pat A. K13 (**17**-19). Work 1st row of Panel Pat. K14 (**16**-19).
2nd row: P14 (**16**-19). Work 2nd row of Panel Pat. P13 (**17**-19). Work 2nd row of Panel Pat. P14 (**16**-19).
Panel Pat is now in position.

Cont in pat until work from beg measures 12 ins [30.5 cm] ending with right side facing for next row.

Armhole shaping: Keeping cont of pat cast off 7 (**8**-9) sts beg next 2 rows. Dec 1 st each end of needle on next and every row to 87 (**89**-91) sts.

Cont even in pat until work from beg measures 19 (**19½**-20) ins [48 (**49.5**-51) cm] ending with right side facing for next row.

Shoulder shaping: Cast off 9 sts beg next 6 rows. Cast off rem 33 (**35**-37) sts.

LEFT FRONT

With smaller needles, cast on 57 (61**-65) sts.
1st row: (Right side). K1. *P1. K1. Rep from * to end of row.
2nd row: P1. *K1. P1. Rep from * to end of row.
Rep these 2 rows in (K1. P1) ribbing for 3½ ins [9 cm] ending on 2nd row and inc 4 sts across last row. 61 (**65**-69) sts.**

Change to larger needles and proceed as follows:
1st row: (Right side). K14 (**16**-19). Work 1st row of Panel Pat. K6 (**8**-9). (P1. K1) 3 times.
2nd row: (P1. K1) 3 times. P6 (**8**-9). Work 2nd row of Panel Pat. P14 (**16**-19). Panel Pat is now in position.

Cont in pat until work from beg measures 12 ins [30.5 cm] ending with right side facing for next row.

Armhole shaping: Next row: Cast off 7 (**8**-9) sts (armhole edge). Pat to end of row.
Dec 1 st at armhole edge on next and every row to 49 (**50**-52) sts.

Work even in pat until work from beg measures 16½ (**16¾**-17) ins [42 (**42.5**-43) cm] ending with **wrong** side facing for next row.

Neck shaping: Next row: Cast off 11 sts. Pat to end of row.
Dec 1 st at neck edge on next 3 rows, then on every alt row to 27 sts.

Cont even in pat until work from beg measures same length as Back to beg of shoulder shaping, ending with right side facing for next row.

Shoulder shaping: Cast off 9 sts beg next and following alt row. Work 1 row even. Cast off rem 9 sts.

On Left Front mark positions for buttons. Buttons are placed in groups of 2 spaced 4 rows apart. Place marker for upper button of top group 1 inch [2.5 cm] down from upper edge and 1½ inch [4 cm] up from lower edge for upper button of bottom group. Place markers for upper buttons of rem 5 groups of 2 buttons evenly spaced.

Note: Buttonholes are worked to correspond to buttonholes on Right Front as follows:
Next row: (Right side). K1. P1. K1. yfwd. K2tog. Pat to end of row.

RIGHT FRONT

Work from ** to ** as given for Left front.

Change to larger needles and proceed as follows:
1st row: (Right side). (K1. P1) 3 times. K6 (**8**-9). Work 1st row of Panel Pat. K14 (**16**-19).
2nd row: P14 (**16**-19). Work 2nd row of Panel Pat A. P6 (**8**-9). (K1. P1) 3 times.
Panel Pat is now in position.

Cont in pat until work from beg measures 12 ins [30.5 cm], ending with **wrong** side facing for next row.

Armhole shaping: Next row: Cast off 7 (**8**-9) sts (armhole edge). Pat to end of row.
Dec 1 st at armhole edge on next and every row to 49 (**50**-52) sts.

Work even in pat until work from beg measures 16½ (**16¾**-17) ins [42 (**42.5**-43) cm] ending with right side facing for next row.

Neck shaping: Next row: Cast off 11 sts. Pat to end of row.
Dec 1 st at neck edge on next 2 rows, then on every alt row to 27 sts.

Cont even in pat until work from beg measures same length as Back to beg of shoulder shaping ending with **wrong** side facing for next row.

Shoulder shaping: Cast off 9 sts beg next and following alt row. Work 1 row even. Cast off rem 9 sts.

SLEEVES

With smaller needles, cast on 55 (**61**-67) sts. Work 1 inch [2.5 cm] in (K1. P1) ribbing as given for Back ending on a 2nd row and inc 2 sts evenly across last row. 57 (**63**-69) sts.

Change to larger needles and proceed as follows:
1st row: (Right side). Inc 1 st in first st. K10 (**13**-16). Work 1st row of Panel Pat. Knit to last 2 sts. Inc 1 st in next st. K1. 59 (**65**-71) sts.
2nd row: P12 (**15**-18). Work 2nd row of Panel Pat. Purl to end of row.
3rd row: K12 (**15**-18). Work 3rd row of Panel Pat. Knit to end of row.
4th row: P12 (**15**-18). Work 4th row of Panel Pat. Purl to end of row.
Panel Pat is now in position.

Keeping cont in pat, inc 1 st each end of needle on next and following 4th rows to 67 (**73**-79) sts, taking inc sts into stocking st.
Cont even in pat until sleeve from beg measures 5¼ ins [13 cm] ending with right side facing for next row.

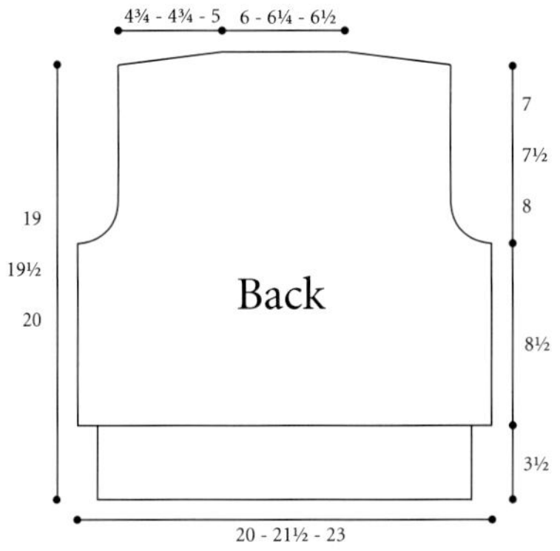
4¾ - 4¾ - 5
6 - 6¼ - 6½
19
19½
20
Back
7
7½
8
8½
3½
20 - 21½ - 23

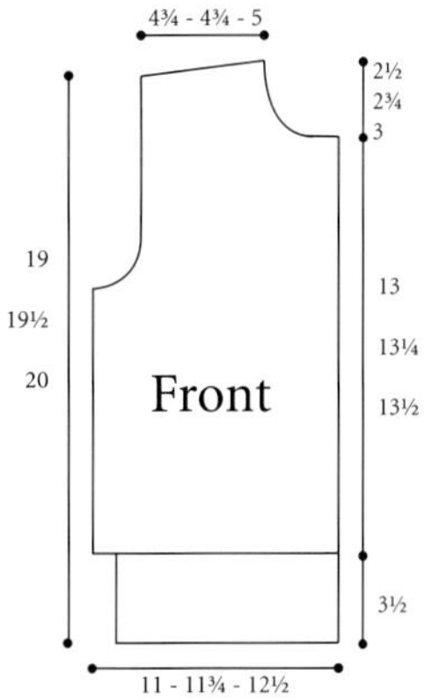
4¾ - 4¾ - 5
2½
2¾
3
19
19½
20
Front
13
13¼
13½
3½
11 - 11¾ - 12½

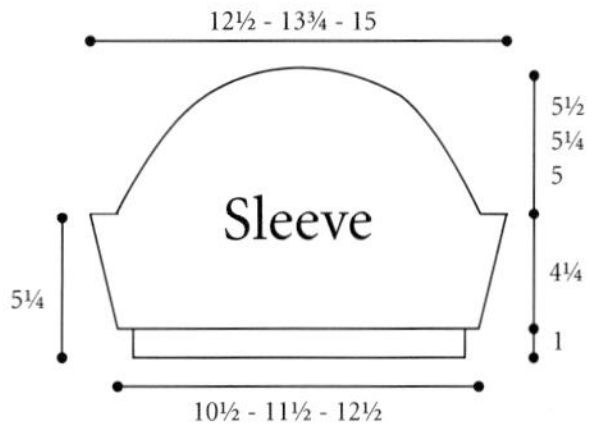
12½ - 13¾ - 15
5½
5¼
5
Sleeve
4¼
1
5¼
10½ - 11½ - 12½

Top shaping: Keeping cont of pat, cast off 2 sts beg next 2 rows.
Dec 1 st each end of needle on next and every alt row to 43 (**51**-53) sts, ending with right side facing for next row. Cast off 2 sts beg every row to 19 sts. Cast off rem 19 sts.

COLLAR

With larger needles, cast on 24 sts.
1st row: (Right side). K2. *P1. K1. Rep from * to end of row.
Rep last row 4 times more.

Proceed as follows:
1st row: K1. (K1. P1) twice. K2togtbl. yfwd. K4. yfwd. K3tog. yfwd. K2. K2togtbl. yfwd. K6.
2nd and alt rows: K1. P3. P2tog. yfwd. P9. P2tog. yfwd. P2. (K1. P1) twice. K1.
3rd row: K1. (K1. P1) twice. K2togtbl. yfwd. K2. K2togtbl. yfwd. K3. yfwd. (K2togtbl) twice. yfwd. K6.
5th row: As 1st row.
7th and 9th rows: K1. (K1. P1) twice. K2togtbl. yfwd. K9. K2togtbl. yfwd. K6.
10th row: As 2nd row.
Rep 1st to 10th rows 11 times more, then 1st to 6th rows once more.
Next row: (Right side). K2. *P1. K1. Rep from * to end of row.
Rep last row 4 times more. Cast off in ribbing.

FINISHING

Pin garment pieces to measurements. Cover with a damp cloth and leave to dry.

Sew shoulder seams. Sew in sleeves. Sew side and armband seams. Sew collar around neck. Sew buttons to correspond to buttonholes. ♠

FORSYTHIA

1930s

as shown on page 4

SIZES

Bust measurement

Small	30–32 ins	[76–81 cm]
Medium	34–36 "	[86–91 "]
Large	38–40 "	[97–102 "]

Finished bust

Small	41	ins	[104	cm]
Medium	44	"	[112	"]
Large	47	"	[119.5	"]

MATERIALS

Patons Cotton DK (50 g)

Size		S	M	L	
6307		8	9	11	balls

Sizes 3¼ mm (U.S. 4) and 4 mm (U.S. 6) knitting needles **or size needed to obtain tension**.

TENSION

22 sts and 30 rows = 4 ins [10 cm] with larger needles in stocking st.

INSTRUCTIONS

The instructions are written for smallest size. If changes are necessary for larger sizes the instructions will be written thus ( ).

BACK

With smaller needles, cast on 105 (111**-117) sts.
1st row: (Right side). K1. *P1. K1. Rep from * to end of row.
2nd row: P1. *K1. P1. Rep from * to end of row.
Rep these 2 rows in (K1. P1) ribbing for 3½ ins [9 cm] ending on 1st row, inc 9 (**10**-11) sts across last row. 114 (**121**-128) sts.

Change to larger needles and proceed as follows:
1st row: (Wrong side). Knit.
2nd row: Purl.
3rd row: K1. *yfwd. K1. Rep from * to end of row.
4th row: P1. *Drop extra st from needle. P1. Rep from * to end of row.
5th row: Knit.
6th row: P1. *yfwd. P1. Rep from * to last st. yfwd. P1.
7th row: K1. Drop extra st st from needle. K1. Rep from * to end of row.
8th row: Purl.
9th and 10th rows: Knit.
11th, 13th, 15th and 17th rows: Purl.
12th row: K2. *K2tog. yfwd. K1. yfwd. Sl1. K1. psso. K2. Rep from * to end of row.
14th row: K1. *K2tog. yfwd. K3. yfwd. Sl1. K1. psso. Rep from * to last st. K1.

16th row: K2. *K1. yfwd. K3tog. yfwd. K3. Rep from * to end of row.
18th row: Knit.
These 1st to 18th rows form pat.

Cont in pat until work from beg measures 12 ins [30.5 cm] ending with right side facing for next row.

Armhole shaping: Keeping cont of pat cast off 7 (**8**-9) sts beg next 2 rows. Dec 1 st each end of needle on next and every row to 86 (**93**-100) sts.**

Cont even in pat until work from beg measures 19 (**19½**-20) ins [48 (**49.5**-51) cm] ending with right side facing for next row.

Shoulder shaping: Cast off 9 (**10**-10) sts beg next 4 rows, then 8 (**9**-11) sts beg following 2 rows. Cast off rem 34 (**35**-38) sts.

FRONT

Work from ** to ** as given for Back.

Cont even in pat until work from beg measures 16 (**16¼**-16½) ins [40.5 (**41.5**-42) cm] ending with right side facing for next row.

Neck shaping: Next row: Pat across 33 (**36**-38) sts (neck edge). **Turn.** Leave rem sts on a spare needle. Keeping cont of pat, dec 1 st at neck edge on next 4 rows, then on every alt row to 26 (**29**-31) sts.

Cont even in pat until work from beg measures same length as Back to beg of shoulder shaping ending with right side facing for next row.

Shoulder shaping: Cast off 9 (**10**-10) sts beg next and following alt row. Work 1 row even. Cast off rem 8 (**9**-11) sts.

With right side of work facing cast off next 20 (**21**-24) sts from spare needle. Join yarn to rem sts and pat to end of row.
Keeping cont of pat, dec 1 st at neck edge on next 4 rows, then on every alt row to 26 (**29**-31) sts.

Cont even in pat until work from beg measures same length as Back to beg of shoulder shaping ending with **wrong** side facing for next row.

Shoulder shaping: Cast off 9 (**10**-10) sts beg next and following alt row. Work 1 row even. Cast off rem 8 (**9**-11) sts.

SLEEVES

With smaller needles, cast on 55 (**61**-61) sts. Work 1 inch [2.5 cm] in (K1. P1) ribbing as given for Back ending on a 2nd row and inc 3 (**4**-4) sts evenly across last row. 58 (**65**-65) sts.

Change to larger needles and work in pat as given for Back, inc 1 st each end of needle on next and following 4th rows to 68 (**73**-79) sts, taking inc sts into pat.
Cont even in pat until sleeve from beg measures 5¼ ins [13 cm] ending with right side facing for next row.

Top shaping: Keeping cont of pat, cast off 2 sts beg next 2 rows.
Dec 1 st each end of needle on next and every alt row to 43 (**51**-53) sts ending with right side facing for next row. Cast off 2 sts beg every row to 19 sts. Cast off rem 19 sts.

TIE

With smaller needles, cast on 3 sts.
1st row: (Right side). Inc 1 st in first st. Inc 1 st in next st. K1.
2nd row: K1. (P1. K1) twice.
3rd row: K1. Inc 1 st in next st. K1. Inc 1 st in next st purlwise. K1.
4th row: K1. (P1. K1) twice. K2.
5th row: K1. Inc 1 st in next st. P1. K1. P1. Inc 1 st in next st. K1.
Cont in seed st inc 1 st each end of needle every alt row as before to 19 sts.
Cont even in seed st until work from beg measures 29 ins [73.5 cm].
Dec 1 st each end of needle every alt row to 3 sts.
Next row: K3tog. Fasten off.

FINISHING

Pin garment pieces to measurements. Cover with a damp cloth and leave to dry.

Sew shoulder seams. Sew in sleeves. Sew side and sleeve seams. Sew collar around neck. ♠

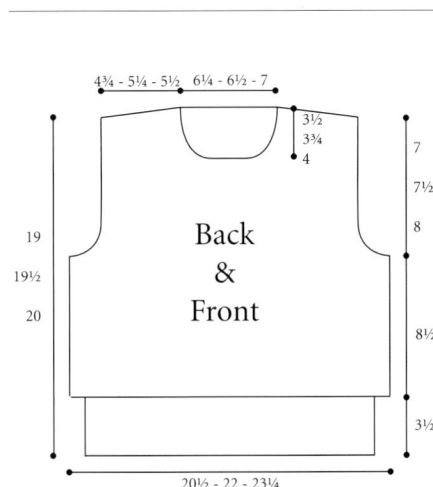

4¾ - 5¼ - 5½   6¼ - 6½ - 7
3½
3¾
4
7
7½
8
19
19½
20
8½
3½
Back & Front
20½ - 22 - 23¼

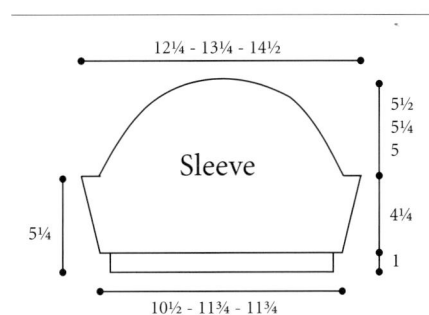

12¼ - 13¼ - 14½
5½
5¼
5
Sleeve
5¼
4¼
1
10½ - 11¾ - 11¾

BABY SLIPPERS

1930s

as shown on page 5

as shown on page 5

LEFT SLIPPER

Work from ** to ** as given for Right Slipper.
Next row: Knit to last 5 sts. Cast off 3 sts. K2.
Next row: K2. Cast on 3 sts. Knit to end of row.
Knit 3 rows. Cast off.

Pom-poms (make 2)
Wind yarn around 2 fingers approx 60 times. Remove from fingers and tie tightly in centre. Cut through each side of loops. Trim to a smooth round shape.

Sew buttons to correspond to buttonholes. Sew pom-pon to top of Slipper. ♠

MATERIALS

Patons Beehive Baby (50 g)

Size	6 mos	
3351	1	ball

Size 2 mm (U.S. 0) knitting needles **or size needed to obtain tension.** 2 buttons.

TENSION

36 sts and 44 rows = 4 ins [10 cm] in stocking st.

INSTRUCTIONS

RIGHT SLIPPER

**Sole: Cast on 24 sts.
Proceed in garter st (knit every row) inc 1 st each end of needle every alt row until there are 40 sts.
Dec 1 st each end of needle every alt row until there are 24 sts.
Next row: Cast on 8 sts for heel. Knit to end of row. 32 sts.

Toe: Cont in garter st on these 32 sts keeping the heel edge even and inc 1 st at other end every alt row until there are 40 sts.
Next row: Cast off 22 sts at heel. Knit to end of row. 18 sts.

On rem 18 sts proceed in pat as follows:
1st row: *K3. P3. Rep from * to end of row.
2nd and 3rd rows: As 1st row.
4th to 6th rows: *P3. K3. Rep from * to end of row.
Rep these 6 rows twice more.
Next row: Cast on 22 sts at heel. Knit to end of row. 40 sts.

Cont in garter st on these 40 sts keeping the heel edge even and dec 1 st at other end every alt row until there are 32 sts. Cast off.

Sew tog the 2 straight edges of the heel and sew tog the edges round the sole, easing in pat at toe.

Strap: Pick up and knit 20 sts across top of heel (10 sts at each side of seam).
Cast on 16 sts beg next 2 rows. 52 sts.
Knit 2 rows.**
Next row: K2. Cast off 3 sts. Knit to end of row.
Next row: Knit to last 5 sts. Cast on 3 sts. K2.
Knit 3 rows.
Cast off.

KNIT TRIANGULAR SHAWL

1930s

as shown on page 5

as shown on page 5

MEASUREMENT

Finished Size: Approx 29 ins across [73.5 cm]

MATERIALS

Patons Kroy 3 ply **or** Beehive Baby (50 g)

Main color (MC) White	2	balls
Contrast A Blue	2	balls

Size 3¾ mm (U.S. 5) knitting needles **or size needed to obtain tension.**

TENSION

28 sts and 36 rows = 4 ins [10 cm] in stocking st.

STITCH GLOSSARY

K3S = K3. Slip first st over 2nd and 3rd sts.

INSTRUCTIONS

With MC, cast on 3 sts.
1st row: Knit.
2nd row: Purl.
3rd row: yrn. (K1. yfwd) twice. K1. 6 sts.
4th row: Purl.
5th row: yrn. K1. yfwd. K3S. (yfwd. K1) twice. 9 sts.
6th row: Purl.
7th row: yrn. K1. *yfwd. K3S. Rep from * to last 2 sts. (yfwd. K1) twice.
8th row: Purl.
9th row: With A, as 7th row.
10th row: Purl.
7th to 10th rows form pat.

Cont in this manner, changing color every 3rd row, working 3 more sts into pat on next and following alt rows to 303 sts. Cast off.

Border: With MC, cast on 5 sts.
1st row: Knit.
2nd row: K2. (yfwd. K1) twice. K1. 7 sts.
3rd and alt rows: Knit.
4th row: K3. yfwd. K2tog. yfwd. K2. 8 sts.
6th row: K4. yfwd. K2tog. yfwd. K2. 9 sts.
8th row: K5. yfwd. K2tog. yfwd. K2. 10 sts.
10th row: K10.
11th row: Cast off 5 sts loosely. K5.
Rep 2nd to 11th rows of pat.

Cont in pat until Border fits along both diagonal edges of Shawl ending with 11th row of pat. Cast off.

Sew Border to Shawl. Roll Shawl in a damp towel for several hours, then spread out flat, pin into shape and leave to dry. ♠

COBWEB AFGHAN

1930s

as shown on page 6

MEASUREMENT

Finished Size: Approx 49 x 61 ins [124.5 x 155 cm]

MATERIALS

Patons Decor (100 g)

Main color (MC) (1803)	5	balls
Contrast A (1729)	4	balls
Contrast B (1728)	4	balls

Size 5.00 mm (U.S. H or 8) crochet hook **or size needed to obtain tension.**

TENSION

Each motif = 6 ins [15 cm] wide.

INSTRUCTIONS

Motif One (make 40).
With A, ch 4. Join with ss into ring.
1st round: Ch 3 (counts as first dc). 23 dc in ring. Join with ss to top of ch 3. 24 dc.
2nd round: (Ch 3. 1 dc. Ch 2. 2 dc) all in same sp as last ss (counts as first shell). *Miss next dc. (Yoh and draw up a loop around post. Yoh and draw through 2 loops on hook) 3 times around next dc. Yoh and draw through all 4 loops on hook – cluster made. Miss next dc.** (2 dc. Ch 2. 2 dc) in next dc - shell made. Rep from * 4 times more, then from * to ** once. Join with ss to top of ch 3.
3rd round: Ss in next dc and in next ch 2 sp. (Ch 3. 2 dc. Ch 2. 3 dc) all in same sp (counts as first shell). *Cluster around cluster of last round.** (3 dc. Ch 2. 3 dc) all in ch 2 sp of next shell. Rep from * 4 times more, then from * to ** once. Join with ss to top of ch 3. Fasten off.
4th round: Join MC with ss to ch 2 sp of any shell. (Ch 3. 3 dc. Ch 2. 4 dc) in same sp (counts as first shell). *Cluster around cluster of last round.** (4 dc. Ch 2. 4 dc) all in ch 2 sp of next shell. Rep from * 4 times more, then from * to ** once. Join with ss to top of ch 3. Fasten off.

Motif Two (make 40)
Work as given for Motif One substituting B for A.

Join Afghan tog 8 motifs wide by 10 motifs long, alternating Motif One and Motif Two as illustrated.

Joining sides of Motifs: Place motifs right side sides tog and join with ss through corresponding corner ch 2 sps. Ss through corresponding front loops only of each of next 4 dc. Ss through corresponding clusters. Ss through corresponding front loops only of each of next 4 dc. Ss through next corresponding corner ch 2 sps. Fasten off.

Edging: 1st round: With right side of Afghan facing and A, work 1 row sc evenly around outer edge of Afghan, working 3 sc in ch 2 sps of each shell on outer points and 1 sc in joining sp between 2 Motifs. Join with ss to first sc. Fasten off.
2nd round: Join MC with ss in back loop only of centre sc of any 3 sc group on outer edge. Ch 1. 3 sc in same sp. Working into back loop **only** of each st, proceed as follows: *1 sc in each sc to next 3 sc group. 1 sc in next sc. 3 sc in next sc. 1 sc in next sc. Rep from * around. Join with ss to first sc. Fasten off.
3rd round: With B, as 2nd round. ♠

DAHLIA AFGHAN

1930s

as shown on page 6

MEASUREMENT

Finished Size: Approx 49 x 57 ins
[124.5 x 144.5 cm]

MATERIALS

Patons Decor (100 g)

Main color (MC) (1642)	5	**balls**
Contrast A (1608)	3	**balls**
Contrast B (1612)	5	**balls**

Size 5.00 mm (U.S. H or 8) crochet hook
or size needed to obtain tension.

TENSION

Large motif = 4½ ins [11.5 cm] wide.

INSTRUCTIONS

Large Motif (make 120).
With A, ch 5. Join with ss into ring.
1st round: Ch 1. 12 sc in ring. Join with ss to first sc. Fasten off.
2nd round: Join B with ss in any sc. Ch 4. *(Yoh and draw up a loop 1 inch [2.5 cm] high. Yoh and draw through 2 loops on hook) twice in same sc as last ss. Yoh and draw through all loops on hook (counts as first petal). *Ch 3. (Yoh and draw up a loop 1 in [2.5 cm] high.*

*Yoh and draw through 2 loops on hook) 3 times in next sc. Yoh and draw through all loops on hook – counts as petal. Rep from * around ending with ch 3. Join with ss to top of ch 4. Fasten off.*
3rd round: Join MC with ss in any ch 3 sp. Ch 1. (1 sc. 1 dc. 1 tr. 1 dc. 1 sc) in same sp. *(1 sc. 1 dc. 1 tr. 1 dc. 1 sc) in next ch 3 sp. Rep from * around. Join with ss to first sc. Fasten off.

Join Large Motifs into 30 groups of 4 by sewing 3 points tog of each side to corresponding points of adjoining motifs, thus leaving center of group open.

Small Motif
With A, ch 4. Join with ss into ring.
1st round: Ch 1. 8 sc in ring. Join with ss to first sc.
2nd round: *Ch 3. Join with ss to corresponding point of Large Motif group inside of square. Ch 3. 1 sc in next sc of Small Motif. Rep from * 7 times more. Fasten off.

Join Large Motif groups tog into Afghan having 10 motifs wide by 12 motifs long and working Small Motif between adjoining groups.

Edging: 1st round: With right side of Afghan facing, join A with ss to top of last petal before join of any Large Motif on outer edge. *Ch 3. [(1 tr. Ch 2) twice. 1 tr] all in next joining sp between 2 Large Motifs. Ch 3. Ss in top of petal of next Large Motif. (Ch 2. Ss in top of next petal) twice. Rep from * to next corner petal. Ch 3. [(1 tr. Ch 3) twice. 1 tr] all in between corner petals. Ch 3. Ss in top of next petal. (Ch 2. Ss in top of next petal) twice. Rep from * around. Join with ss to first ss.
2nd round: Ss in next ch 3 sp. Ch 1. 1 sc in same sp. *Ch 1. [(1 dc. Ch 1) 4 times. 1 dc] all in center tr of next 3 tr group. Ch 1. 1 sc in next ch 3 sp. Ch 1. [(1 sc. Ch 1) twice] in each of next 2 ch 2 sps. 1 sc in next ch 3 sp. Rep from * to next corner tr group. Ch 1. [(1 dc. Ch 2) 4 times. 1 dc] all in center tr of corner tr group. Ch 1. 1 sc in next ch 3 sp. Ch 1. [(1 sc. Ch 1) twice] in each of next 2 ch 2 sps.** 1 sc in next ch 3 sp. Rep from * around ending at **. Join with ss to first sc. Fasten off.
3rd round: Join B with ss in next ch 1 sp before 5 dc group. Ch 5. 1 tr in same sp. Ch 1. [(1 tr. Ch 1) twice] in each of next 5 ch 1 sps. *Miss next sc, ch 1 sp and next sc. 1 sc in next ch 1 sp. (Ch 1. Miss next sc. 1 sc in next ch 1 sp) twice. Ch 1.** [(1 tr. Ch 1) twice] in each of next 6 ch 1 sps. Rep from * to next corner Motif. Miss next sc, ch 1 sp and next sc. 1 sc in next ch 1 sp. (Ch 1. Miss next sc. 1 sc in next ch 1 sp) twice. Ch 1. [(1 tr. Ch 1) twice] in each of next 6 ch 2 sps. Rep from * around, ending at **. Join with ss to 4th ch of ch 5. Fasten off.
4th round: Join MC with ss in center sc of any 3 sc group between tr groups on side edge. Ch 1. 1 sc in same sp. *Ch 1. 1 tr in ch 1 sp between next 2 tr. Ch 3. Ss in top of tr – picot made. [(Ch 1. 1 tr. Picot) in next ch 1 sp] 10 times. Ch 1.** 1 sc in center sc of next 3 sc group. Rep from * around, ending at **. Join with ss to first sc. Fasten off. ◆

WINDBREAKER

1930s

as shown on pages 6-7

as shown on pages 6-7

SIZES

Chest measurement

2 – 4	22 – 24 ins	[56 – 61 cm]
6 – 8	26 – 28 "	[66 – 71 "]

Finished chest

2 – 4	29 ins	[73.5 cm]
6 – 8	32 "	[81 "]

MATERIALS

Patons Classic Merino Wool (100 g)

Size	2-4	6-8	
213	4	4	balls

Sizes 3¾ mm (U.S. 5) and 4½ mm (U.S. 7) knitting needles **or size needed to obtain tension**. 4 st holders. One separating zipper. 2 buttons.

TENSION

20 sts and 26 rows = 4 ins [10 cm] with larger needles in stocking st.

INSTRUCTIONS

The instructions are written for smallest size. If changes are necessary for larger sizes the instructions will be written thus ( ).

BACK

With smaller needles, cast on 65 (**71**) sts.
1st row: (Right side). K1. *P1. K1. Rep from * to end of row.
2nd row: P1. *K1. P1. Rep from * to end of row. Rep these 2 rows (K1. P1) ribbing for 3 ins [7.5 cm] ending on a 2nd row and inc 7 sts evenly across last row. 72 (**78**) sts.

Change to larger needles and proceed in stocking st until work from beg measures 10 (**11½**) ins [25 (**28.5**) cm] ending with right side facing for next row.

Armhole shaping: Cast off 4 sts beg next 2 rows.
Dec 1 st at each end of needle every alt row 4 times. 56 (**62**) sts.

Cont even until armhole measures 5¾ (**7**) ins [14.5 (**18**) cm] ending with right side facing for next row.

Shoulder shaping: Cast off 6 (**7**) sts beg next 6 rows. Cast off rem 20 sts.

Pocket Lining (make 2)
With larger needles, cast on 21 sts. Work 3 ins [7.5 cm] in stocking st, ending with right side facing for next row. Leave these 21 sts on a st holder.

Pocket Flap (make 2)
With larger needles, cast on 3 sts.
1st row: Inc 1 st in each of first 2 sts. K1.
2nd row: Inc 1 st in first st. K2. Inc 1 st in next st. K1.

3rd row: Inc 1 st in first st. K4. Inc 1 st in next st. K1.
Cont in this manner, inc 1 st at each end of needle, as before, until there are 15 sts.
7th row: Inc 1 st in first st. K6. yfwd. K2tog. K4. Inc 1 st in next st. K1.
8th and 9th rows: Inc 1 st in first st. Knit to last 2 sts. Inc 1st in next st. K1. 21 sts.
Work 5 rows garter st (knit every row). Leave these 21 sts on a st holder.

LEFT FRONT

With smaller needles, cast on 33 (**35**) sts.
1st row: (Right side). *K1. P1. Rep from * to last 3 sts. K3.
2nd row: K3. *K1. P1. Rep from * to end of row.
Rep these 2 rows for 3 ins [7.5 cm] ending on a 2nd row and inc 3 (**5**) sts evenly across last row. 36 (**40**) sts.

Change to larger needles and proceed as follows:
1st row: (Right side). Knit.
2nd row: K3. Purl to end of row.
These 2 rows form stocking st and garter border.

Cont even until work from beg measures 5 (**6**) ins [12.5 (**15**) cm] ending with **wrong** side facing for next row.
Next row: K3. P6 (**8**). Cast off 21 sts.

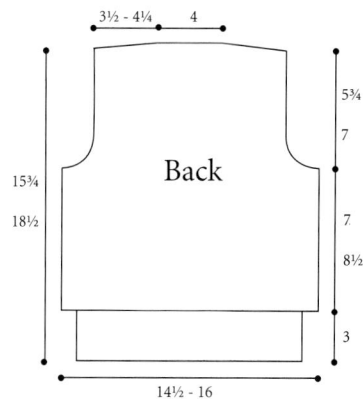

Back diagram

3½ - 4¼ 4

5¾
7

15¾

18½

Back

7

8½

3

14½ - 16

Purl to end of row.
Next row: K6 (**8**). Placing needle with pocket lining behind needle with pocket flap, (knit tog 1 st from each needle) 21 times in place of the cast off sts of Front. K9 (**11**).

Keeping cont of garter st border, cont in stocking st until work from beg measures 10 (**11½**) ins [25.5(**28.5**) cm] ending with right side facing for next row.

Armhole shaping: Cast off 4 sts beg next row. Work 1 row even.
Dec 1 st at armhole edge on next and every alt row 4 times. 28 (**32**) sts.

Cont even in stocking st until armhole measures 3¾ (**5**) ins [9.5 (**12.5**) cm] ending with **wrong** side facing for next row.

Neck shaping: Cast off 6 sts beg next row. Dec 1 st at neck edge on every row to 18 (**21**) sts.

Cont even until armhole measures 5¾ (**7**) ins [14.5 (**18**) cm] ending with right side facing for next row.

Shoulder shaping: Cast off 6 (**7**) sts beg next and following alt row. Work 1 row even. Cast off rem 6 (**7**) sts.

RIGHT FRONT

With smaller needles cast on 33 (**35**) sts.
1st row: (Right side). K3. *K1. P1. Rep from * to end of row.
2nd row: *K1. P1. Rep from * to last 3 sts. K3.

Rep these 2 rows for 3 ins [7.5 cm] ending on a 2nd row and inc 3 (**5**) sts evenly across last row. 36 (**40**) sts.

Change to larger needles and proceed as follows:
1st row: (Right side). Knit.
2nd row: Purl to last 3 sts. K3.
These 2 rows form stocking st and garter border.

Cont even until work from beg measures 5 (**6**) ins [12.5 (**15**) cm] ending with **wrong** side facing for next row.
Next row: P6 (**8**). Cast off 21 sts. P6 (**8**). K3.
Next row: K9 (**11**). Placing needle with pocket lining behind needle with pocket flap, (knit tog 1 st from each needle) 21 times in place of the cast off sts of Front. K6 (**8**).

Keeping cont of garter st border, cont in stocking st until work from beg measures 10 (**11½**) ins [25.5 (**28.5**) cm] ending with **wrong** side facing for next row.

Armhole shaping: Cast off 4 sts beg next row. Work 1 row even.
Dec 1 st at armhole edge on next and every alt row 4 times. 28 (**32**) sts.

Cont even in stocking st until armhole measures 3¾ (**5**) ins [9.5 (**12.5**) cm] ending with right side facing for next row.

Neck shaping: Cast off 6 sts beg next row. Dec 1 st at neck edge on next and every row to 21 sts.

Cont even until armhole measures 5¾ (**7**) ins [14.5 (**18**) cm] ending with **wrong** side facing for next row.

Shoulder shaping: Cast off 6 (**7**) sts beg next and following alt row. Work 1 row even. Cast off rem 6 (**7**) sts.

SLEEVES

With smaller needles, cast on 37 (**41**) sts. Work 3 ins [7.5 cm] in (K1. P1) ribbing as given for Back ending on a 2nd row and inc 1 st in center of last row. 38 (**42**) sts.

Change to larger needles and proceed in stocking st inc 1 st each end of needle on 7th and every following 6th row to 52 (**58**) sts.

Cont even until Sleeve from beg measures 13 (**14½**) ins [33 (**37**) cm] ending with right side facing for next row.

Shape top: *Cast off 2 sts beg next 2 rows. Dec 1 st beg next 2 rows. Rep from * to 20 (**22**) sts. Cast off.

FINISHING

Pin garment pieces to measurements. Cover with a damp cloth and leave to dry.

Collar: With larger needles cast on 2 sts.
1st row: (Right side). Inc 1 st in first st. K1.
2nd row: K1. Inc 1 st in next st. K1.
3rd row: K1. Inc 1 st in next st. Knit to end of row.
4th row: Knit to last 3 sts. Inc 1 st in next st. K2.
Rep 3rd and 4th rows to 16 sts, placing a marker at end (neck edge) of last row.
Cont even in garter st until Collar measures 11½ (**12½**) ins [29 (**32**) cm] from marker ending with **wrong** side facing for next row. Place a marker at neck edge of last row.
Next row: Knit to last 3 sts. K2tog. K1.
Next row: K1. K2tog. Knit to end of row.
Rep last 2 rows to 4 sts.
Next row: K1. K2tog. K1.
Next row: K2tog. K1. Cast off.

Sew shoulder, side and sleeve seams. Sew in sleeves. Sew neck edge of Collar between markers in position to neck edge. Sew zipper in position under front border. Sew on buttons to correspond to buttonholes on pocket flaps. Sew pocket linings in position on wrong side. ♠

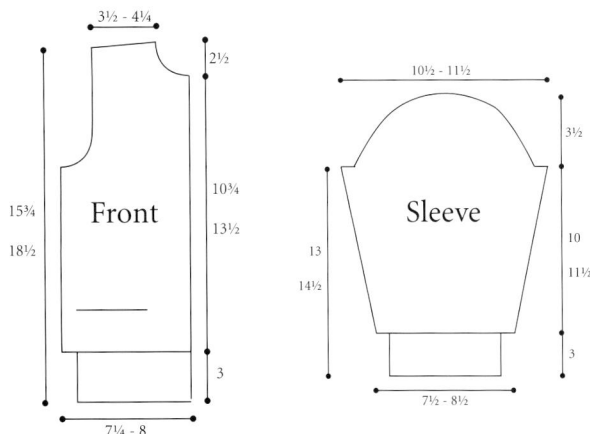

Front
3½ - 4¼
2½
15¾
18½
10¾
13½
3
7¼ - 8

Sleeve
10½ - 11½
3½
13
14½
10
11½
3
7½ - 8½

ANCASTER

1930s

as shown on page 7

as shown on page 7

SIZES

Chest measurement

Small	30-32 ins	[76-81	cm	]
Medium	34-36 "	[86-91	"	]
Large	38-40 "	[97-102	"	]

Finished chest

Small	37½ ins	[95	cm	]
Medium	42 "	[106.5	"	]
Large	47 "	[119.5	"	]

MATERIALS

Patons Classic Merino Wool (100 g)

Size	S	M	L	
225	4	5	5	balls

Sizes 3¾ mm (U.S. 5) and 4½ mm (U.S. 7) knitting needles **or size needed to obtain tension**. One cable needle.

TENSION

20 sts and 26 rows = 4 ins [10 cm] with larger needles in stocking st.

STITCH GLOSSARY

C6B = slip next 3 sts onto a cable needle and leave at back of work. K3, then K3 from cable needle.

C5B = slip next 2 sts onto a cable needle and leave at back of work. K3, then K2 from cable needle.

INSTRUCTIONS

The instructions are written for smallest size. If changes are necessary for larger sizes the instructions will be written thus ( ).

FRONT

**With smaller needles, cast on 97 (111-125) sts.
1st row: (Right side). K1. *P1. K1. Rep from * to end of row.
2nd row: P1. *K1. P1. Rep from * to end of row. Rep these 2 rows (K1. P1) ribbing for 4 ins [10 cm] ending on a 2nd row and inc 16 sts evenly across last row. 113 (**127**-141) sts.

Change to larger needles and proceed in pat as follows:
1st row: (Right side). K1. *K6. P1. Rep from * to last 7 sts. K7.
2nd row: K1. *P6. K1. Rep from * to end of row.
3rd and 4th rows: As 1st and 2nd rows.
5th row: K1. *K6. P1. C6B. P1. Rep from * to last 14 sts. K6. P1. C6B. K1.
6th row: As 2nd row.
7th to 10th rows: As 1st and 2nd rows twice.
11th row: K1. *C6B. P1. K6. P1. Rep

from * to last 14 sts. C6B. P1. K7.
12th row: As 2nd row.
These 12 rows form pat.
Cont in pat until work from beg measures approx 12½ ins [32 cm] ending with 12th row of pat.

Proceed as follows:
1st row: (Right side). K2. (P1. K1) 7 times. K5. Pat to last 21 sts. K5. (K1. P1) 7 times. K2.
2nd row: (K1. P1) 8 times. K5. Pat to last 21 sts. P5. (P1. K1) 8 times.
3rd and 4th rows: As 1st and 2nd rows.
5th row: K2. (P1. K1) 7 times. K5. Pat to last 21 sts. C5B. (K1. P1) 7 times. K2.
6th row: As 2nd row.

Armhole shaping: 1st row: Cast off 8 sts. K2. (P1. K1) 3 times. K5. Pat to last 21 sts. K5. (K1. P1) 7 times. K2.
2nd row: Cast off 8 sts. (K1. P1) 4 times. P5. Pat to last 13 sts. P5. (P1. K1) 4 times.
3rd row: K2. (P1. K1) 3 times. K2tog. K3. Pat to last 13 sts. K3. K2tog. (K1. P1) 3 times. K2.
4th row: (K1. P1) 4 times. Pat to last 8 sts. (P1. K1) 4 times.

Keeping cont of pat, and working 8 side sts in ribbing, dec 1 st at each armhole edge, as before every alt row 4 times more. 87 (**101**-115) sts.**

Work 5 rows even in pat.

Neck shaping: Next row: (Right side). Pat across 37 (**43**-49) sts. Cast off next 13 (**15**-17) sts. Pat to end of row.
Cont on these 37 (**43**-49) sts, dec 1 st

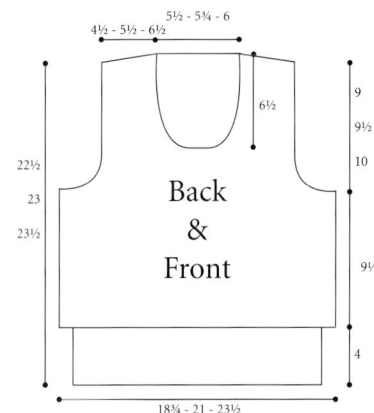

Back & Front

at neck edge every row 7 times, then every alt row 3 times. 27 (**33**-39) sts. Cont even in pat until armhole measures 9 (**9½**-10) ins [23 (**24**-25.5) cm] ending with **wrong** side facing for next row.

Shoulder shaping: Keeping cont of pat cast off 9 (**11**-13) sts beg next and following alt row. Work 1 row even. Cast off rem 9 (**11**-13) sts.

With **wrong** side of work facing, join yarn to rem 37 (**43**-49) sts. Dec 1 st at neck edge every row 7 times, then every alt row 3 times. 27 (**33**-39) sts.

Cont even in pat until armhole measures 9 (**9½**-10) ins [23 (**24**-25.5) cm] ending with right side facing for next row.

Shoulder shaping: Keeping cont of pat cast off 9 (**11**-13) sts beg next and following alt row. Work 1 row even. Cast off rem 9 (**11**-13) sts.

BACK

Work from ** to ** as given for Front.

Cont even in pat until work from beg measure same length as Front to beg of shoulder shaping, ending with right side facing for next row.

Shoulder shaping: Keeping cont of pat cast off 9 (**11**-13) sts beg next 6 rows. Cast off rem 33 (**35**-37) sts.

FINISHING

Pin garment pieces to measurements. Cover with a damp cloth and leave to dry.

Neckband: Sew right shoulder seam. With right side of work facing and smaller needles, pick up and knit 25 (**27**-29) sts down left front neck edge. 13 (**15**-17) sts across center front, 25 (**27**-29) sts up right front neck edge and 33 (**35**-37) sts across center back, dec 3 sts evenly across. 93 (**101**-109) sts.

Beg and ending on a 2nd row, work 5 rows in (K1. P1) ribbing as given for Front. Cast off loosely in ribbing. Sew left shoulder and neckband seam. Sew side seams. ▲

RESTIGOUCHE

1930s

as shown on page 7

SIZES

Chest measurement

Small	34-36	ins	[86.5-91.5	cm]
Medium	38-40	"	[96.5-101.5	"]
Large	42-44	"	[106.5-112	"]

Finished chest

Small	38	ins	[96.5	cm]
Medium	44	"	[112	"]
Large	48½	"	[123	"]

MATERIALS

Patons Classic Merino Wool (100 g)

Sizes	S	M	L	
218	10	11	13	**balls**

Sizes 4 mm (U.S. 6) and 5 mm (U.S. 8) knitting needles **or size needed to obtain tension**. One cable needle. 2 st holders.

TENSION

19 sts and 25 rows = 4 ins [10 cm] with larger needles in stocking st.

STITCH GLOSSARY

C6B = slip next 3 sts onto a cable needle and leave at back of work. K3, then K3 from cable needle.

INSTRUCTIONS

The instructions are written for smallest size. If changes are necessary for larger sizes the instructions will be written thus ( ).

FRONT

With smaller needles, cast on 103 (119**-135) sts.
1st row: (Right side). K1. *P1. K1. Rep from * to end of row.
2nd row: P1. *K1. P1. Rep from * to end of row.
Rep these 2 rows (K1. P1) ribbing for 3½ ins [9 cm] ending on a 2nd row and inc 11 sts evenly across last row. 114 (**130**-146) sts.

Change to larger needles and proceed in pat as follows:
1st row: (Right side). K1. *K3. P2. K3. Rep from * to last st. K1.
2nd row: Purl.
3rd and 4th rows: As 1st and 2nd rows once.
5th row: K1. *K3. P2. C6B. P2. K3. Rep from * to last st. K1.
6th row: As 2nd row.
7th and 8th rows: As 1st and 2nd rows once.
These 8 rows form pat.

Cont in pat until work from beg measures 15½ (**16**-17) ins [39.5 (**40.5**-43) cm] ending with right side facing for next row.
Armhole shaping: Keeping cont of pat, cast off 4 sts beg next 2 rows.
Dec 1 st at each end of needle every alt row 12 times. 82 (**98**-114) sts.**

Cont even in pat until armhole measures 8 (**8**-8½) ins [20.5 (**20.5**-21.5) cm] ending with right side facing for next row.

Neck shaping: Next row: Pat across 27 (**35**-43) sts (neck edge). **Turn.** Leave rem sts on a spare needle.
Work 1 row even.
Keeping cont of pat dec 1 st at neck edge every alt row to 24 (**30**-36) sts.
Cont even in pat until armhole measures 10 (**10**-10½) ins [25.5 (**25.5**-26.5) cm] ending with right side facing for next row.

Shoulder shaping: Keeping cont of pat, cast off 8 (**10**-12) sts beg next and following alt row. Work 1 row even. Cast off rem 8 (**10**-12) sts.

With right side of work facing, slip next 28 sts from spare needle onto a st holder. Join yarn to rem sts and pat to end of row.

Work 1 row even.
Keeping cont of pat, dec 1 st at neck edge every alt row to 24 (**30**-36) sts.

Cont even in pat until armhole measures 10 (**10**-10½) ins [25.5 (**25.5**-26.5) cm] ending with **wrong** side facing for next row.
Shoulder shaping: Keeping cont of pat, cast off 8 (**10**-12) sts beg next and following alt row. Work 1 row even. Cast off rem 8 (**10**-12) sts.

B A C K

Work from ** to ** as given for Front.

Cont even in pat until work from beg measure same length as Front to beg of shoulder shaping, ending with right side facing for next row.

Shoulder shaping: Keeping cont of pat, cast off 8 (**10**-12) sts beg next 6 rows. Leave rem 34 (**38**-42) sts on a st holder.

S L E E V E S

With smaller needles, cast on 47 sts. Work 3½ ins [9 cm] in (K1. P1) ribbing as given for Front ending on a 2nd row and inc 19 sts evenly across last row. 66 sts.

Change to larger needles and proceed in pat as given for Front inc 1 st each end of needle on 5th and every following 6th row to 90 (**90**-96) sts, taking inc sts into pat.

Cont even in pat until sleeve from beg measures 18½ (**19**-19½) ins [47 (**48**-49.5) cm] ending with right side facing for next row

Shape top: *Keeping cont of pat, cast off 2 sts beg next 2 rows, then dec 1 st at beg of next 2 rows. Rep from * to 24 sts. Cast off.

F I N I S H I N G

Pin garment pieces to measurements. Cover with a damp cloth and leave to dry.

Neckband: Sew right shoulder seam. With right side of work facing and smaller needles, pick up and knit 19 sts down left front neck edge. Knit across 28 sts from front st holder, dec 3 sts evenly across. Pick up and knit 19 sts up right front neck edge. Knit across 34 (**38**-42) sts from back st holder dec 4 sts evenly across. 93 (**97**-101) sts.

Beg and ending on a 2nd row, work 6 ins [15 cm] in (K1. P1) ribbing as given for Front. Cast off **loosely** in ribbing. Sew left shoulder and neckband seam. ▲

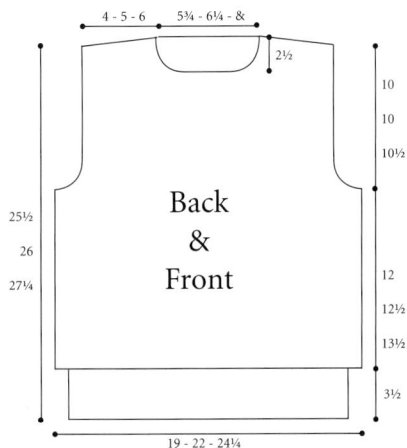

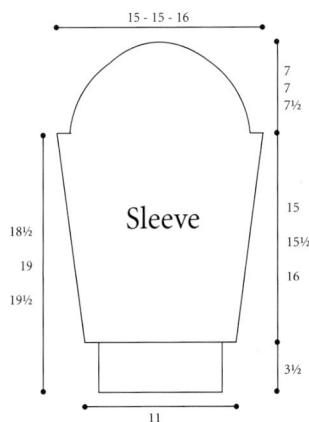

Back & Front

4 - 5 - 6   5¾ - 6¼ - &
2½
10
10
10½
25½
26
27¼
12
12½
13½
3½
19 - 22 - 24¼

Sleeve

15 - 15 - 16
7
7
7½
18½
19
19½
15
15½
16
3½
11

CROCHET SHAWL

1940s

Beehive

as shown on page 8

MEASUREMENT

Finished Size: Length from point to base
23½ ins [59.5 cm]

MATERIALS

Patons Kroy 3 ply or **Beehive Baby** (50 g)
Aran   4   **balls**

Size 2.25 mm (U.S. B or 1) crochet hook **or size needed to obtain tension.**

TENSION

11 sps and 20 rows = 4 ins [10 cm] in pat.

INSTRUCTIONS

Ch 9. Join with ss to first ch to form ring. Ch 7. Turn.

1st row: (1 dc. Ch 4. 1 dc) all in ring. Ch 7. Turn.

2nd row: 1 sc in first sp. 1 sc in next dc. 1 sc in next sp. Ch 4. 1 dc in 3rd ch of turning ch. Ch 7. Turn.

3rd row: 1 sc in first sp. 1 sc in each of next 3 sc. 1 sc in next sp. Ch 4. 1 dc in 3rd ch of turning ch. Ch 7. Turn.

4th row: 1 sc in first sp. 1 sc in each of next 5 sc. 1 sc in next sp. Ch 4. 1 dc in 3rd ch of turning ch. Ch 7. Turn.

5th row: 1 sc in first sp. Ch 4. Miss next sc. 1 sc in each of next 5 sc. Ch 4. Miss next sc. 1 sc in next sp. Ch 4. 1 dc in 3rd ch of turning ch. Ch 7. Turn.

6th row: 1 sc in first sp. Ch 4. Miss next sc. 1 sc in next sp. Ch 4. Miss next sc. 1 sc in each of next 3 sc. (Ch 4. Miss next sc. 1 sc in next sp) twice. Ch 4. 1 dc in 3rd ch of turning ch. Ch 7. Turn.

7th row: 1 sc in first sp. (Ch 4. Miss next sc. 1 sc in next sp) twice. Ch 4. Miss next sc. 1 dc in next sc. (Ch 4. Miss next sc. 1 sc in next sp) 3 times. Ch 4. 1 dc in 3rd ch of turning ch. Ch 7. Turn.

8th row: 1 dc in first sp. *(Ch 4. Miss next sc. 1 sc in next sp) 3 times. Ch 4. Miss next dc. 1 sc in next sp. (Ch 4. Miss next sc. 1 sc in next sp) twice. Ch 4. Miss next sc. 1 dc in next sp.* Ch 4. 1 dc in 3rd ch of turning ch. Ch 7. Turn.

9th row: 1 sc in first sp. 1 sc in next dc. 1 sc in next sp. *(Ch 4. Miss next sc. 1 sc in next sp) 5 times. Ch 4. Miss next sc. 1 sc in next sp. 1 sc in next dc. 1 sc in next sp.* Ch 4. 1 dc in 3rd ch of turning ch. Ch 7. Turn.

10th row: 1 sc in first sp. 1 sc in each of next 3 sc. 1 sc in next sp. *(Ch 4. Miss next sc. 1 sc in next sp) 4 times. Ch 4. Miss next sc. 1 sc in next sp. 1 sc in each of next 3 sc. 1 sc in next sp.* Ch 4. 1 dc in 3rd ch of turning ch. Ch 7. Turn.

11th row: 1 sc in first sp. 1 sc in each of next 5 sc. 1 sc in next sp. *(Ch 4. Miss next sc. 1 sc in next sp) 3 times. Ch 4. Miss next sc. 1 sc in next sp. 1 sc in each of next 5 sc. 1 sc in next sp.* Ch 4. 1 dc in 3rd ch of turning ch. Ch 7. Turn.

12th row: 1 sc in first sp. Ch 4. Miss next sc. 1 sc in each of next 5 sc. *(Ch 4. Miss next sc. 1 sc in next sp) 4 times. Ch 4. Miss next sc. 1 sc in each of next 5 sc.* Ch 4. Miss next sc. 1 sc in next sp. Ch 4. 1 dc in 3rd ch of turning ch. Ch 7. Turn.

13th row: 1 sc in first sp. Ch 4. Miss next sc. 1 sc in next sp. Ch 4. Miss next sc. 1 sc in each of next 3 sc. *(Ch 4. Miss next sc. 1 sc in next sp) 5 times. Ch 4. Miss next sc. 1 sc in each of next 3 sc.* (Ch 4. Miss next sc. 1 sc in next sp) twice. Ch 4. 1 dc in 3rd ch of turning ch. Ch 7. Turn.

14th row: 1 sc in first sp. (Ch 4. Miss next sc. 1 sc in next sp) twice. Ch 4. Miss next sc. 1 dc in next sc. *(Ch 4. Miss next sc. 1 sc in next sp) 6 times. Ch 4. Miss next sc. 1 dc in next sc.* (Ch 4. Miss next sc. 1 sc in next sp) 3 times. Ch 4. 1 dc in 3rd ch of turning ch. Ch 7. Turn.

Rep 8th to 14th rows for pat noting that on next 7 rows instructions from * to * will be worked twice, on following 7 rows they will be worked 3 times and so on until 112 rows of pat have been worked in total, ending last row with ch 5. Turn.

Next row: 1 sc in first sp. *Ch 2. 1 sc in next sp. Rep from * to last sp. Ch 2. 1 sc in last sp. Ch 2. 1 dc in 3rd ch of turning ch. Ch 7. Turn.

Edging: 1st round: 1 dc in first sp. 1 dc in next sc. 1 dc in next sp. *Ch 2. Miss next 2 sts. 1 dc in next sp. 1 dc in next sc. 1 dc in next sp. Rep from * to corner loop. Ch 2. (3 dc. Ch 3. 3 dc) in corner loop. Work around side of Shawl as follows: Ch 2. Miss next sp. 1 dc in next sp. 1 dc in next dc. 1 dc in next sp. **Ch 2. Miss next dc. 1 dc in next sp. 1 dc in next dc. 1 dc in next sp. Rep from ** to corner loop. Ch 2. (3 dc. Ch 3. 3 dc) in corner loop. Rep from ** to corner loop on other side of Shawl. Ch 2. (3 dc. Ch 2. 2 dc) in corner loop. Ss in 3rd ch of turning ch. Ch 5.
2nd round: 1 dc in first sp. (Ch 2. 1 dc in same sp) twice. Miss next 3 dc. *[(1 dc. Ch 2) 3 times. 1 dc] all in next sp – shell made. Rep from * to next corner sp. [(1 dc. Ch 2) 5 times. 1 dc] all in next sp – corner shell made.** Rep from * to ** twice more. Join with ss to 3rd ch of ch 5.
3rd round: Ss in next sp. Ss in next dc. Ss in next sp (center sp of first shell). Ch 5. (1 dc. Ch 4. 1 sc in 4th ch from hook – picot made. 1 dc. Ch 2. 1 dc) all in same sp. *(1 dc. Ch 2. 1 dc. Picot. 1 dc. Ch 2. 1 dc) all in center sp of next shell. Rep from * to next corner shell. (1 dc. Ch 2. 1 dc. Picot. 1 dc. Ch 2. 1 dc) all in 2nd sp of next corner shell. (1 dc. Ch 2. 1 dc. Picot. 1 dc. Ch 2. 1 dc) all in 4th sp of next corner shell.** Rep from * to ** twice more. Join with ss to 3rd ch of ch 5.
Fasten off.

Roll Shawl in a damp towel for several hours, then spread out flat, pin into shape and leave to dry. ◆

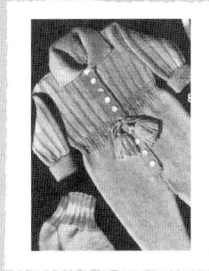

S L E E P S U I T

1940s
Beehive

as shown on page 8

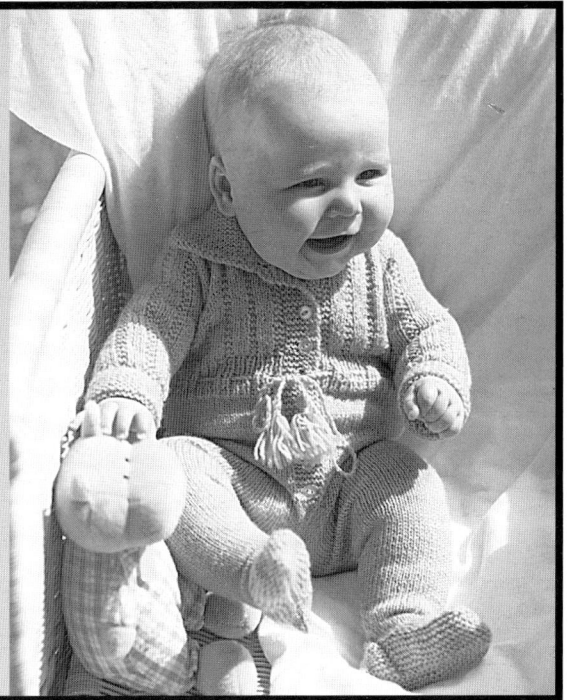

SIZES

Chest measurement

3–6 mos	16 ins	[40.5 cm]
Finished chest		
3-6 mos	18 ins	[45.5 cm]

MATERIALS

Patons Beehive Baby or **Kroy 3 ply** (50 g)

Size	3-6 mos	
Baby Blue	3	**balls**

Size 3¼ mm (U.S. 3) knitting needles **or size needed to obtain tension**. Size 3¼ mm (U.S. 3) circular knitting needle 70 cm long. 10 buttons. 2 st holders.

TENSION

32 sts and 40 rows = 4 ins [10 cm] in stocking st.

INSTRUCTIONS

Note: Garment is worked from shoulders down.

BACK

Cast on 50 sts.
1st row: (Right side). K4. *P2. K3. Rep from * to last st. K1.
2nd row: K1. Purl to last st. K1.
These 2 rows form pat.

Cont in pat until work from beg measures 2 ins [5 cm] ending with right side facing for next row.

Shape armholes: Keeping cont of pat, inc 1 st at each end of needle on next and every alt row to 62 sts.
Cast on 5 sts beg next 2 rows. 72 sts.

Cont in pat until work from beg measures 5 ins [12.5 cm] ending with right side facing for next row.

Proceed as follows:
1st row: (Right side). K2. *P1. K1. Rep from * to end of row.
Rep this row 5 times more.
7th row: (Eyelets). K2. *yfwd. K2tog. P1. K1. Rep from * to last 2 sts. yfwd. K2tog.
Rep 1st row 5 times more.

Shape back: 1st row: K42. **Turn.**
2nd row: P12. **Turn.**
3rd row: K20. **Turn.**
4th row: P28. **Turn.**
5th row: K36. **Turn.**
6th row: P44. **Turn.**
7th row: Knit.
8th row: K1. Purl to last st. K1.
Leave these sts on a st holder.

LEFT FRONT

Cast on 16 sts.
1st row: (Right side). K1. P1. (K3. P2) twice. K4.

2nd row: K1. Purl to last st. K1.
These 2 rows form pat.
Work 2 more rows in pat.

Shape neck: 1st row: K1. Inc 1 st in next st (neck edge). Pat to end of row.
Work 1 row even in pat.
Rep last 2 rows once more.
Work 3 rows even in pat.
8th row: K1. Purl to end of row. **Turn.**
Cast on 10 sts.
9th row: K7. Pat to end of row.
10th row: K1. Purl to last 7 sts. K7.
Rep 9th and 10th rows until work from beg 2 ins [5 cm] ending with right side facing for next row.

Shape armhole: Keeping cont of pat, inc 1 st at end (armhole edge) of next and every alt row 5 times.
Cast on 5 sts. 39 sts.

Cont even in pat until work from beg measures 5 ins [12.5 cm] ending with right side facing for next row.

Proceed as follows:
1st row: K8. *P1. K1. Rep from * to last st. K1.
2nd row: *K1. P1. Rep from * to last 7 sts. K7.
Rep these 2 rows twice more.
7th row: (Eyelets). K8. *yfwd. K2tog. P1. K1.
Rep from * to last 3 sts. yfwd. K2tog. K1.
Rep 2nd row once, then 1st and 2nd rows twice more.
Next row: Knit. Leave sts on a st holder.

RIGHT FRONT

Cast on 16 sts.
1st row: (Right side). K4. (P2. K3) twice. P1. K1.
2nd row: K1. Purl to last st. K1.
These 2 rows form pat.
Work 2 more rows in pat.

Shape neck: 1st row: Pat to last 3 sts.
Inc 1 st in next st (neck edge). P1. K1.
Work 1 row even in pat.
Rep last 2 rows once more.
Work 2 rows even in pat.
7th row: Pat to end of row. **Turn.**
Cast on 10 sts.
8th row: K7. *Purl to last st. K1.
9th row: Pat to last 7 sts. K3. yfwd. K2tog (buttonhole). K2.
10th row: As 8th row.
11th row: K1. *K3. P2. Rep from * to last 7 sts. K7.

Keeping cont of pat and working a buttonhole in border at front edge every 10th row, as before, work to correspond to Left Front reversing armhole shaping until work from beg 5 ins [12 cm] ending with right side facing for next row.

Proceed as follows:
1st row: (Right side). K2. *P1. K1. Rep from * to last 7 sts. K7.
2nd row: K7. *P1. K1. Rep from * to end of row.
Rep these 2 rows twice more.
7th row: (Eyelets). K2. *yfwd. K2tog.
P1. K1. Rep from * to last 9 sts. yfwd.
K2tog. K3. yfwd. K2tog. K2.
Rep 2nd row once, then 1st and 2nd rows twice more.
Next row: Knit.

Join Fronts and Back: With **wrong** side of work facing proceed as follows with circular needle:
1st row: (K7. P32) from Right Front.
P72 of Back. (P32. K7) from Left Front. 150 sts.
2nd row: Knit.
3rd row: K7. Purl to last 7 sts. K7.
Cont in stocking st, keeping borders in garter st, working buttonholes every 10th row, as before, until work from joining measures 4 ins [10 cm] ending with **wrong** side facing for next row.
Next row: Cast off 3 sts. Purl to last 7 sts. K7.
Next row: Cast off 3 sts. Knit to end of row. 144 sts.
Next row: Purl.

Cont in stocking st until work from joining measures 6 ins [15 cm] ending with right side facing for next row.

Shape left leg: Next row: K72. **Turn.**
Leave rem 72 sts on a spare needle.
Cont in stocking st, dec 1 st at each end of needle on next and every following 4th row to 40 sts. Cont even until leg seam measures 7 ins [18 cm] ending with right side facing for next row.

Shape foot: 1st row: K19. **Turn.** Leave rem 21 sts on a spare needle.
2nd row: K1. P13. K1. **Turn.**
3rd row: K15. **Turn.**
Rep 2nd and 3rd rows 8 times more, then 2nd row once.

21st row: K1. K2tog. K9. K2tog. K1.
22nd row: K1. P11. K1.
23rd row: K1. K2tog. K7. K2tog. K1.
Break yarn. Join yarn to rem 21 sts and knit to end of row.

Next row: K21. Pick up and knit 14 sts along side of foot. Knit across 11 sts at toe.
Pick up and knit 14 sts along other side of foot. Knit 4 sts that were left. 64 sts.
Work 9 rows garter st (knit every row).

Shape toe: Next row: K23. (K2tog) twice.
K28. (K2tog) twice. K5.
2nd row: Knit.
3rd row: K22. (K2tog) twice. K26.
(K2tog) twice. K4.
Knit 2 rows. Cast off.

Shape right leg: Join yarn to rem 72 sts. Work from ** to ** as given for Left Leg.

Shape foot: 1st row: K36. **Turn.** Leave rem 4 sts on a spare needle.
2nd row: K1. P13. K1. **Turn.**
3rd row: K15. **Turn.**
Rep 2nd and 3rd rows 8 times more, then 2nd row once.
21st row: K1. K2tog. K9. K2tog. K1.
22nd row: K1. P11. K1.
23rd row: K1. K2tog. K7. K2tog. K1.
Break yarn. Join yarn to rem 4 sts and knit to end of row.

Next row: K4. Pick up and knit 14 sts along side of foot. Knit across 11 sts at toe.
Pick up and knit 14 sts along other side of foot. Knit 21 sts that were left. 64 sts.
Work 9 rows garter st.

Shape toe: Next row: K5. (K2tog) twice.
K28. (K2tog) twice. K23.
2nd row: Knit.
3rd row: K4. (K2tog) twice. K26.
(K2tog) twice. K22.
Knit 2 rows. Cast off.

SLEEVES

Cast on 32 sts. Work 18 rows in garter st, thus ending with right side facing for next row. Place a marker at each end of last row.
Next row: K2. *P1. K1. Rep from * to end of row.
Rep this row 13 times more.
Next row: K1. *Inc 1 st in next st purlways. P2. Rep from * to last 4 sts.
P1. Inc 1 st in each of next 2 sts purlways. K1. 43 sts.

Proceed in pat as follows:
1st row: (Right side). *K3. P2. Rep from * to last 3 sts. K3.
2nd row: K1. Purl to last st. K1.
These 2 rows form pat.

Cont even in pat until work from marker measures 5 ins [12.5 cm] ending with right side facing for next row.

Shape top: *Keeping cont of pat, cast off 2 sts beg next 2 rows, dec 1 st at each end of next row. Work 1 row even.* Rep from * to * until 13 sts rem. Cast off.

FINISHING

Collar: Cast on 16 sts. Work 8 ins [20.5 cm] in garter st. Cast off.

Sew shoulder and sleeve seams. Sew in sleeves. Sew Collar in position placing each end 2 sts from edge of each front. Sew leg and crotch seams. Place the cast off sts of Right Front over cast off sts of Left Front and sew in position. Sew buttons to correspond to buttonholes. Thread twisted cord through eyelets at waist. Sew tassels to each end of cord.

Twisted cord: Cut 2 strands of yarn 80 ins [203 cm] long. With both strands together hold one end and with someone holding other end, twist strands to the right until they begin to curl. Fold the 2 ends together and tie in a knot so they will not unravel. The strands will now twist themselves together. Adjust length if desired.

Tassel: Cut a piece of cardboard 3 x 3 ins [7.5 x 7.5 cm]. Wind yarn around the cardboard 8 times. Break yarn, leaving a long end and thread through a blunt ended needle. Slip needle through all the loops on the cardboard and tie tightly at on end. Slip off cardboard and wind the yarn several times around the loops ½ inch [1 cm] from the fold. Draw needle through the top and sew the tassel in position. Cut through the other fold and trim evenly. ♠

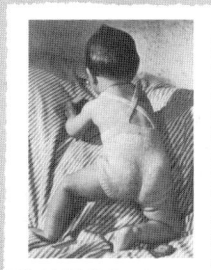

PLAYING IN
THE SUN

1940s

Beehive

as shown on page 9

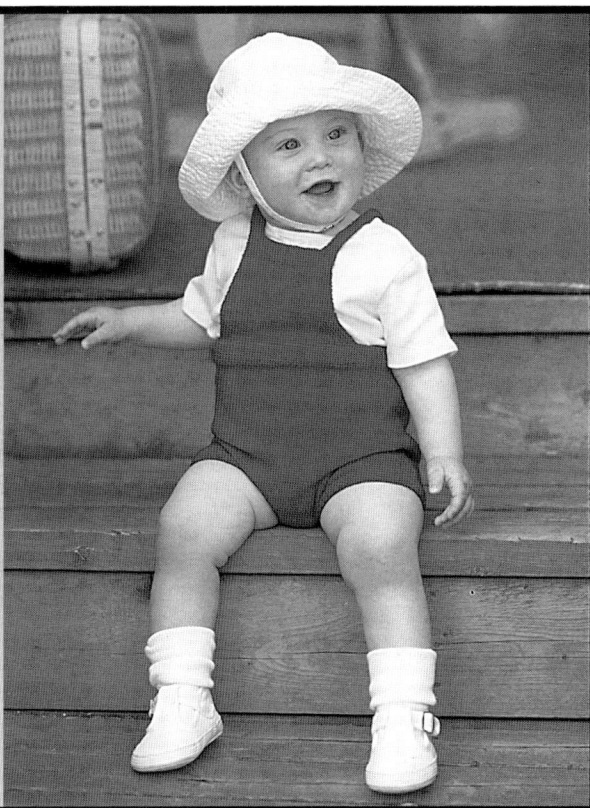

SIZES

Finished length from top of bib to crotch

12 mos	12¼ ins	[32 cm]

MATERIALS

Patons Beehive Baby or **Kroy 3 Ply** (50 g)

Size	12 mos	
Red	2	balls

Size 2¾ mm (U.S. 2) knitting needles **or size needed to obtain tension**.

TENSION

36 sts and 44 rows = 4 ins [10 cm] in stocking st.

INSTRUCTIONS

FRONT

**Cast on 18 sts (lower edge).

Shape legs: Proceed in stocking st casting on 5 sts beg every row until there are 98 sts.
Work 12 rows even.
Cont in stocking st, dec 1 st at each end of needle on next and every 12th row to 86 sts.

Cont even until work from beg measures 7½ ins [19 cm] ending with **wrong** side facing for next row.**
Work 1 inch [2.5 cm] in (K1. P1) ribbing ending with right side facing for next row.
Cast off 16 sts in ribbing beg next 2 rows. 54 sts.

PRICE
45¢
SERIES NO. 50

Make bib: 1st row: (Right side). Rib 8 (border). Knit to last 8 sts. Rib 8 (border).
2nd row: Rib 8. Purl to last 8 sts. Rib 8. Keeping cont of borders, cont in stocking st, dec 1 st inside each border on next and every following 6th row to 40 sts ending with right side facing for next row.

Work ¾ inch [2 cm] in (K1. P1) ribbing ending with right side facing for next row.

Next row: (Right side). Rib 8. Cast off 24 sts in ribbing. Rib 8.

Make shoulder straps: Working on these last 8 sts, rib 10 ins [25.5 cm]. Cast off in ribbing.
Join yarn to rem 8 sts and work as given for 1st strap.

BACK

Work from ** to ** as given for Front.

Shape back: 1st row: K1. P49. **Turn.**
2nd row: K14. **Turn.**
3rd row: P20. **Turn.**
4th row: K26. **Turn.**
5th row: P32. **Turn.**
6th row: K38. **Turn.**
Cont in this manner working 6 more sts every row before turning, until all sts have been worked.

Beg with wrong side facing, work 1 inch [2.5 cm] in (K1. P1) ribbing ending with right side facing for next row. Cast off in ribbing.

FINISHING

Sew tog cast on sts at crotch.

Leg bands: With right side of work facing pick up and knit 84 sts evenly across leg opening. Work ¾ inch [2 cm] in (K1. P1) ribbing. Cast off **loosely** in ribbing.

Sew side seams. Cross straps at back and sew to top of ribbing 2 ins [5 cm] from side seams. Adjust length of straps if desired. ♠

TWINKLE
TOES
———
1940s

Beehive

as shown on page 9

MATERIALS

Patons Astra or Look at Me! (50 g)

Size	2	4	6	
Main Color (blue)	1	1	1	ball
Contrast A (red)	1	1	1	ball

Size 4.00 mm (U.S. G or 6) crochet hook **or size needed to obtain tension.**

TENSION

16 dc and 6½ rows = 4 ins [10 cm] with single strand of yarn.

INSTRUCTIONS

The instructions are written for smallest size. If changes are necessary for larger sizes the instructions will be written thus ( ).

Upper: With MC, ch 44 (**48**-52). Join with ss to form a ring.
1st round: Ch 3. 1 dc in first ch. 1 dc in each ch to end of round. Join with ss in top of ch 3 at beg of round. 45 (**49**-53) dc.
2nd round: Ch 1. 1 sc in same sp as last ss. 1 sc in each of next 20 (**22**-24) dc. *Draw up a loop in each of next 3 dc. Yoh and draw through 4 loops on hook – sc3tog made at center front of foot.* 1 sc in each dc to end of round. Join with ss to first sc.
3rd round: Ch 3. 1 dc in each of next 18 (**20**-22) sc. *[(Yoh. Draw up a loop in next sc. Yoh and draw through 2 loops on hook) twice. Yoh and draw through 3 loops on hook – dc2tog made at center front of foot] twice.* 1 dc in each sc to end of round. Join with ss to top of ch 3.
4th round: Ch 1. 1 sc in same sp as last ss. 1 sc in each of next 17 (**19**-21) dc. Sc3tog. 1 sc in each dc to end of round. Join with ss to first sc.
5th round: Ch 1. 1 sc in same sp as last ss. 1 sc in each of next 16 (**18**-22) sc. Sc3tog. 1 sc in each sc to end of round. Join with ss to first sc. Fasten off.
Sew center 7 (**8**-9) sts tog at center front.

Sole: With 2 strands of A, ch 11 (**13**-15).
1st round: 1 sc in 2nd ch from hook. 1 sc in each ch to last ch. 3 sc in last ch (toe). Working along other side of ch, work 1 sc in each st to last st. 2 sc in last ch (heel). Join with ss to first sc.
2nd round: Ch 1. 3 sc in first st. 1 sc in each of next 8 (**10**-12) sts. 2 sc in each of center 3 sts. 1 sc in each st to last st. 2 sc in last st. Join with ss to first sc.
3rd round: Ch 1. 2 sc in first st. 1 sc in each of next 3 sts. 1 ss in each of next 4 sts. 1 sc in each of next 5 (**7**-9) sts. 2 sc in each of center 3 sts. 1 sc in each of next 5 (**7**-9) sts. 1 ss in each of next 4 sts. 1 sc in each st to last st of round. 2 sc in last st. Join with ss to first sc.
4th round: Ch 1. 2 sc in first st. 1 sc in each of next 3 sts. 1 ss in each of next 4 sts. 1 sc in each of next 7 (**9**-11) sts. 2 sc in each of center 3 sts. 1 sc in each of next 7 (**9**-11) sts. 1 ss in each of next 4 sts. 1 sc in each st to last st of round. 2 sc in last st. Join with ss to first sc.
5th round: Ch 1. 2 sc in each of first 2 sts. 1 sc in each of next 16 (**18**-20) sts. 2 sc in each of center 3 sts. 1 sc in each st to last st. 2 sc in last st. **Do not break yarn.**

FINISHING

Join Upper and Sole: Place Upper on Sole matching heel to heel. With 2 strands of A, work 1 round of sc working through 1 st from Upper and 1 st from Sole. Join with ss to first sc. Fasten off.

Pom-poms (make 2)
Wind MC around 2 fingers approx 60 times. Remove from fingers and tie tightly in center. Cut through each side of loops. Trim to a smooth round shape. Sew to top of Slipper as illustrated. ♠

PHILLIP'S CABLE PULLOVER

1940s
Beehive

as shown on page 10

SIZES

Chest measurement

Size 4	23¼ ins	[59 cm	]
Size 6	26 "	[66 "	]
Size 8	28 "	[71 "	]

Finished chest

Size 4	26 ins	[66 cm	]
Size 6	32 "	[81 "	]
Size 8	37½ "	[93 "	]

MATERIALS

Patons Classic Merino Wool (100 g)

Sizes	4	6	8	
238	3	3	4	balls

Sizes 4 mm (U.S. 6) and 5 mm (U.S. 8) knitting needles **or size needed to obtain tension**. 1 cable needle.

TENSION

19 sts and 25 rows = 4 ins [10 cm] with larger needles in stocking st.

STITCH GLOSSARY

C4B = slip next 2 sts onto a cable needle and leave at back of work. K2, then K2 from cable needle.

INSTRUCTIONS

The instructions are written for smallest size. If changes are necessary for larger sizes the instructions will be written thus ( ).

BACK

With smaller needles, cast on 61 (75**-89) sts.
1st row: (Right side). K1. *P1. K1. Rep from * to end of row.
2nd row: P1. *K1. P1. Rep from * to end of row.
Rep these 2 rows (K1. P1) ribbing for 3 ins [8 cm] ending on a 1st row and inc 5 sts evenly across last row. 66 (**80**-94) sts.

Change to larger needles and proceed in pat as follows:
1st row: (Wrong side). *K1. P1. K1. P4. Rep from * to last 3 sts. K1. P1. K1.
2nd row: K2. P1. K4. *P1. K1. P1. K4. Rep from * to last 3 sts. P1. K2.
3rd and 8th rows: As 1st and 2nd rows 3 times.
9th row: As 1st row.
10th row: K2. P1. C4B. *P1. K1. P1. C4B. Rep from * to last 3 sts. P1. K2.
These 10 rows form pat.

Work a further 40 (**50**-50) rows pat, then rep 1st row once, thus ending with right side facing for next row.

Armhole shaping: Keeping cont of pat, cast off 3 sts beg next 2 rows.**
Dec 1 st at each end of needle on next and every following alt row to 52 (**66**-80) sts.

Cont even in pat until armhole from beg measures 6 (**6½**-7) ins [15 (**16.5**-18) cm] ending with right side facing for next row.

Shoulder shaping: Keeping cont of pat, cast off 5 (**7**-9) sts beg next 4 rows, then 6 (**8**-10) sts beg following 2 rows. Cast off rem 20 (**22**-24) sts.

FRONT

Work from ** to ** as given for Back.

Dec 1 st each end of needle on next and following alt row. 56 (**72**-86)sts. Work 1 row even in pat, thus ending with right side facing for next row.

Neck shaping: 1st row: Work 2tog. Pat across 24 (**32**-39) sts. K2 (neck edge). **Turn.** Leave rem sts on a spare needle.
2nd row: P2. Pat to end of row.
3rd row: Work 2tog. Pat to last 7 sts. K2tog. P1. K1. P1. K2.
4th row: P2. K1. P1. K1. P3. Pat to end of row.
5th row: Pat to last 7 sts. K2tog. P1. K1. P1. K2.
6th row: P2. K1. P1. K1. P2. Pat to end of row.
7th row: As 5th row.
8th row: P2. (K1. P1) twice. Pat to end of

row.
Rep last 2 rows 1 (**3**-4) time(s) more. 22 (**28**-34) sts.
Next row: (Right side). Pat to last 6 sts. (K1. P1) twice. K2.
Next row: P2. (K1. P1) twice. Pat to end of row.
Rep last 2 rows until armhole measures same length as Back to beg of shoulder shaping, ending with right side facing for next row.

Shoulder shaping: Keeping cont of pat, cast off 5 (**7**-9) sts beg next and following alt row.
Work 1 row even. Cast off 6 (**8**-10) sts beg next row. 6 sts.
Next row: P2. (K1. P1) twice.
Next row: (K1. P1) twice. K2.
Rep last 2 rows for 2 ins [5 cm]. Cast off in pat.

With right side of work facing, join yarn to rem sts
1st row: K2. Pat to last 2 sts. Work 2tog.
2nd row: Pat to last 2 sts. P2.
3rd row: K2. P1. K1. P1. Sl1. K1. psso. Pat to last 2 sts. Work 2tog.
4th row: Pat to last 8 sts. P3. K1. P1. K1. P2.
5th row: K2. P1. K1. P1. Sl1. K1. psso. Pat to end of row.
6th row: Pat to last 7 sts. P2. K1. P1. K1. P2.
7th row: As 5th row.
8th row: Pat to last 6 sts. (P1. K1) twice. P2.
Rep last 2 rows 1 (**3**-4) time(s) more. 22 (**28**-34) sts.

Next row: (Right side). K2. (P1. K1) twice. Pat to end of row.

Next row: Pat to last 6 sts. P1. K1. P1. K1. P2.
Rep last 2 rows until armhole measures same length as Back to beg of shoulder shaping ending with **wrong** side facing for next row.

Shoulder shaping: Keeping cont of pat, cast off 5 (**7**-9) sts beg next and following alt row.
Work 1 row even. Cast off 6 (**8**-10) sts beg next row. 6 sts.
Next row: K2. (P1. K1) twice.
Next row: (P1. K1) twice. P2.
Rep last 2 rows for 2 ins [5 cm]. Cast off in pat.

SLEEVES

With smaller needles, cast on 37 sts. Work 2½ ins [6 cm] in (K1. P1) ribbing as given for Back inc 8 sts evenly across last row. 45 sts.

Change to larger needles and proceed in pat as given for Back inc 1 st each end of needle on 4th and following 6th rows until there are 63 (**65**-69) sts, taking inc sts into pat.

Work even until sleeve measures 12 (**13**-14½) ins [30.5 (**33**-37) cm] ending with right side facing for next row.

Shape top: Cast off 2 sts beg every row until there are 17 sts. Cast off.

FINISHING

Pin garment pieces to measurements. Cover with a damp cloth and leave to dry.

Sew shoulder, side and sleeve seams. Sew in sleeves. Sew ends of ribbing extensions tog. Sew across back neck edge having seam at center back neck. ♠

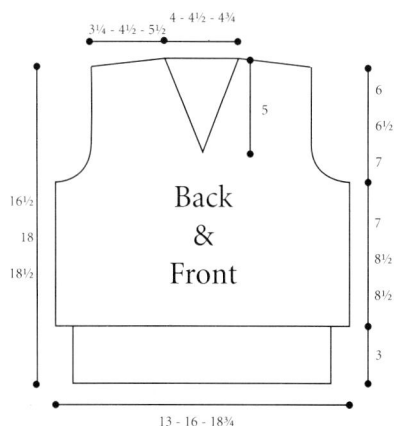

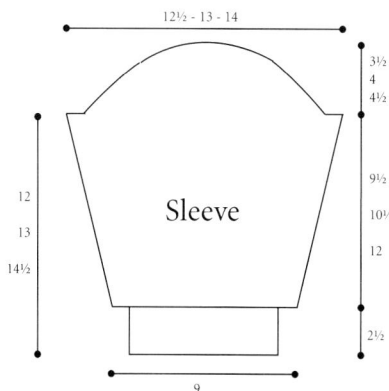

Back & Front

3¼ - 4½ - 5½
4 - 4½ - 4¾
6
5
6½
7
16½
18
18½
7
8½
8½
3
13 - 16 - 18¾

Sleeve

12½ - 13 - 14
3½
4
4½
12
13
14½
9½
10½
12
2½
9

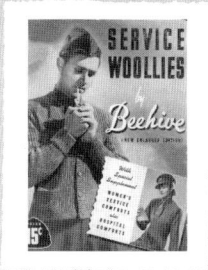

SERVICE CARDIGAN

1940s

Beehive

as shown on page 10

SIZES

Chest measurement

Small	38	ins	[97	cm	]
Medium	40	"	[102.5	"	]
Large	42	"	[107	"	]

Finished chest

Small	40	ins	[102.5	cm	]
Medium	43	"	[109	"	]
Large	45	"	[114.5	"	]

MATERIALS

Patons Classic Merino Wool (100 g)

Size	S	M	L	
228	7	7	8	balls

Sizes 3¾ mm (U.S. 5) and 4½ mm (U.S. 7) knitting needles **or size needed to obtain tension**. 5 buttons. 2 st holders.

TENSION

20 sts and 26 rows = 4 ins [10 cm] with larger needles in stocking st.

INSTRUCTIONS

The instructions are written for smallest size. If changes are necessary for larger sizes the instructions will be written thus ( ).

BACK
With larger needles, cast on 89 (**95**-101) sts.
Work 12 rows garter st (knit every row), noting that first row is wrong side.
Next row: K1 (**4**-7). *K4. Inc 1 st in next st. K3. Rep from * 11 times more. Knit to end of row. 101 (**107**-113) sts.

Proceed in pat as follows:
1st row: (Right side). K2. *P1. K1. Rep from * to last st. K1.
2nd row: K1. Purl to last st. K1.
These 2 rows form pat.

Cont in pat until work from beg measures 14 ins [35.5 cm] ending with right side facing for next row.

Armhole shaping: Keeping cont of pat, cast off 6 (**7**-8) sts beg next 2 rows. Dec 1 st at each end of needle every alt row until 67 (**67**-71) sts rem.

Cont even in pat until armhole measures 9 (**9½**-9½) ins [23 (**24**-24) cm] ending with right side facing for next row.

Shoulder shaping: Keeping cont of pat, cast off 7 (**7**-8) sts beg next 4 rows, then 7 sts beg following 2 rows. Cast off rem 25 sts.

Pocket Lining (make 2)
With larger needles, cast on 23 sts. Work 4 ins [10 cm] in pat as given for Back ending with right side facing for next row. Leave these 23 sts on a st holder.

RIGHT FRONT

With larger needles, cast on 49 (**51**-53) sts. Work 12 rows in garter st noting that first row is wrong side.
Next row: K5. *K4. Inc 1 st in next st. K3. Rep from * 5 times. Knit to end of row. 55 (**57**-59) sts.

Proceed in pat as follows:
1st row: (Right side). K8. *P1. K1. Rep from * to last st. K1.
2nd row: K1. Purl to last 7 st. K7.
These 2 rows form pat and front garter st border.

Cont even in pat until work from beg measures 4½ ins [11.5 cm] ending with **wrong** side facing for next row.

Pocket border: 1st row: K1. P7 (**9**-11). K23. P17. K7.
2nd row: K8. (P1. K1) 8 times. K23. (K1. P1) 3 (**4**-5) times. K2.
3rd to 6th rows: As 1st and 2nd rows twice.
7th row: K1. P7 (**9**-11). Cast off 23 sts. P17. K7.
8th row: K8. (P1. K1) 8 times. Pat across 23 sts from pocket lining. (K1. P1) 3 (**4**-5) times. K2.

Keeping cont of garter st border, cont in stocking st until work from beg measures 14 ins [35.5 cm] ending with **wrong** side facing for next row.

Armhole and front shaping: Next row: Cast off 6 (**7**-8) sts. Pat to end of row.
Next row: K8. K2tog (front edge). Pat to last 2 sts. K2tog.
Work 1 row even in pat.
Dec 1 st at armhole edge on next and every alt row 10 (**11**-10) times more, **at the same time**, dec 1 st at neck edge inside border, as before, on every following 6th row from previous dec until 28 (**28**-30) sts rem.

Cont even in pat until armhole measures 9 (9½-9½) ins [23 (24-24) cm] ending with **wrong** side facing for next row.

Shoulder shaping: Keeping cont of pat, cast off 7 (**7**-8) sts beg next and following alt row. Work 1 row even in pat. Cast off 7 sts. Cont in garter st on rem 7 sts for 2½ ins [6 cm] ending with right side facing for next row. Cast off.

Place markers for buttons along front edging, having bottom button 4 rows above cast on edge, top button ½ inch [1 cm] below first front dec and rem 3 buttons spaced evenly between.

LEFT FRONT

With larger needles, cast on 49 (**51**-53) sts. Work 3 rows garter st, noting that first row is wrong side.
4th row: (Buttonhole row). Knit to last 5 sts. Cast off 2 sts. K3.
5th row: Knit, casting on 2 sts over cast off sts. Work 7 rows in garter st.
Next row: K5. *K4. Inc 1 st in next st. K2. Rep from * 5 times. Knit to end of row. 55 (**57**-59) sts.

Proceed in pat as follows:
1st row: (Right side). K2. *P1. K1. Rep from * to last 7 sts. K7.
2nd row: K7. Purl to last st. K1.
These 2 rows form pat and front garter st border.

Cont even in pat until work from beg measures 4½ ins [11.5 cm] ending with **wrong** side facing for next row

and working buttonhole to correspond to marker, as before.

Pocket border: 1st row: K7. P17. K23. Purl to last st. K1.
2nd row: K2. (P1. K1) 3 (**4**-5) times. K23. (K1. P1) 8 times. K8.
3rd to 6th rows: As 1st and 2nd rows twice.
7th row: K7. P17. Cast off 23 sts. Purl to last st. K1.
8th row: K2. (P1. K1) 3 (**4**-5) times. Pat across 23 sts from pocket lining. (K1. P1) 8 times. K8.

Keeping cont of garter st border, cont in stocking st until work from beg measures 14 ins [35.5 cm] ending with right side facing for next row and working buttonholes to correspond to markers, as before.

Armhole and front shaping: Next row: Cast off 6 (**7**-8) sts. Pat to end of row.
Work 1 row even in pat.
Next row: Work 2tog. Pat to last 10 sts. K2togtbl (front edge). K8.
Work 1 row even in pat.
Dec 1 st at armhole edge on next and every alt row 10 (**11**-10) times more, **at the same time**, dec 1 st at neck edge inside border, as before, on every following 6th row from previous dec until 28 (**28**-30) sts rem.

Cont even in pat until armhole measures 9 (9½-9½) ins [23 (**24**-24) cm] ending with right side facing for next row.

Shoulder shaping: Keeping cont of pat, cast off 7 (**7**-8) sts beg next and following alt row. Work 1 row even in pat. Cast off 7 sts.
Cont in garter st on rem 7 sts for 2½ ins [6 cm] ending with right side facing for next row. Cast off.

SLEEVES

With smaller needles, cast on 47 sts.
1st row: (Right side). K1. *P1. K1. Rep from * to end of row.
2nd row: P1. *K1. P1. Rep from * to end of row.
Rep these 2 rows (K1. P1) ribbing for 7 ins [18 cm] ending on a 2nd row and inc 8 sts evenly across last row. 55 sts.

Change to larger needles and proceed in pat as given for Back inc 1 st each end of needle on 7th and every following 6th row to 83 (**87**-87) sts.

Cont even in pat until sleeve from beg measures 21 ins [53.5 cm], allowing for 3 ins [7.5 cm] cuff turnback, ending with right side facing for next row.

Shape top: Cast off 2 sts beg next 2 rows. Keeping cont of pat, dec 1 st each end of needle on next and every alt row until 23 sts rem. Cast off.

FINISHING

Pin garment pieces to measurements. Cover with a damp cloth and leave to dry.

Sew shoulder, side and sleeve seams. Sew in sleeves. Sew cast off sts of neckband tog and placing this seam at center back neck sew in position to back neck edge.
Sew pocket linings in position on wrong side. Sew buttons to correspond to buttonholes. ▲

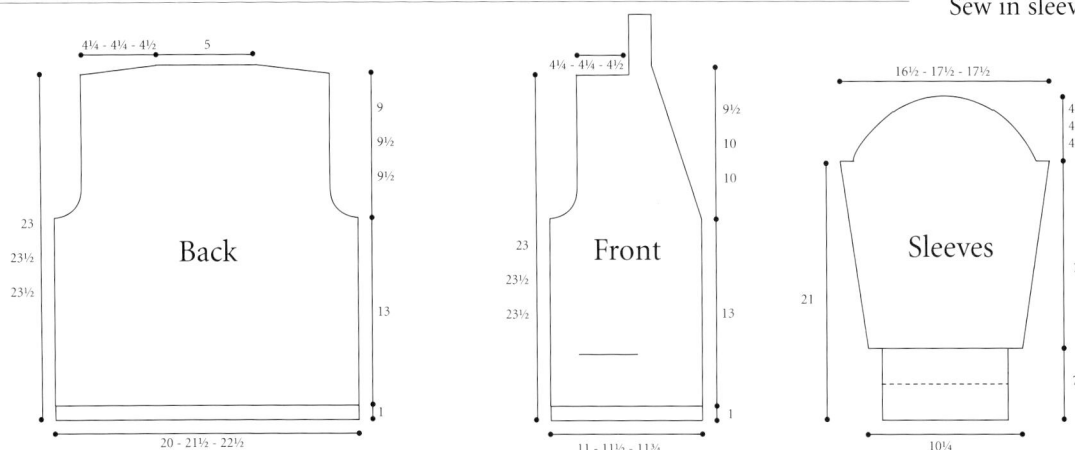

Back

4¼ - 4¼ - 4½   5
9
9½
9½
23
23½
23½
13
20 - 21½ - 22½

Front

4¼ - 4¼ - 4½
9½
10
10
23
23½
23½
13
1
11 - 11½ - 11¾

Sleeves

16½ - 17½ - 17½
4¼
4½
4½
14
21
7
10¼

SNOW TRAIN AND ACCESSORIES

1940s *Beehive*

as shown on page 11

SNOW TRAIN

SIZES

Bust measurement

Petite	29 ins	[73.5 cm]
Small	31 "	[78.5 "]
Medium	33 "	[84 "]

Finished bust

Petite	30 ins	[76 cm]
Small	32 "	[81 "]
Medium	34 "	[86 "]

MATERIALS

Patons Classic Merino Wool (100 g)

Size	P	S	M	
216	4	5	5	balls

Sizes 3¾ mm (U.S. 5) and 4½ mm (U.S. 7) knitting needles **or size needed to obtain tension**. One separating zipper.

TENSION

20 sts and 26 rows = 4 ins [10 cm] with larger needles in stocking st.

INSTRUCTIONS SWEATER

The instructions are written for smallest size. If changes are necessary for larger sizes the instructions will be written thus ( ).

BACK

With smaller needles cast on 65 (**73**-73) sts.
1st row: (Right side). *K1. P1. (K1. P1) in next st. P1. Rep from * to last st. K1.
2nd row: K1. *K1. P2tog. K1. P1. Rep from * to last 5 sts. K1. P2tog. K2.
Rep these 2 rows rib pat for 3½ ins [9 cm] ending on a 2nd row.
Next row: (Right side). K2 (**5**-5). *Inc 1 st in next st. K4 (**5**-5). Rep from * to last 3 (**2**-2) sts. (Inc 1 st in next st) 1 (**0**-0) time. K2. 78 (**84**-84) sts.
Next row: Knit.

Change to larger needles and proceed in pat as follows:
1st row: (Right side). *K3. P3. Rep from * to end of row.
2nd and 3rd rows: As 1st row.
4th row: Knit.
5th, 6th and 7th rows: *P3. K3. Rep from * to end of row.
8th row: Knit.
These 8 rows form check pat.

Cont even in check pat until work from beg measures 13 ins [33 cm] ending with right side facing for next row.

Armhole shaping: Keeping cont of pat, cast off 3 sts beg next 2 rows.
Dec 1 st at each end of needle on next and every alt row until there are 60 (**66**-66) sts.

Cont even in pat until armhole measures 7½ (**7½**-8) ins [19 (**19**-20.5) cm] ending with right side facing for next row.

Shoulder shaping: Cast off 6 (**7**-7) sts beg next 6 rows. Cast off rem 24 sts.

LEFT FRONT

With smaller needles cast on 37 (**37**-41) sts and work 3½ ins [9 cm] in rib pat as given for Back ending on a 2nd row.
Next row: (Right side). K0 (**0**-4). *K1 (**1**-0). Inc 1 st in next st. K2. Rep from * to last 13 sts. Rib pat to end of row. 43 (**43**-49) sts.
Next row: Rib pat across first 13 sts. Knit to end of row.

Change to larger needles and proceed in check pat as given for Back, keeping 13 sts at front edge in rib pat, until work from beg measures same length as Back to beg of armhole shaping ending with right side facing for next row.

Armhole shaping: Keeping cont of check pat, cast off 6 sts beg next row.
Work 1 row even in pat.
Dec 1 st at armhole edge on next and every alt row until 31 (**34**-34) sts rem.

Keeping cont of rib pat at front edge and check pat, cont even until armhole measures same length as Back to beg of shoulder shaping ending with right side facing for next row.

Shoulder shaping: Cast off 6 (**7**-7) sts beg next and following 2 alt rows.
Cont in rib pat on rem 13 sts for 2 (**2**-2½) ins [5 (**5**-6) cm] ending with right side facing for next row. Cast off.

RIGHT FRONT

With smaller needles, cast on

37 (**37**-41) sts and work 3½ ins [9 cm] in rib pat as given for Back ending on a 2nd row.
Next row: (Right side). Rib pat across 13 sts. K0 (**0**-4). *K1 (**1**-0). Inc 1 st in next st. K2. Rep from * to end of row. 43 (**43**-49) sts.
Next row: Knit to last 13 sts. Rib pat across last 13 sts.

Change to larger needles and proceed in check pat as given for Back, keeping 13 sts at front edge in rib pat, until work from beg measures same length as Back to beg of armhole shaping ending with **wrong** side facing for next row.

Armhole shaping: Keeping cont of check pat, cast off 6 sts beg next row.
Dec 1 st at armhole edge on next and every alt row until 31 (**34**-34) sts rem.

Keeping cont of rib pat at front edge and check pat, cont even until armhole measures same length as Back to beg of shoulder shaping ending with **wrong** side facing for next row.

Shoulder shaping: Cast off 6 (**7**-7) sts beg next and following 2 alt rows.
Cont in rib pat on rem 13 sts for 2 (**2**-2½) ins [5 (**5**-6) cm] ending with right side facing for next row. Cast off.

SLEEVES

With smaller needles, cast on 33 sts.
Work 2½ ins [6 cm] in rib pat as given for Back ending on a 2nd row.
Next row: (Right side). K4. *Inc 1 st in next st. K2. Rep from * to last 2 sts. K2. 42 sts.
Next row: Knit.
Change to larger needles and proceed in check pat as given for Back inc 1 st each end of needle on 5th and every following 8th row until there are 66 (**66**-72) sts, taking inc sts into check pat.

Cont even in pat until sleeve from beg measures 17 ins [43 cm] ending with right side facing for next row.

Shape top: Dec 1 st each end of needle on next and every alt row until there are 18 (**18**-20) sts. Cast off.

FINISHING

Pin garment pieces to measurements. Cover with a damp cloth and leave to dry.

Sew shoulder, side and sleeve seams. Sew in sleeves. Sew ribbed border across back neck. Sew ends tog. Sew zipper in position under front border.

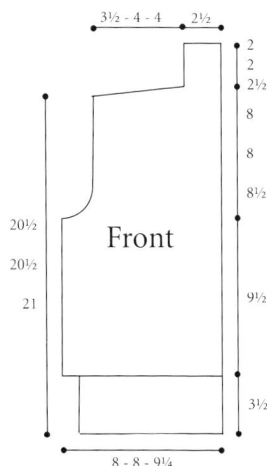

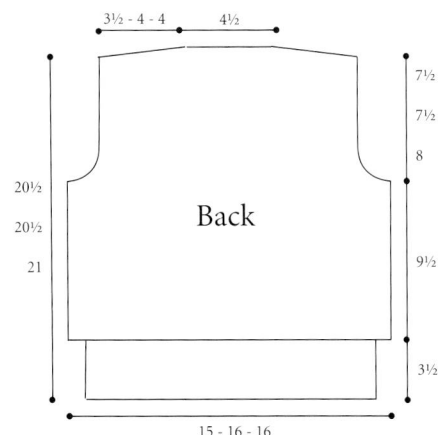

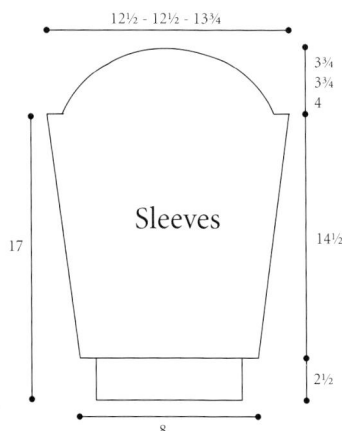

Front diagram:
3½ - 4 - 4   2½
2
2
2½
8
8
8½
20½
20½
Front
21
9½
3½
8 - 8 - 9¼

Back diagram:
3½ - 4 - 4   4½
7½
7½
8
20½
20½
Back
21
9½
3½
15 - 16 - 16

Sleeves diagram:
12½ - 12½ - 13¾
3¾
3¾
4
17
Sleeves
14½
2½
8

Chart I

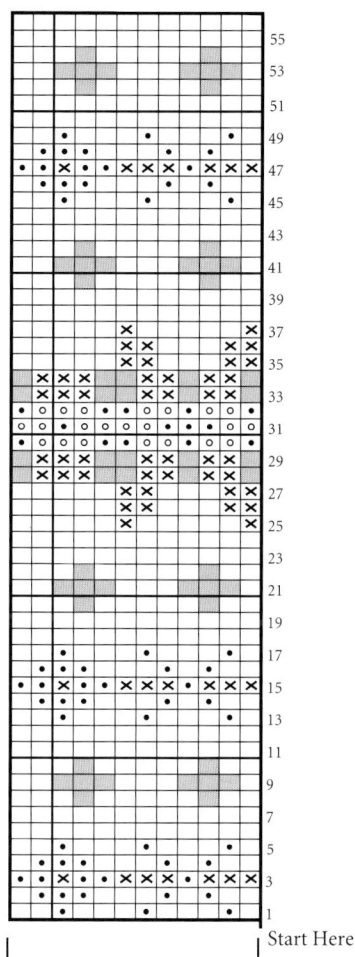

12 st rep

Key

☐ = MC
⊠ = Contrast A
▨ = Contrast B
⊡ = Contrast C
⊙ = Contrast D

Chart II

Earflaps: (Make 2)
With A, cast on 40 sts. Divide sts into 12, 16 and 12 on 3 needles. Join in round, placing a marker on first st. Knit 2 ins [5 cm].
Slip 2 sts from first and third needles onto second needle. Sts are now divided 10, 20 and 10 on 3 needles.

Proceed as follows:
1st round: *1st needle:* Knit to last 3 sts. K2tog. K1. **2nd needle:** K1. Sl1. K1. psso. Knit to last 3 sts. K2tog. K1. **3rd needle:** K1. Sl1. K1. psso. Knit to end of needle.
2nd round: Knit.
Rep last 2 rounds to 12 sts divided as 3, 6 and 3 on 3 needles.
Knit 6½ ins [16.5 cm] even. Knit sts from first needle onto 3rd needle. Break yarn, leaving an end 8 ins [20.5 cm] long. Graft 2 sets of 6 sts tog. (See Helpful Hints).

Sew cast on edge of Earflap tog and sew Earflaps to Headband as illustrated.
Tie ends of Earflaps as illustrated.

INSTRUCTIONS SCARF

With MC, cast on 108 sts. Divide sts into 36, 36 and 36 on 3 needles. Join in round. Knit 4 rounds.

Work 8th to 39th rows of Chart I 10 times, noting the 12 st rep will be worked 9 times, then work 8th to 22nd rows once.

With MC, knit 4 rounds. Cast off. Sew ends closed.

Fringe: Cut 5 ins [12.5 cm] lengths of A. Taking 3 strands tog knot into fringe across cast on and cast off edges. (See Helpful Hints).

INSTRUCTIONS MITTS

With A, cast on 52 sts. Divide sts into 16, 20 and 16 on 3 needles. Join in round.
1st round: *K2. P2. Rep from * around. Work 3½ ins [9 cm] in (K2. P2) ribbing.
Next round *K5. Inc 1 st in next st. Rep from * to last 4 sts. K4. 60 sts. Break A.
Next round: With MC, knit to last 5 sts. Slip last 5 sts onto a safety pin. **Turn.**
Next round: Work across 55 sts, K1. Purl to last st. K1.

Working back and forth on 3 needles, proceed as follows:
Work Chart II to end of chart, reading **knit** rows from **right** to left and **purl** rows from **left** to right.
Next row: With MC, K1. Purl to last st. K1.

Next row: With MC, knit across 3 needles, casting on 5 sts at end of 3rd needle. Divide sts into 20, 20 and 20 on 3 needles. Join in round. 60 sts.
Next round: Knit.

Proceed as follows:
Work 20th to 42nd rows of Chart I reading rows from **right** to left noting 12 st rep will be worked 5 times.

Next round: With MC, knit.

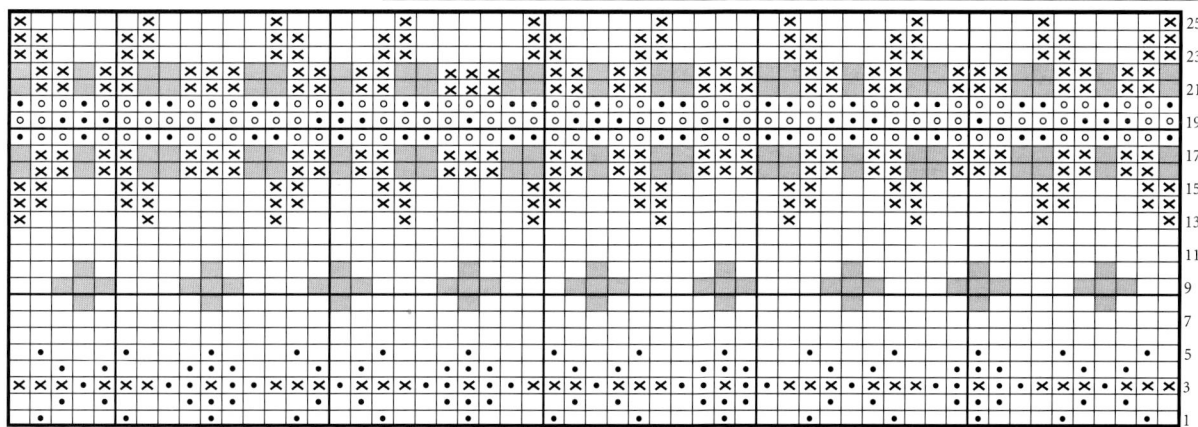

Start Here

Next round: *K3. K2tog. Rep from * around. 48 sts.

Work 1st to 6th rows of Chart I noting 12 st rep will work 4 times.

Next round: With MC, *K2. K2tog. Rep from * around. 36 sts. Break MC.

With A, knit 5 rounds even.

Next round: *K1. K2tog. Rep from * around. 24 sts.

Knit 5 rounds even.

Next round: *K2tog. Rep from * around. 12 sts. Break A.

Thread yarn through rem sts. Draw up and fasten securely.

Thumb gusset and Thumb: Slip 5 sts from safety pin onto needle. With right side of work facing, join A.

Working back and forth, proceed as follows:

1st and 3rd rows: (K1. P1) twice. K1.
2nd and 4th rows: K2. P1. K2.
5th row: K1. P1 (seam st). Knit into front, back and front of next st. P1 (seam st). K1. 7 sts.
6th row: K2. P3. K2.
7th row: K1. P1. K3. P1. K1.
8th row: K2. P3. K2.
9th row: K1. P1. Inc 1 st in each of next 2 sts. K1. P1. K1. 9 sts.
10th and alt rows: K2. Purl to last 2 sts. K2.
11th row: K1. P1. K5. P1. K1.
13th row: K1. P1. Inc 1 st in next st. K2. Inc 1 st in next st. K1. P1. K1. 11 sts.
15th row: K1. P1. K7. P1. K1.
17th row: K1. P1. Inc 1 st in next st. K4. Inc 1 st in next st. K1. P1. K1. 13 sts.

Cont increasing in this manner, every 4th row, until there are 17 sts.

Next row: K2. Purl to last 2 sts. K2.
Next row: Knit, casting on 5 sts at end of row. 22 sts. Divide sts into 6, 6 and 10 on 3 needles. Join in round.

Proceed as follows:

1st round: Knit to last 4 sts. (K2tog) twice. 20 sts.
2nd round: As 1st round. 18 sts.
Rearrange sts into 6, 6 and 6 on 3 needles. Knit 2¼ ins [5.5 cm] even.
Next round: (K2tog) 9 times. Break A. Thread yarn through rem sts. Draw up and fasten securely.

LEFT MITT

Work as given for Right Mitt. ♠

CABLE AND POPCORN

1950s

Patons Beehive
for perfect knitting

as shown on page 12

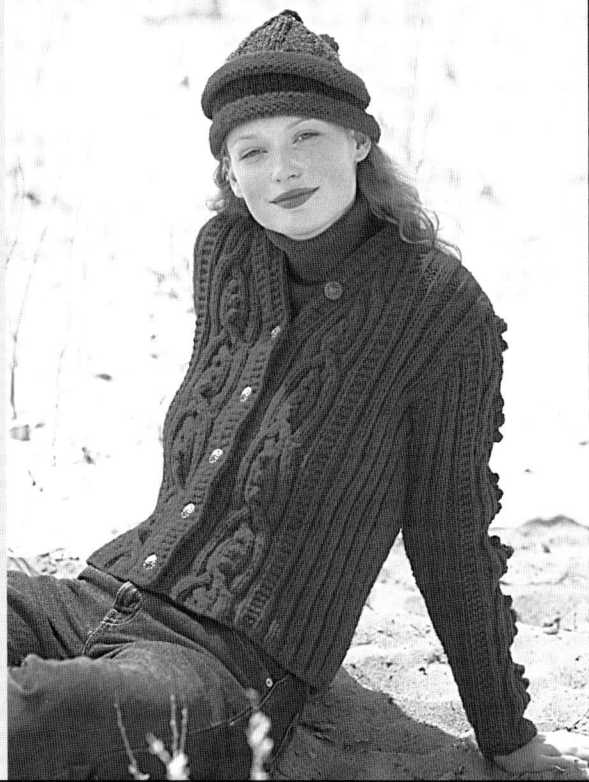

SIZES

Bust measurement

8	32	ins	[81 cm]
10	34	"	[86 "]
12	36	"	[91 "]

Finished bust

8	35	ins	[89 cm]
10	37	"	[94 "]
12	39	"	[99 "]

MATERIALS

Patons Shetland Chunky (50 g)

Size	8	10	12	
2272	11	12	13	balls

Size 6 mm (U.S. 10) knitting needles **or size needed to obtain tension**. One cable needle. 6 buttons.

TENSION

15 sts and 20 rows = 4 ins [10 cm] in stocking st.

STITCH GLOSSARY

T6F = slip next 2 sts onto a cable needle and leave at front of work. K2. P2, then K2 from cable needle.

T6B = slip next 4 sts onto a cable needle and leave at back of work. K2, then P2. K2 from cable needle.

MB = (Make bobble). [(P1. K1) twice] all in next st. **Turn**. K4. **Turn**. P4. Slip 2nd, 3rd and 4th sts over first st.

INSTRUCTIONS

The instructions are written for smallest size. If changes are necessary for larger sizes the instructions will be written thus ( ).

Panel Pat (worked over 26 sts)
1st row: (Right side). K4. P2. K2. P2. T6F. P2. K2. P2. K4.
2nd and alt rows: (P1. K2) twice. (P2. K2) 4 times. P1. K2. P1.
3rd row: K4. (P2. K2) 4 times. P2. K4.
5th row: K4. P2. T6F. P2. T6B. P2. K4.
7th row: As 3rd row.
9th row: As 1st row.
11th row: K4. (P2. K2) twice. MB. P1. (K2. P2) twice. K4.
13th row: As 3rd row.
15th row: As 11th row.
17th row: As 3rd row.
19th row: As 11th row.
20th row: As 2nd row.
These 20 rows form Panel Pat.

50

BACK

Cast on 68 (**76**-76) sts.
1st row: (Right side). K3. P2. (K2. P2) 4 (**5**-5) times. K4. (P2. K2) 4 times. P2. K4. *P2. K2. Rep from * to last st. K1.
2nd row: K1. (P2. K2) 5 (**6**-6) times. (P1. K2) twice. (P2. K2) 4 times. P1. K2. P1. *K2. P2. Rep from * to last st. K1.
3rd row: K3. P2. (K2. P2) 4 (**5**-5) times. Work 1st row of panel pat. *P2. K2. Rep from * to last st. K1.
4th row: K1. (P2. K2) 5 (**6**-6) times. Work 2nd row of panel pat. *K2. P2. Rep from * to last st. K1.
These 4 rows form side rib pat. Panel pat is now in position.

Cont in rib pat, working appropriate rows of panel pat, until work from beg measures 13½ ins [34.5 cm] ending with right side facing for next row.

Armhole shaping: Keeping cont of pat, cast off 1 (**3**-1) st(s) beg next 2 rows. Dec 1 st at each end of needle on next and every alt row until there are 60 (**60**-64) sts.

Cont even in pat until armhole measures 7½ (**7½**-8) ins [19 (**19**-20.5) cm] ending with right side facing for next row.

Shoulder shaping: Keeping cont of pat, cast off 6 sts beg next 4 rows, then 7 (**7**-8) sts beg following 2 rows. Cast off rem 22 (**22**-24) sts.

LEFT FRONT

Cast on 55 (**55**-59) sts.

1st row: (Right side). K3. P2. (K2. P2) 4 (**4**-5) times. K4. (P2. K2) 4 times. P2. K12.
2nd row: K2. (P1. K2) 4 times. (P2. K2) 4 times. P1. K2. P1. *K2. P2. Rep from * to last st. K1.
3rd row: K3. P2. (K2. P2) 4 (**4**-5) times. Work 1st row of panel pat. K8 (front edge).
4th row: K2. (P1. K2) twice. Work 2nd row of panel pat. *K2. P2. Rep from * to last st. K1.
These 4 rows form side rib and front edge pat. Panel pat is now in position.

Cont in pat, working appropriate rows of panel pat until work from beg measures same length as Back to beg of armhole shaping ending with right side facing for next row.

Armhole shaping: Keeping cont of pat, cast off 6 (**4**-6) sts beg next row. Work 1 row even in pat.
Dec 1 st at armhole edge on next and every alt row until there are 43 (**47**-49) sts.

Work 9 rows even in pat.

Front shaping: 1st row: (Right side). Pat to last 14 sts. P2tog. K12.
2nd row: (K2. P1) 4 times. K2tog. Pat to end of row.
Rep these 2 rows until 30 (**30**-31) sts rem.

Cont even in pat until work from beg measure same length as Back to beg of shoulder shaping, ending with right side facing for next row.

Shoulder shaping: Keeping cont of pat cast off 6 sts beg next and following alt row. Work 1 row even. Cast off 7 (**7**-8) sts. Cont even in pat on rem 11 sts for 2 (**2½**-2½) ins [5 (**6**-6) cm] to sew across of back neck edge. Cast off.

Place button markers on front band having first button 4 rows above cast on edge and rem 5 buttons spaced 2½ ins [6 cm] apart.

RIGHT FRONT

Cast on 55 (**55**-59) sts.

1st row: (Right side). K12. (P2. K2) 4 times. P2. K4. *P2. K2. Rep from * to last st. K1.
2nd row: K1. (P2. K2) 5 (**5**-6) times. (P1. K2) twice. (P2. K2) 4 times. (P1. K2) 4 times.

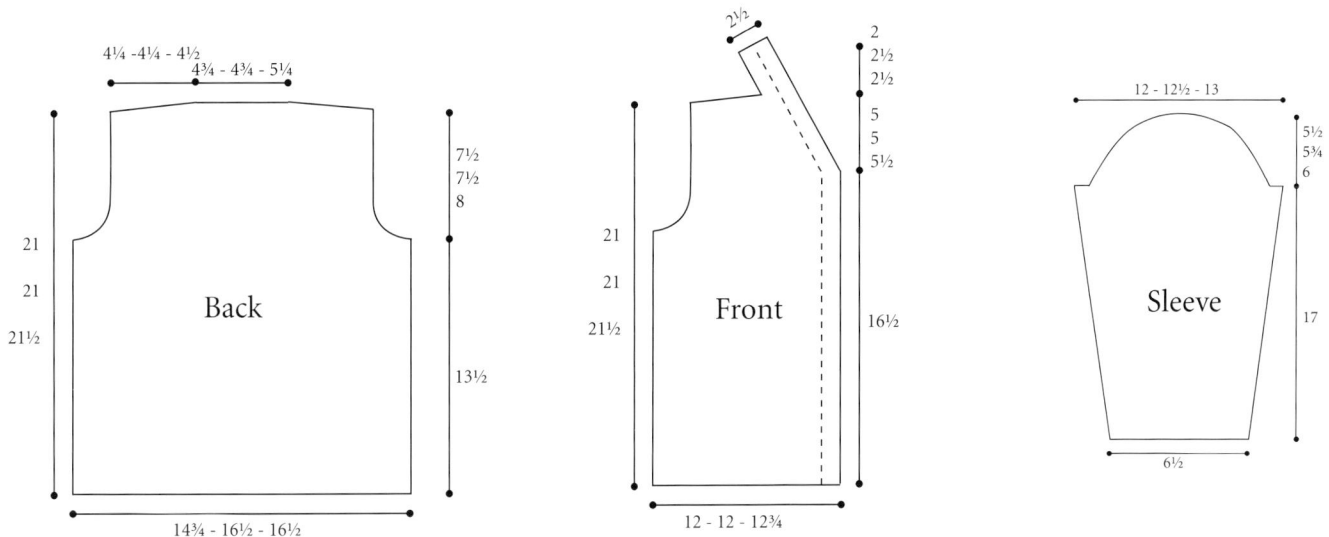

4¼ -4¼ - 4½
4¾ - 4¾ - 5¼

7½
7½
8

21
21
21½

Back

13½

14¾ - 16½ - 16½

2½

2
2½
2½

5
5
5½

21
21
21½

Front

16½

12 - 12 - 12¾

12 - 12½ - 13

5½
5¾
6

Sleeve

17

6½

51

3rd row: K8 (front edge). Work 1st row of panel pat. *P2. K2. Rep from * to last st. K1.

4th row: K1. (P2. K2) 5 (**5**-6) times. Work 2nd row of panel pat. K2. (P1. K2) twice.

These 4 rows form side rib and front edge pat. Panel pat is now in position.

Next row: (Buttonhole row). K2. yfwd. K2tog (buttonhole in facing). K4. yfwd. K2tog (buttonhole in front). K2. (P2. K2) 4 times. P2. K4. *P2. K2. Rep from * to last st. K1.

Cont in pat, working appropriate rows of panel pat and working buttonholes as before to correspond to markers on Left Front, until work from beg measures same length as Back to beg of armhole shaping ending with **wrong** side facing for next row.

Armhole shaping: Keeping cont of pat, cast off 6 (**4**-6) sts beg next row. Dec 1 st at armhole edge on next and every alt row until there are 43 (**47**-49) sts.
Work 9 rows even in pat.

Front shaping: 1st row: (Right side). K12. P2togtbl. Pat to end of row.
2nd row: Pat to last 14 sts. Sl1. K1. psso. (P1. K2) 4 times.
Rep these 2 rows until 30 (**30**-31) sts rem.

Cont even in pat until work from beg measure same length as Back to beg of shoulder shaping, ending with **wrong** side facing for next row.

Shoulder shaping: Keeping cont of pat cast off 6 sts beg next and following alt row. Work 1 row even. Cast off 7 (**7**-8) sts.
Cont even in pat on rem 11 sts for 2 (**2½**-2½) ins [5 (6-6) cm] to sew across of back neck edge. Cast off.

SLEEVES

Cast on 30 sts.
1st row: (Right side). K1. P1. K4. (P2. K2) 4 times. P2. K4. P1. K1.
2nd row: K2. (P1. K2) twice. (P2. K2) 4 times. (P1. K2) twice.

3rd row: K1. P1. Work 1st row of panel pat. P1. K1.
4th row: K2. Work 2nd row of panel pat. K2.
These 4 rows form side rib pat. Panel pat is now in position.

Cont in pat, inc 1 st each end of needle on next and every following 6th row until there are 48 (**46**-44) sts, then every following 4th row until there are 56 (**58**-60) sts, taking inc sts into (K2. P2) rib pat.

Cont even in pat until Sleeve from beg measures 17 ins [43 cm] ending with right side facing for next row.

Shape top: Keeping cont of pat, cast off 2 sts beg next 2 rows, then dec 1 st at each end of needle on next and every alt row until there are 36 sts, then on every row until there are 18 sts. Cast off.

FINISHING

Pin garment pieces to measurements. Cover with a damp cloth and leave to dry.

Sew shoulder side and sleeve seams. Sew in sleeves. Sew cast off sts of neckband tog and placing this seam at center back neck, sew in position to back neck edge. Turn in a 5 st facing at each front edge and sew in position being careful to lineup buttonholes on Right Front facing and front edge. Stitch around buttonholes through all thicknesses. Sew on buttons to correspond to buttonholes. ♠

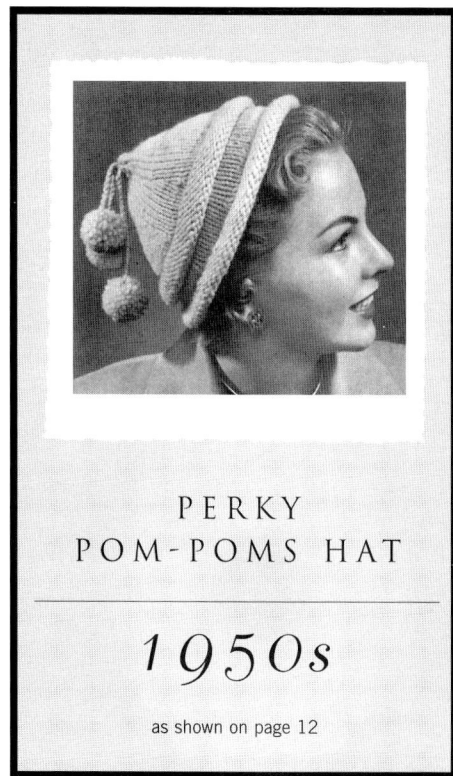

PERKY POM-POMS HAT

1950s

as shown on page 12

SIZE

To fit average woman

MATERIALS

Patons Shetland Chunky (50 g)
Main Color (MC) (2096)   1   ball
Contrast A (2272)   1   ball

Size 6 mm (U.S. 10) knitting needles **or size needed to obtain tension.**

TENSION

15 sts and 20 rows = 4 ins [10 cm] in stocking st.

INSTRUCTIONS

With A, cast on 73 sts.
1st row: (Wrong side). Knit.
2nd row: Purl.
Rep last 2 rows 3 times more.
9th row: (Tuck row). Place cast on st below first st onto left hand needle and knit it tog with first st. *Place cast on st below next st onto left hand needle and knit it tog with next st. Rep from * to end of row.
With MC, beg with a knit row, work 10 rows stocking st.
Next row: (Right side). With A, knit.
Next row: Knit.
Next row: Purl.

Rep last 2 rows 3 times more.
Next row: (Wrong side. Tuck row). Place horizontal bar of st 9 rows below first st onto left hand needle and knit it tog with first st. *Place horizontal bar of st 9 rows below next st onto left hand needle and knit it tog with next st. Rep from * to end of row.
With MC, beg with a knit row, work 3 rows stocking st.

Shape top: Next row: K1. *K2tog. K6. Rep from * to end of row. 64 sts. Work 3 rows even.
Next row: K1. *K2tog. K5. Rep from * to end of row. 55 sts.
Work 3 rows even.
Next row: K1. *K2tog. K4. Rep from * to end of row. 46 sts.
Work 1 row even.
Next row: K1. *K2tog. K3. Rep from * to end of row. 37 sts.
Work 1 row even.
Next row: K1. *K2tog. K2. Rep from * to end of row. 28 sts.
Work 1 row even.
Next row: K1. *K2tog. K1. Rep from * to end of row. 19 sts.
Work 1 row even.
Next row: K1. *K2tog. Rep from * to end of row. 10 sts. Break yarn leaving a long end. Draw end through rem sts and fasten securely. Sew center back seam. Make 2 twisted cords 3½ ins [9 cm] long and one twisted cord 5 ins [12.5 cm] long. Sew one pom-pom to each twisted cord. Attach cords to center of Hat.

Pom-poms: Wind A around 2 fingers approx 45 times. Remove from fingers and tie tightly in center. Cut through each side of loops. Trim to a smooth round shape.

Twisted cord: (Make 3). Cut 2 strands of yarn 12 ins [30.5 cm] long. With both strands tog hold one end and with someone holding other end, twist strands to the right until they begin to curl. Fold the 2 ends tog and tie in a knot so they will not unravel. The strands will now twist themselves together. Adjust lengths as indicated above. ●

MAN'S SWEATER COAT

1950s

PATONS
Beehive
for perfect knitting

as shown on page 12

SIZES

Bust/chest measurement

Small	34–36 ins	[86–91 cm]
Medium	38–40 "	[97–102 "]
Large	42 "	[107 "]

Finished bust/chest

Small	43½ ins	[110.5 cm]
Medium	45½ "	[115.5 "]
Large	47½ "	[120 "]

MATERIALS

Patons Shetland Chunky (50 g)

Size	S	M	L	
2118	15	16	17	balls

Sizes 5 mm (U.S. 8) and 6 mm (U.S. 10) knitting needles **or size needed to obtain tension.** One cable needle. 2 st holders. 8 buttons.

TENSION

15 sts and 20 rows = 4 ins [10 cm] with larger needles in stocking st.

STITCH GLOSSARY

C4B = slip next 2 sts onto a cable needle and leave at back of work. K2, then K2 from cable needle.
C4F = slip next 2 sts onto a cable needle and leave at front of work. K2, then K2 from cable needle.

INSTRUCTIONS

The instructions are written for smallest size. If changes are necessary for larger sizes the instructions will be written thus ( ).

Panel Pat *(worked over 23 sts)*
1st row: (Right side). P1. K4. P1. K11. P1. K4. P1.
2nd row: K1. P4. K1. P11. K1. P4. K1.
3rd row: P1. C4B. (P1. K5) twice. P1. C4F. P1.
4th row: K1. P4. (K1. P5) twice. K1. P4. K1.
5th row: (P1. K4) twice. P1. K1. P1. (K4. P1) twice.
6th row: (K1. P4) twice. K1. P1. K1. (P4. K1) twice.
7th row: P1. C4B. P1. K3. (P1. K1) twice. P1. K3. P1. C4F. P1.
8th row: K1. P4. K1. P3. (K1. P1) twice. K1. P3. K1. P4. K1.
9th row: P1. K4. P1. K2. (P1. K1) 3 times. P1. K2. P1. K4. P1.
10th row: K1. P4. K1. P2. (K1. P1) 3 times. K1. P2. K1. P4. K1.
11th row: P1. C4B. (P1. K1) 6 times. P1. C4F. P1.
12th row: K1. P4. (K1. P1) 6 times. K1. P4. K1.
13th and 14th rows: As 9th and 10th rows.
15th and 16th rows: As 7th and 8th rows.
17th and 18th rows: As 5th and 6th rows.

19th and 20th rows: As 3rd and 4th rows. These 20 rows form panel pat.

BACK

With smaller needles, cast on 77 (**81**-85) sts.
1st row: (Right side). K1. *P1. K1. Rep from * to end of row.
2nd row: P1. *K1. P1. Rep from * to end of row.
Rep these 2 rows (K1. P1) 6 times more. 14 rows in all.

Change to larger needles and proceed in pat as follows:
1st row: (Right side). K27 (**29**-31). Work 1st row panel pat. Knit to end of row.
2nd row: P27 (**29**-31). Work 2nd row panel pat. Purl to end of row.
Panel pat is now in position.

Cont working appropriate rows panel pat until work from beg measures 17½ (**18**-18½) ins [44.5 (**45.5**-47) cm] ending with right side facing for next row.

Armhole shaping: Keeping cont of pat, cast off 3 (**4**-4) sts beg next 2 rows.
Dec 1 st each end of needle on next and following alt rows until there are 61 (**63**-65) sts.

Cont even in pat until armhole measures 9½ (**10**-10) ins [24 (**25.5**-25.5) cm] ending with right side facing for next row.

Shoulder shaping: Keeping cont of pat, cast off 7 sts beg next 4 rows, then 7 (**7**-8) sts beg following 2 rows. Cast off rem 19 (**21**-21) sts.

Pocket linings (Make 2)
With larger needles cast on 19 sts and work 20 rows in stocking st.
Proceed as follows:
1st row: (Right side). K3. P1. (K5. P1) twice. K3.
2nd row: P3. K1. (P5. K1) twice. P3.
3rd row: K3. P1. K4. P1. K1. P1. K4. P1. K3.
4th row: P3. K1. P4. K1. P1. K1. P4. K1. P3.
5th row: (K3. P1) twice. K1. P1. K1. (P1. K3) twice.
6th row: (P3. K1) twice. P1. K1. P1. (K1. P3) twice.
Break yarn. Leave these sts on a st holder.

RIGHT FRONT

With smaller needles, cast on 44 (**46**-48) sts.
1st row: (Right side). *K1. P1. Rep from * to last 2 sts. K2.
2nd row: *K1. P1. Rep from * to end of row.
3rd row: K2. P1. K1. P1. K2. *P1. K1. Rep from * to last st. K1.
4th row: *K1. P1. Rep from * to last 8 sts. K1. P2. (K1. P1) twice. P1.
These 4 rows form ribbing and 6 sts of Irish moss st pat for front band.
Rep last 4 rows twice more, then 1st and 2nd rows once. 14 rows in all.

Change to larger needles and proceed in pat as follows:
1st row: (Right side). K2. P1. K1. P1. K6 (**8**-8). Work 1st row of panel pat. K10 (**10**-12).
2nd row: P10 (**10**-12). Work 2nd row of panel pat. P6 (**8**-8). (K1. P1) twice. P1. Panel pat is now in position.

Work a further 20 rows of panel pat, thus ending on a 2nd row of panel pat and working Irish moss st pat for 6 sts of front band, as before.

Pocket Edging: 1st row: (Right side). Pat across 11 (**13**-13) sts. P1. K2. (P1. K1) 8 times. P1. K2. P1. Knit to end of row.
2nd row: P10 (**10**-12). K1. P2. (K1. P1) 8 times. K1. P2. K1. Pat to end of row.
3rd and 4th rows: As 1st and 2nd rows.
5th row: As 1st row.
6th row: P10 (**10**-12). K1. P1. Cast off next 19 sts in ribbing. P1. K1. Pat to end of row.
7th row: Pat across 11 (**13**-13) sts. P1. K1. Work [K3. P1. K2. (P1. K1) 3 times. P1. K2. P1. K3] across 19 sts of pocket lining. K1. P1. Knit to end of row.

Beg on a 10th row of panel pat, cont even until work from beg measures same length as Back to beg of armhole shaping, ending with **wrong** side facing for next row.

Armhole shaping: Keeping cont of pat, cast off 3 (**4**-4) sts beg next row.
Dec 1 st at armhole edge on next and following alt rows until there are 36 (**37**-38) sts.

Cont even in pat until armhole measures 7 (**7½**-7½) ins [18 (**19**-19) cm] ending with right side facing for next row.

Neck shaping: Next row: Cast off 9 sts (neck edge). Pat to end of row. Dec 1 st at neck edge on next 6 (**7**-7) rows. 21 (**21**-22) sts.

Cont even in pat until

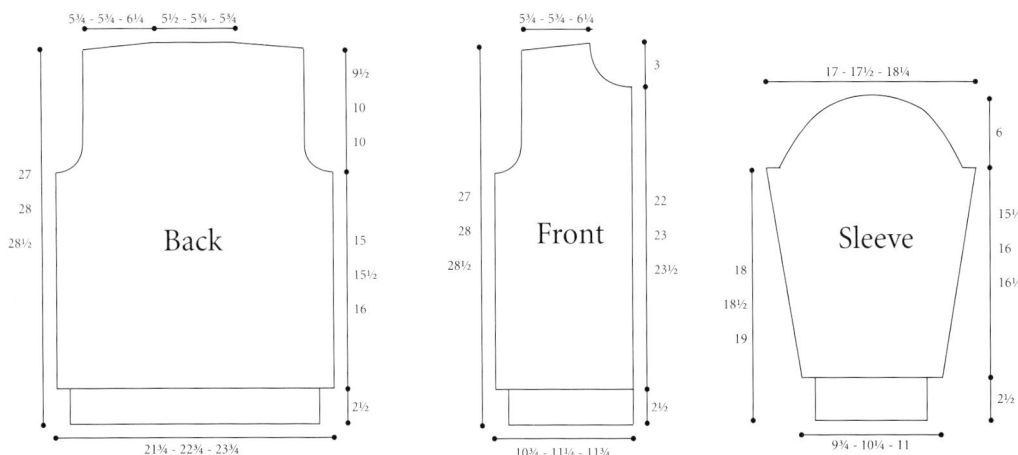

Back: 5¾ - 5¾ - 6¼   5½ - 5¾ - 5¾
9½ 10 10 27 28 28½ 15 15½ 16 2½
21¾ - 22¾ - 23¾

Front: 5¾ - 5¾ - 6¼
3 27 28 28½ 22 23 23½ 2½
10¾ - 11¼ - 11¾

Sleeve: 17 - 17½ - 18¼
6 18 18½ 19 15½ 16 16½ 2½
9¾ - 10¼ - 11

armhole measures same length as back to beg of shoulder shaping ending with **wrong** side facing for next row.

Shoulder shaping: Keeping cont of pat, cast off 7 sts beg next and following alt row. Work 1 row even. Cast off rem 7 (**7**-8) sts.

Place button markers on front band having first button 6 rows above cast on edge, top button 2 rows below cast off edge at neck and rem 6 buttons spaced evenly between.

LEFT FRONT

With smaller needles, cast on 44 (**46**-48) sts.
1st row: (Right side). K2. *P1. K1. Rep from * to end of row.
2nd row: *P1. K1. Rep from * to end of row.
3rd row: K2. *P1. K1. Rep from * to last 8 sts. P1. K2. (P1. K1) twice. K1.
4th row: P2. K1. P1. K1. P2. K1. *P1. K1. Rep from * to end of row.
These 4 rows form ribbing and 6 sts of Irish moss st pat for front band.
Work a further 2 rows.
7th row: (Buttonhole row). Pat to last 5 sts. Cast off 2 sts. Pat to end of row.
8th row: Pat across 3 sts. Cast on 2 sts. Pat to end of row.
Work a further 6 rows in ribbing and Irish moss st pat.

Change to larger needles and proceed in pat as follows:
1st row: (Right side). K10 (**10**-12). Work 1st row of panel pat. K6 (**8**-8). (P1. K1) twice. K1.
2nd row: P2. K1. P1. K1. P6 (**8**-8). Work 2nd row of panel pat. P10 (**10**-12). Panel pat is now in position.

Working buttonholes, as before, to correspond to button markers on Right Front, work a further 20 rows of panel pat, thus ending on a 2nd row of panel pat and working Irish moss st pat for 6 sts of front band, as before.

Pocket Edging: 1st row: (Right side). K10 (**10**-12). P1. K2. (P1. K1) 8 times. P1. K2. P1. Pat to end of row.
2nd row: Pat across 11 (**13**-13) sts. K1. P2. (K1. P1) 8 times. K1. P2. K1. Purl to end of row.
3rd and 4th rows: As 1st and 2nd rows.
5th row: As 1st row.
6th row: Pat across 11 (**13**-13) sts. K1. P1. Cast off next 19 sts in pat. P1. K1. Purl to end of row.
7th row: K10 (**10**-12). P1. K1. Work [K3. P1. K2. (P1. K1) 3 times. P1. K2. P1. K3] across 19 sts of Pocket Lining. K1. P1. Pat to end of row.

Beg on a 10th row of panel pat, cont even until work from beg measures same length as Back to beg of armhole shaping, ending with right side facing for next row.

Armhole shaping: Keeping cont of pat, cast off 3 (**4**-4) sts beg next row.
Work 1 row even in pat.
Dec 1 st at armhole edge on next and following alt rows until there are 36 (**37**-38) sts.
Cont even in pat until armhole measures 7 (7½-7½) ins [18 (**19**-19) cm] ending with right side facing for next row, ending with **wrong** side facing for next row.

Neck shaping: Next row: Pat across 6 sts. Leave these sts on a st holder. Cast off next 3 sts (neck edge). Pat to end of row. Dec 1 st at neck edge on next 6 (**7**-7) rows. 21 (**21**-22) sts.

Cont even in pat until armhole measures same length as back to beg of shoulder shaping ending with right side facing for next row.

Shoulder shaping: Keeping cont of pat, cast off 7 sts beg next and following alt row. Work 1 row even. Cast off rem 7 (**7**-8) sts.

COLLAR

With **wrong** side of work facing and larger needles, join yarn to 6 sts on

Left Front st holder.
1st row: Inc 1 st in first st. K1. (P1. K1) twice.
2nd row: (P1. K1) 3 times. Inc 1 st in last st.
3rd row: Inc 1 st in first st. (P1. K1) twice. P1. Inc 1 st in next st. K1 (outside edge).
4th row: (P1. K1) 4 times. P1. Inc 1 st in last st (neck edge). 11 sts.
Keeping cont of Irish moss st pat, inc 1 st at neck edge every row, **at same time**, inc 1 st at outside edge on next and every alt row until there are 23 sts.

Proceed as follows:
1st row: (P1. K1) 7 times. K9 (neck edge).
2nd row: K10. (P1. K1) 6 times. K1 (outside edge).
3rd row: P2. (K1. P1) 6 times. K9.
4th row: K9. (P1. K1) 7 times.
5th and 6th rows: As 1st and 2nd rows.
7th row: P2. (K1. P1) 6 times. **Turn.**
8th row: With yarn at back of work, slip last st on right hand needle back onto left hand needle. Bring yarn to front of work and slip this slipped st back onto right hand needle. (P1. K1) 7 times.
Rep last 8 rows 9 times more, then 1st to 6th rows once.

Next row: P1. K2tog. *P1. K1. Rep from * to last 2 sts. K2tog (neck edge).
Working all sts in Irish moss st pat, dec 1 st at neck edge on every row, **at same time**, dec 1 st at outside edge on next and every alt row, as before, until there are 7 sts.
Next row: P1. K2tog. Pass first st over 2nd st, then cast off all sts in pat.

SLEEVES

With smaller needles, cast on 35 (**37**-39) sts. Work 14 rows in ribbing as given for Back.

Change to larger needles and proceed in pat as follows:
1st row: (Right side). K6 (**7**-8). Work 1st row of panel pat. Knit to end of row.
2nd row: P6 (**7**-8). Work 2nd row of panel pat. Purl to end of row.
Panel pat is now in position.

Keeping cont of panel pat, inc 1 st each end of needle on next and following 6th rows until there are 47 (**51**-51) sts, then every following 4th row until there are 61 (**65**-67) sts, taking inc sts into stocking st.

Cont even in pat until work from beg measures 18 (**18½**-19) ins [45.5 (**47**-48) cm] ending with right side facing for next row.

Shape top: Keeping cont of pat, cast off 3 sts beg next 2 rows. Dec 1 st each end of needle on next and every alt row until there are 29 (**33**-33) sts, then on every row until there are 23 sts. Cast off in pat.

FINISHING

Pin garment pieces to measurements. Cover with a damp cloth leaving to dry. Sew side, shoulder and sleeve seams. Sew Collar to neck edge. Sew pocket linings in position to wrong side. Sew in Sleeves. Sew buttons to correspond to buttonholes. If desired, sew twill tape along shoulder seams and across back neck edge to prevent stretching with wear. ♠

CARRIAGE SET

1950s

PATONS
Beehive
for perfect knitting

as shown on page 13

SIZES

Layette Set: To fit chest measurement

6–9 mos	18–20 ins [45.5–51 cm]

Toy Horse:

Approx 8 ins [20.5 cm] high.

MATERIALS

Layette: Patons Kroy 4 ply (50 g)
Coat

Main Color (MC) (436)	3	**balls**
Contrast A (437)	1	**ball**
Contrast B (438)	1	**ball**

Leggings: Patons Kroy 4 ply (50 g)

437	3	**balls**

Mitts: Patons Kroy 4 ply (50 g)

Contrast A (437)	1	**ball**
Contrast B (438)	1	**ball**

Helmet: Patons Kroy 4 ply (50 g)

Main Color (MC) (436)	1	**ball**
Contrast A (437)	1	**ball**

Toy Horse: Patons Look at Me! (50 g)

Main Color (MC) (6365)	1	**ball**
Contrast A (6367)	1	**ball**

Layette Set: Sizes 2¾ mm (U.S. 2) and 3¼ mm (U.S. 3) knitting needles **or size needed to obtain tension**. Cable needle. 5 buttons for Coat. Length of ¾ inch [2 cm] wide elastic for Leggings.

Toy Horse: Size 3¾ mm (U.S. 5) knitting needles **or size needed to obtain tension**. Size 3.50 mm (U.S. E or 4) crochet hook. Stuffing.

TENSION

Layette Set: 28 sts and 36 rows = 4 ins [10 cm] in stocking st with larger needles.

Toy Horse: 21 sts and 38 rows = 4 ins [10 cm] in garter st.

STITCH GLOSSARY

C6B = slip next 3 sts onto a cable needle and leave at back of work. K3, then K3 from cable needle.

Sl1wrap = with yarn at front of work, slip first st off right hand needle onto left hand needle. Take yarn to back of work and slip slipped st back onto right hand needle. This prevents a hole at edge of short-turn rows.

COAT

BACK: With MC and larger needles, cast on 92 sts.
Work 7 rows garter st (knit every row), noting that first row is wrong side.
Beg with a knit row, cont in stocking st until work from beg measures 8½ ins [21.5 cm] ending with right side facing for next row.

Shape armholes: Cast off 2 sts beg next 2 rows. 88 sts.
Work 6 rows even, thus ending with right side facing for next row.

Shape Yoke Opening: 1st row: K38. (K2tog. K1) 3 times. K2tog. K39. 84 sts.
2nd row: P38. Cast off 8 sts. P38.

Working on last 38 sts, proceed as follows:
**1st row: Knit to last 6 sts. (K2tog) 3 times.
2nd row: Cast off 3 sts. Purl to end of row.
Rep last 2 rows until there are 2 sts. Cast off.**

With right side of work facing, join yarn to rem 38 sts. Knit to end of row. Proceed as follows:
***1st row: Purl to last 6 sts. (P2tog) 3 times.
2nd row: Cast off 3 sts. Knit to end of row.
Rep last 2 rows until there are 2 sts. Cast off.***

LEFT FRONT: With MC and larger needles, cast on 48 sts.
Work 7 rows garter st noting that first row is wrong side.
1st row: (Right side). Knit.
2nd row: K4. Purl to end of row.
Rep last 2 rows until work from beg measures 8½ ins [21.5 cm], ending with right side facing for next row.

Shape armhole and yoke opening: 1st row: Cast off 2 sts. Knit to end of row.

2nd row: Cast off 8 sts. Purl to end of row. 38 sts.
Rep from ** to ** as given for Back.

RIGHT FRONT: With MC and larger needles, cast on 48 sts.
Work 7 rows garter st noting that first row is wrong side.
1st row: (Right side). Knit.
2nd row: Purl to last 4 sts. K4.
Rep last 2 rows until work from beg measures 8½ ins [21.5 cm], ending with **wrong** side facing for next row.

Shape armhole and yoke opening: 1st row: Cast off 2 sts. Purl to last 4 sts. K4.
2nd row: Cast off 8 sts. Knit to end of row. 38 sts.
Rep from *** to *** as given for Back

LEFT SLEEVE: ****With MC and smaller needles, cast on 32 sts.
Work 15 rows garter st, noting that first row is wrong side.

Change to larger needles and proceed as follows:
1st row: (Right side). K2. *Inc 1 st in next st. K2. Rep from * to end of row. 42 sts.
Cont in stocking st inc 1 st each end of needle on 3rd and following 6th rows until there are 56 sts.

Cont even until Sleeve from beg measures 7 ins [18 cm], ending with right side facing for next row.

Shape top: Cast off 2 sts beg next 2 rows.****
Work 13 rows even, thus ending with **wrong** side facing for next row.
Next row: Cast off 2 sts. Purl to end of row.
Next row: Knit to last 16 sts. (K2tog) 8 times.
Next row: Cast off 8 sts. Purl to end of row.
Rep last 2 rows until there are 2 sts. Cast off.

RIGHT SLEEVE: Work from **** to **** as given for Left Sleeve.
Work 12 rows even, thus ending with right side facing for next row.
Next row: Cast off 2 sts. Knit to end

of row.
Next row: Purl to last 16 sts. (P2tog) 8 times.
Next row: Cast off 8 sts. Knit to end of row.
Rep last 2 rows until there are 2 sts. Cast off.

YOKE: With A and smaller needles, cast on 28 sts.
Work 5 rows garter st noting that first row is wrong side.

Change to larger needles and proceed as follows:
1st row: (Right side). K3. (yfwd. K2tog. K6) twice. yfwd. K2tog. K1. Inc 1 st in each of next 2 sts. K2. yfwd. K2tog. 30 sts. (4 buttonholes).
2nd row: K3. P6. K21.
3rd row: Knit.
4th row: K3. P6. K21.

Proceed as follows:
1st row: (Right side). Knit to last 9 sts. C6B. K3.
2nd row: K3. P6. K1. **Turn.**
3rd and alt rows: Sl1 wrap. Knit to end of row.
4th row: K3. P6. K9. **Turn.**
6th row: K3. P6. K17. **Turn.**
8th row: K3. P6. Knit to end of row.
Rep last 8 rows 37 times more, then 1st row once.

Next row: (Wrong side). K3. P6. K21.
Work 5 rows garter st. Cast off knitways (wrong side).

COLLAR: With B and larger needles, cast on 72 sts.
Work 20 rows garter st. Cast off.

FINISHING: Pin garment pieces to measurements and cover with a damp cloth leaving to dry. Sew side and sleeve seams. Sew armhole edges of Sleeves and Body tog. Sew Yoke to Coat matching 1 ridge at long edge of Yoke to each cast off st along top edge of Coat. Sew Collar in position to neck edge placing edges of Collar ½ inch [1 cm] in from edge of Yoke. Sew buttons to correspond to buttonholes.

LEGGINGS

RIGHT LEG: **With larger needles, cast on 75 sts.
1st row: (Right side). K1. *P1. K1. Rep from * to end of row.
2nd row: P1. *K1. P1. Rep from * to end of row.**
Rep these 2 rows (K1. P1) ribbing for 2 ins [5 cm] ending on a 2nd row and inc 1 st in center of last row. 76 sts.

Shape back: 1st row: (Right side). K8. **Turn**.
2nd and alt rows: Sl1 wrap. Purl to end of row.
3rd row: K16. **Turn**.
5th row: K24. **Turn**.
7th row: K32. **Turn**.
9th row: K40. **Turn**.
11th row: K48. **Turn**.
12th row: As 2nd row.
Cont in stocking st across all 76 sts, inc 1 st at beg of next and following 6th rows until there are 86 sts.

Cont even until work from cast on edge at center front (short end) measures 9½ ins [24 cm] ending with right side facing for next row. Place a marker at each end of last row.

Shape leg: Dec 1 st each end of needle on next and every alt row until there are 54 sts, then on following 4th rows until there are 42 sts.
Cont even until Leg from markers measures 9½ ins [24 cm] ending with right side facing for next row.

Shape foot: 1st row: K35. **Turn**.
2nd row: K12. **Turn**.
Work 29 rows garter st (knit every row) across these 12 sts for toe flap.
Next row: Pick up and knit 15 sts along side of toe flap. Knit rem 7 sts.
Next row: K34. Pick up and knit 15 sts along other side of toe flap. Knit rem 23 sts. 72 sts.
Work 14 rows even in garter st.

Proceed as follows:
1st row: K6. (K2tog) twice. K32. (K2tog) twice. Knit to end of row.
2nd and alt rows: Knit.

3rd row: K5. (K2tog) twice. K30. (K2tog) twice. Knit to end of row.
5th row: K4. (K2tog) twice. K28. (K2tog) twice. Knit to end of row.
7th row: K3. (K2tog) twice. K26. (K2tog) twice. Knit to end of row.
Cast off.

LEFT LEG: Work from ** to ** as given for Right Leg.

Rep these 2 rows (K1. P1) ribbing for 2 ins [5 cm] ending on a 1st row and inc 1 st in center of last row. 76 sts.

Shape back: 1st row: (Wrong side). P8. **Turn**.
2nd and alt rows: Sl1 wrap. Knit to end of row.
3rd row: P16. **Turn**.
5th row: P24. **Turn**.
7th row: P32. **Turn**.
9th row: P40. **Turn**.
11th row: P48. **Turn**.
12th row: As 2nd row.
Beg with a purl row, cont in stocking st across all 76 sts, inc 1 st at end of 2nd and following 6th rows until there are 86 sts.

Cont even until work from cast on edge at center front (short end) measures 9½ ins [24 cm] ending with right side facing for next row. Place a marker at each end of last row.

Shape leg: Dec 1 st each end of needle on next and every alt row until there are 54 sts, then on following 4th rows until there are 42 sts.
Cont even until Leg from markers measures 9½ ins [24 cm] ending with right side facing for next row.

Shape foot: 1st row: K19. **Turn**.
2nd row: K12. **Turn**.
Work 29 rows garter st across these 12 sts for toe flap.
Next row: Pick up and knit 15 sts along side of toe flap. Knit rem 23 sts.
Next row: K50. Pick up and knit 15 sts along other side of toe flap. Knit rem 7 sts. 72 sts.

Work 14 rows even in garter st.

Proceed as follows:
1st row: K26. (K2tog) twice. K32. (K2tog) twice. Knit to end of row.
2nd and alt rows: Knit.
3rd row: K25. (K2tog) twice. K30. (K2tog) twice. Knit to end of row.
5th row: K24. (K2tog) twice. K28. (K2tog) twice. Knit to end of row.
7th row: K23. (K2tog) twice. K26. (K2tog) twice. Knit to end of row.
Cast off.

FINISHING: Pin garment pieces to measurements and cover with a damp cloth leaving to dry. Sew inseams. Sew crotch seam. Fold waistband in half to wrong side and sew in position leaving an opening to insert elastic. Cut elastic to waist measurement and insert through waistband. Sew ends tog securely. Sew opening of waistband closed.

MITTENS

With B and larger needles, cast on 35 sts.
Work 2 ins [5 cm] in (K1. P1) ribbing as given for Right Leg of Leggings ending on a 2nd row and inc 1 st in center of last row. 36 sts.
Next row: (Right side. Eyelet row). K2. *yfwd. K2tog. Rep from * to end of row.
Beg with a purl row, cont in stocking st until work from beg measures 5 ins [12.5 cm] ending with right side facing for next row.
Next row: *K1. K2tog. Rep from * to end of row.
Purl 1 row.
Next row: (K2tog) 12 times.
Purl 1 row. Break yarn leaving a long end. Draw end through rem sts and fasten securely. Sew seam. Thread twisted cord through eyelet row.

Twisted cord: Cut 2 strands of A, 28 ins [71 cm] long. With both strands tog hold one end and with someone holding other end, twist strands to the right until they begin to curl. Fold the 2 ends tog and tie in a knot so they will not unravel. The strands will now twist themselves tog. Adjust length if desired.

HELMET

SIDES: With A and smaller needles, cast on 22 sts.
1st row: (Wrong side). K3. P6. K13.
2nd row: K13. C6B. P3.
3rd row: K3. P6. K1. **Turn.**
4th and following alt rows: Sl1 wrap. Knit to end of row.
5th row: K3. P6. K5. **Turn.**
7th row: K3. P6. K9. **Turn.**
9th row: K3. P6. Knit to end of row.
Rep 2nd to 9th rows 19 times more, then 2nd to 6th rows once.
Cast off in pat. Draw yarn around shorter edge and gather into a tight circle. Sew cast on and cast off edges tog.

CENTER SECTION: With MC and smaller needles cast on 18 sts.
Work 5 rows garter st (knit every row) noting that first row is wrong side.
Next row: (Right side). K3. *Inc 1 st in next st. K4. Rep from * to end of row. 21 sts.
Change to larger needles and beg with a purl row, cont in stocking st until work from beg measures 8¼ ins [21 cm] ending with right side facing for next row.

Shape back: Next row: Knit to center 3 sts. Sl1. K2tog. psso. Knit to end of row.
Work 3 rows even.
Rep last 4 rows until there are 13 sts.

Change to smaller needles and work 5 rows garter st. Cast off.

CHIN STRAP: With A and smaller needles, cast on 26 sts.
Work 2 rows garter st.
3rd row: K2. K2tog. yfwd. Knit to end of row.
Work 2 rows garter st. Cast off.

FINISHING: Sew center section to sides between markers along larger side of Sides. (See Diagram I).
Sew Chin Strap and button in position

SIDE (Make 2 noting that 1st row of First Side is right side and 1st row of Second Side is wrong side): Beg at rear of Horse, with MC cast on 8 sts.
1st row: Knit.
2nd row: Inc 1 st in first st. Knit to end of row.
3rd row: Cast on 11 sts (Back Leg). Knit to end of row (back edge).
4th row: Inc 1 st in first st. Knit to end of row (front edge).
5th row: Knit.
Rep 4th and 5th rows once more, then 4th row once. 23 sts.
Work 4 rows even in garter st (knit every row), ending at foot edge.
13th row: Cast off 10 sts **loosely**. Knit to end of row.
14th row: Knit.
15th row: (Underbody edge). K2tog. Knit to end of row (back edge). 12 sts.
Work 13 rows even in garter st, ending at underbody edge.

Proceed as follows:
1st row: Inc 1 st in first st. Knit to end of row.
2nd row: Knit.
3rd row: Cast on 12 sts (Front Leg). Knit to last 2 sts. Inc 1 st in next st. K1. 26 sts.
4th row: Knit.
5th row: Knit to last 2 sts. Inc 1 st in next st. K1.
Rep 4th and 5th rows 3 times more, then 4th row once, ending at foot edge. 30 sts.
11th row: Cast off 15 sts. Knit to end of row. 15 sts.
12th row: Knit to last 2 sts. K2tog.
13th row: K2tog. Knit to end of row (back edge).
Rep 12th and 13th rows once more. 11 sts.
Work 2 rows even, ending at back edge.
18th row: K2tog. Knit to last 2 sts. Inc 1 st in next st. K1.
19th row: Knit.
Rep 18th and 19th rows once more, then 18th row once.

Work 1 row even, ending at back edge.
24th row: K2tog. Knit to end of row.
25th row: Knit to last 2 sts. K2tog.
Rep 24th and 25th rows once more.
28th and 29th rows: K2tog. Knit to last 2 sts. K2tog.
Cast off rem 3 sts.

UNDERBODY: Beg at rear of Horse, with MC cast on 1 st.
1st row: Inc 1 st in st. 2 sts.
Work 2 rows even in garter st.
4th row: Inc 1 st in first st. Inc 1 st in last st. 4 sts.
Work 2 rows even.
7th row: Inc 1 st in first st. K1. Inc 1 st in next st. K1. 6 sts.
Work 2 rows even.
Cast on 11 sts beg next 2 rows for Back Legs. 28 sts.
Work 8 rows even.
Cast off 10 sts beg next 2 rows to complete Back Legs. 8 sts.
Dec 1 st each end of needle on next 2 rows. 4 sts.
Work 12 rows even.

Proceed as follows:
1st row: Inc 1 st in first st. K1. Inc 1 st in next st. K1.
2nd row: Knit.
Cast on 12 sts beg next 2 rows for Front Legs. 30 sts.
Work 6 rows even.
Cast off 11 sts beg next 2 rows for Front Legs. 8 sts.
Dec 1 st each end of needle on next and every alt row until there are 2 sts.
Next row: K2tog. Fasten off.

Diagram I

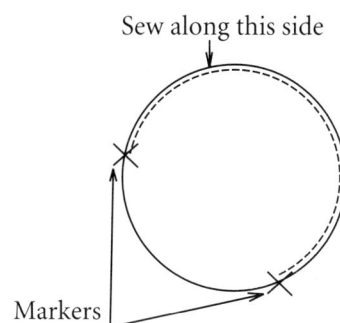

Sew along this side

Markers

Sew Leg seams of Sides and Underbody, leaving center back and center front seams open.

HOOVES: With right side of work facing and A, pick up and knit 13 sts across lower edge of Leg (including both Side and Underbody sections).
1st row: (Wrong side). Knit.
2nd row: K4. Inc 1 st in each of next 5 sts. K4. 18 sts.
Work 2 rows even.
5th row: K4. (K2tog) 5 times. K4. 13 sts.
6th row: Knit. Cast off.

EARS: With MC cast on 8 sts.
Work 8 rows garter st.
Dec 1 st each end of needle on next and following alt row. 4 sts.
Work 2 rows even.
Cast off.

TAIL: Cut 9 strands of A, 5 ins [13 cm] long and braid (using 3 strands for each ply of braid). Knot end. Trim ends evenly.

FINISHING: Sew center back and center front Leg seams leaving an opening 2½ ins [6 cm] long for stuffing at center back. Sew Head seam. Stuff firmly, adjusting stuffing to allow Legs to stand without spreading. Sew opening closed. Fold cast on edge of Ears in half and sew in position to Head. Sew tail in position.

Optional: With A, embroider eyes, nose and mouth using French Knot st and Stem st. Cut lengths of A 2 ins [5 cm] long and knot into fringe through seam edge of Head and upper back (see Helpful Hints). Trim fringe evenly.

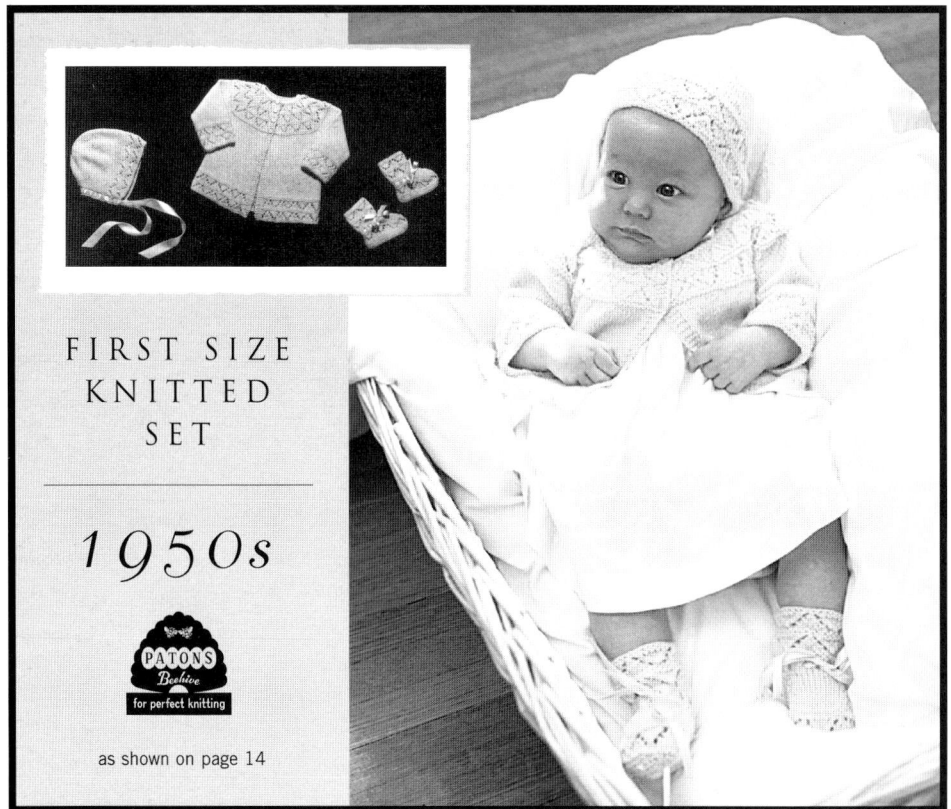

♠

FIRST SIZE
KNITTED
SET

1950s

as shown on page 14

SIZES

Chest measurement

0-6 mos	16 ins	[40.5 cm]

Finished chest

0-6 mos	17 ins	[43 cm]

MATERIALS

Patons Beehive Baby or Kroy 3 ply (50 g)

Pink	2	balls

Size 3¼ mm (U.S. 3) knitting needles **or size needed to obtain tension.** Size 3¼ mm (U.S. 3) circular knitting needle 70 cm long. 4 buttons and 2 st holders for Jacket. ¾ yard [.70 m] of ¼ inch [1 cm] wide ribbon for Bonnet. ⅔ yard [.60 m] of ⅜ inch [5 mm] wide ribbon for Bootees.

TENSION

32 sts and 40 rows = 4 ins [10 cm] in stocking st.

INSTRUCTIONS JACKET

Note: Jacket is worked in one piece to armholes.
With circular needle, cast on 153 sts.

Do not join. Working back and forth across needle, proceed as follows:
Work 3 rows garter st (knit every row).

Proceed in pat as follows:
1st row: (Right side). K5. *yfwd. Sl1. K1. psso. K3. K2tog. yfwd. K1. Rep from * to last 4 sts. K4.
2nd, 4th and 6th rows: K4. Purl to last 4 sts. K4.
3rd row: K6. *yfwd. Sl1. K1. psso. K1. K2tog. yfwd. K3. Rep from * to last 3 sts. K3.
5th row: K7. *yfwd. Sl1. K2tog. psso. yfwd. K5. Rep from * to last 2 sts. K2.
7th to 10th rows: Knit.
These 10 rows form border pat.

Work border pat once more.

Next row: (Right side). Knit.
Next row: K4. Purl to last 4 sts. K4.
Rep these 2 rows until work from beg measures 5½ ins [14 cm] ending with **wrong** side facing for next row.

Next row: K4. P35. P2tog. **Turn** (armhole edge). Leave rem sts on a spare needle. Cont in stocking st on these 40 sts (left front), keeping garter st border as before, dec 1 st at armhole edge on next and every row until there are 35

sts, ending with **wrong** side facing for next row.

Next row: K4. P8. (P2tog. P5) 3 times. P2tog. Break yarn. Leave rem 31 sts on a spare needle for Left Front.

With **wrong** side of work facing join yarn to rem sts. P2tog. P67. P2tog. **Turn.**

Working on these 69 sts (back), cont in stocking st dec 1 st at each end of needle on next and every row until there are 59 sts, ending with **wrong** side facing for next row.
Next row: P2tog. P10. (P2tog. P9) 4 times. P1. P2tog. Break yarn. Leave these 53 sts on a spare needle for Back.

With **wrong** side of work facing join yarn to rem sts. P2tog. P35. K4.

Working on these 40 sts (right front), keeping garter st border as before, dec 1 st at armhole edge every row until there are 35 sts, ending with **wrong** side facing for next row.

Next row: P2tog. (P5. P2tog) 3 times. P8. K4. **Do not break yarn.** Leave these 31 sts on a spare needle for Right Front.

SLEEVES

Cast on 41 sts. Work 3 rows in garter st. Proceed in pat as follows:
1st row: (Right side). K1. *yfwd. Sl1. K1. psso. K3. K2tog. yfwd. K1. Rep from * to end of row.
2nd, 4th and 6th rows: K1. Purl to last st. K1.
3rd row: K2. *yfwd. Sl1. K1. psso. K1. K2tog. yfwd. K3. Rep from * to last 7 sts. yfwd. Sl1. K1. psso. K1. K2tog. yfwd. K2.
5th row: K3. *yfwd. Sl1. K2tog. psso. yfwd. K5. Rep from * to last 6 sts. yfwd. Sl1. K2tog. psso. yfwd. K3.
7th to 10th rows: Knit.
These 10 rows form border pat. Work border pat once more.

Next row: K5. *Inc 1 st in next st. K5. Rep from * to end of row. 47 sts.
Beg with a purl row, cont in stocking st inc 1 st at each end of needle on every following 8th row to 53 sts.

Cont even until work from beg measures 5 ins [12.5 cm] ending with **wrong** side facing for next row.

Dec 1 st at each end of next and every row until there are 41 sts.
Next row: P2tog. P5. (P2tog. P6) 4 times. P2tog. Break yarn. Leave rem 35 sts on a st holder for Sleeve.

YOKE

With right side of work facing and circular needle, knit across 31 sts of Right Front, 35 sts from first sleeve, 53 sts from Back, 35 sts from second sleeve and 31 sts from Left Front. 185 sts.

**Knit 1 row.
Next row: (buttonhole row). K2. yfwd. K2tog. Knit to end of row.
Knit 1 row.
Rep 1st to 6th rows of border pat.**
Next row: K4. *K2tog. K2. K2tog. K3. Rep from * to last st. K1. 145 sts.
Rep from ** to ** once more.
Next row: K3. *K2tog. K1. K2tog. K2. Rep from * to last 2 sts. K2. 105 sts.
Rep from ** to ** once more.
Next row: K3. *(K2tog) twice. K1. Rep from * to last 2 sts. K2. 65 sts.
Next row: Knit.
Next row: K2. yfwd. K2tog. Knit to end of row.
Next row: Knit. Cast off.

Sew sleeve seams. Sew armhole seams. Sew on buttons to correspond to buttonholes.

Cast on 67 sts.
1st row: (Wrong side). Knit.
2nd row: K1. *Inc 1 st in next st. K10. Rep from * to end of row. 73 sts.
3rd row: Knit.

Next 20 rows: Work 2 complete border pats as given for Sleeve of Jacket.
Next row: K3. *Inc 1 st in next st. K9. Rep from * to end of row. 80 sts.
Beg with a purl row, cont in stocking st until work from beg measures 4½ ins

[11.5 cm] ending with right side facing for next row.
Shape crown: 1st row: *K6. K2tog. Rep from * to end of row.
2nd and every alt row: K1. Purl to last st. K1.
3rd row: *K5. K2tog. Rep from * to end of row.
5th row: *K4. K2tog. Rep from * to end of row.
Cont dec in this manner every alt row until there are 20 sts. Break yarn and thread end through rem sts. Fasten securely.

Neckband: Sew back seam for 2½ ins [6 cm] from base of crown. With right side of work facing pick up and knit 54 sts along lower edge of bonnet. Knit 1 row.
Next row: (eyelet row). K2. *yfwd. K2tog. Rep from * to end of row.
Knit 2 rows. Cast off **loosely**. Thread ribbon through eyelet row.

Cast on 33 sts. Work 3 rows in garter st.
Next 20 rows: Work 2 complete border pats as given for Sleeve.
Knit 1 row.
Next row: (Eyelet row). K1. *yrn. P2tog. Rep from * to end of row.

Make foot: K22. **Turn.** K1. P9. K1. **Turn.**
Working on these 11 sts, work 1¾ ins [4.5 cm] in stocking st ending with a knit row.
Pick up and knit 12 sts along side of toe flap. Knit rem 11 sts.
Next row: K34. Pick up and knit 12 sts along other side of toe flap. Knit rem 11 sts. 57 sts.
Knit 2 rows.
Next 10 rows: Work 1 complete border pat as given for Sleeve of Jacket.

Proceed as follows:
1st row: (K1. K2tog. K23. K2tog) twice. K1.
2nd and 3rd rows: Knit.
4th row: (K1. K2tog. K21. K2tog) twice. K1.
5th and 6th rows: Knit.
7th row: (K1. K2tog. K19. K2tog) twice. K1.
8th row: Knit. Cast off.
Sew back seam. Thread ribbon through eyelet row at ankles. ▲

YOUR
CLASSIC
EYELET

1950s

as shown on page 14

as shown on page 14

SIZES

Bust measurement

Small	34–36	ins	[86–91cm	]
Medium	38	"	[97	"]
Large	40	"	[102	"]

Finished bust

Small	39	ins	[99	cm]
Medium	41	"	[104	"]
Large	43	"	[109	"]

MATERIALS

Patons Kroy 3 ply (50 g)

Size	S	M	L	
331	6	6	7	balls

Sizes 2¾ mm (U.S. 2) and 3¼ mm (U.S. 3) knitting needles **or size needed to obtain tension**. 3 st holders. 4 inch [10 cm] zipper.

TENSION

32 sts and 40 rows = 4 ins [10 cm] with larger needles in stocking st.

INSTRUCTIONS

The instructions are written for smallest size. If changes are necessary for larger sizes the instructions will be written thus ( ).

FRONT
With smaller needles, cast on 139 (**147**-155) sts.
1st row: (Right side). K1. *P1. K1. Rep from * to end of row.
2nd row: P1. *K1. P1. Rep from * to end of row.
Rep these 2 rows (K1. P1) ribbing for 4 ins [10 cm] ending on a 2nd row and inc 1 st in center of last row. 140 (**148**-156) sts.

Change to larger needles and proceed in pat as follows:
1st row: (Right side). K62 (**66**-70). Sl1. K1. psso. yfwd. K10. Sl1. K1. psso. yfwd. Knit to end of row.
2nd row: P62 (**66**-70). P2tog. yrn. P10. P2tog. yrn. Purl to end of row.
Rep last 2 rows 3 times more.

Keeping cont of pat, inc 1 st each end of needle on next and following 8th rows until there are 148 (**156**-164) sts, ending with right side facing for next row.

Next row: K54 (**58**-62). *Sl1. K1. psso. yfwd. K10. Rep from * twice more. Sl1. K1. psso. yfwd. Knit to end of row.
Next row: P54 (**58**-62). *P2tog. yrn. P10.

Rep from * twice more. P2tog. yrn. Purl to end of row.
Rep last 2 rows twice more.

Keeping cont of pat, inc 1 st each end of needle on next and following 8th rows until there are 154 (**162**-170) sts, ending with right side facing for next row.

Next row: K45 (**49**-53). *Sl1. K1. psso. yfwd. K10. Rep from * 4 times more. Sl1. K1. psso. yfwd. Knit to end of row.
Next row: P45 (**49**-53). *P2tog. yrn. P10. Rep from * 4 times more. P2tog. yrn. Purl to end of row.
Rep last 2 rows twice more.

Keeping cont of pat, inc 1 st each end of needle on next and following 8th rows until there are 160 (**168**-176) sts, ending with right side facing for next row.

Next row: K36 (**40**-44). *Sl1. K1. psso. yfwd. K10. Rep from * 6 times more. Sl1. K1. psso. yfwd. Knit to end of row.
Next row: P36 (**40**-44). *P2tog. yrn. P10. Rep from * 6 times more. P2tog. yrn. Purl to end of row.
Rep last 2 rows until work from beg measures 14 ins [35.5 cm] ending with right side facing for next row.

Armhole shaping: Keeping cont of pat, cast off 5 (**6**-6) sts beg next 6 (**2**-4) rows.

Sizes M and L only: Cast off 5 sts beg next (**4**-2) rows.

All Sizes: 130 (**136**-142) sts.
Keeping cont of pat, dec 1 st each end of needle on next and following alt rows until there are 108 (**110**-112) sts.

Cont even in pat until armhole measures 6 (**6**-6½) ins [15 (**15**-16.5) cm] ending with right side facing for next row.

Neck shaping: Next row: Pat across 41 (**42**-43) sts (neck edge). **Turn.** Leave rem sts on a spare needle.

Keeping cont of pat, dec 1 st at neck edge on next 9 (**9**-10) rows. 32 (**33**-33) sts.

Cont even in pat until armhole measures 8 (**8**-8½) ins [20.5 (**20.5**-21.5) cm] ending with right side facing for next row.

Shoulder shaping: Cast off 11 sts beg next and following alt row. Work 1 row even. Cast off rem 10 (**11**-11) sts.

With right side of work facing slip next 26 sts from spare needle onto a st holder. Join yarn to rem sts and pat to end of row.

Keeping cont of pat, dec 1 st at neck edge on next 9 (**9**-10) rows. 32 (**33**-33) sts.

Cont even in pat until armhole measures 8 (**8**-8½) ins [20.5 (**20.5**-21.5) cm] ending with **wrong** side facing for next row.

Shoulder shaping: Cast off 11 sts beg next and following alt row. Work 1 row even. Cast off rem 10 (**11**-11) sts.

BACK

With smaller needles, cast on 131 (**139**-147) sts.
Work 4 ins [10 cm] in (K1. P1) ribbing as given for Front ending on a 2nd row and inc 1 st in center of last row.

132 (**140**-148) sts.

Change to larger needles and proceed in stocking st inc 1 st each end of needle on 9th and following 8th rows until there are 152 (**160**-168) sts.

Cont even until work from beg measures same length as Front to beg of armhole shaping, ending with right side facing for next row.

Armhole shaping: Cast off 5 (**6**-7) sts beg next 4 rows.
Dec 1 st each end of needle on next and every alt row until there are 108 (**110**-112) sts.

Cont even until armhole measures 4 (**4**-4½) ins [10 (**10**-11.5) cm] ending with right side facing for next row.

Back Opening: Next row: K54 (**55**-56).
Turn. Leave rem sts on a spare needle.
Cont even until armhole measures same length as front to beg of shoulder shaping, ending with right side facing for next row.

Shoulder shaping: Cast off 11 sts beg next and following alt row.
Work 1 row even. Cast off rem 10 (**11**-11) sts. Leave rem 22 (**22**-23) sts on a st holder.

With right side of work facing, join yarn to rem 54 (**55**-56) sts.

Cont even until armhole measures same length as front to beg of shoulder shaping, ending with **wrong** side facing for next row.

Shoulder shaping: Cast off 11 sts beg next and following alt row. Work 1 row even. Cast off rem 10 (**11**-11) sts. Leave rem 22 (**22**-23) sts on a st holder.

SLEEVES

With smaller needles, cast on 71 (**71**-79) sts. Work 3 ins [8 cm] in (K1. P1) ribbing as given for Front ending on a 2nd row and inc 1 st in center of last row. 72 (**72**-80) sts.

Change to larger needles and proceed in stocking st inc 1 st each end of needle on 9th and following 8th rows until there are 106 (**106**-114) sts.

Cont even until work from beg measures 17 (**17½**-18) ins [43 (**44.5**-45.5) cm] ending with right side facing for next row.

Shape top: Cast off 2 sts beg next 2 rows.
Dec 1 st each end of needle on next row.
Work 1 row even.
Rep last 4 rows until there are 28 (**28**-30) sts. Cast off.

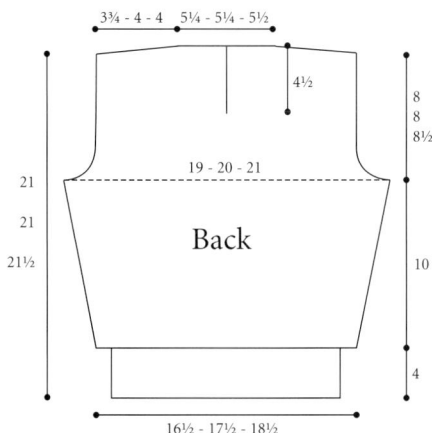

Back

3¾ - 4 - 4   5¼ - 5¼ - 5½
4½
8
8
8½
19 - 20 - 21
21
21
21½
10
16½ - 17½ - 18½
4

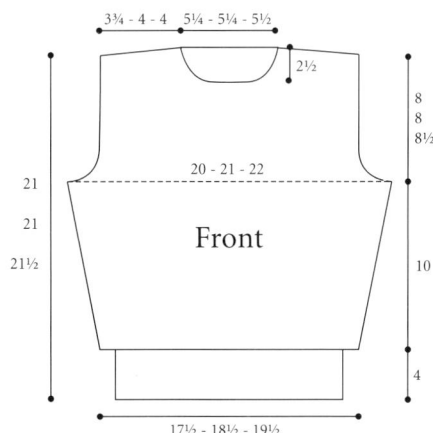

Front

3¾ - 4 - 4   5¼ - 5¼ - 5½
2½
8
8
8½
20 - 21 - 22
21
21
21½
10
17½ - 18½ - 19½
4

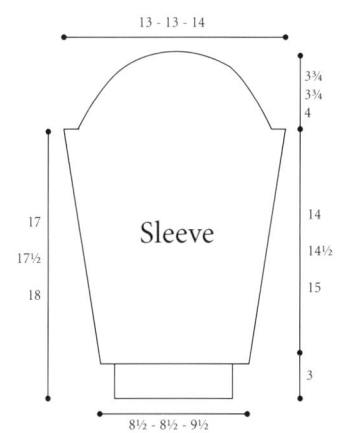

Sleeve

13 - 13 - 14
3¾
3¾
4
17
17½
18
14
14½
15
8½ - 8½ - 9½
3

FINISHING

Pin garment pieces to measurements. Cover with a damp cloth leaving to dry.

Neckband: Sew shoulder seams. With right side of work facing and smaller needles, knit across 22 (**22**-23) sts from left back neck st holder. Pick up and knit 26 (**28**-30) sts down left front neck edge. Knit across 26 sts from front st holder inc 1 st at center. Pick up and knit 26 (**28**-30) sts up right front neck edge. Knit across 22 (**22**-23) sts from right back neck st holder. 123 (**127**-133) sts. Beg and ending on a 2nd row, work 1 inch [2.5 cm] in (K1. P1) ribbing as given for Front. Cast off in ribbing.

Optional
Bow: With larger needles, cast on 2 sts.
1st row: Inc 1 st in first st. K1.
2nd row: Inc 1 st in first st. P1. K1.
3rd row: Inc 1 st in first st. P1. K2.
4th row: Inc 1 st in first st. K1. P1. K2.
5th row: Inc 1 st in first st. K1. (P1. K1) twice.
Moss st pat is now in position.

Keeping cont of moss st pat, inc 1 st beg next and every row until there are 23 sts, taking inc sts into moss st pat, as before.

Work 2 ins [5 cm] even in moss st pat.

Keeping cont of moss st pat, dec 1 st beg next and every row until there are 2 sts.
Next row: K2tog. Fasten off.

Bow Center: With larger needles, cast on 5 sts.
1st row: K1. (P1. K1) twice.
Rep last row for 1½ ins [4 cm]. Cast off in pat. Sew cast off and cast on edges tog. Slip Bow through. Sew in position to Front.
Sew side and sleeve seams. Sew in sleeves. Sew zipper in position in center back opening. ♠

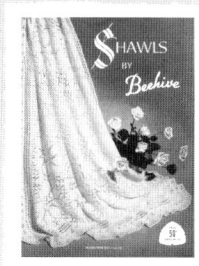

HEIRLOOM SHAWL

1950s

PATONS Beehive
for perfect knitting

as shown on page 15

MEASUREMENT

Finished Size: Approx 44 x 44 ins [112 x 112 cm]

MATERIALS

Patons Kroy 3 ply (50 g)

383	7	balls

Size 3¼ mm (U.S. 3) knitting needles and set of four 3¼ mm (U.S. 3) double pointed knitting needles **or size needed to obtain tension**.

TENSION

32 sts and 40 rows = 4 ins [10 cm] in stocking st.

BEEHIVE
Since 1785
PATONTED
3 PLY
SCOTCH
FINGERING

STITCH GLOSSARY

KB1 = knit into back of next st.

INSTRUCTIONS

MEDALLION *(make 16).*

With double pointed needles, cast on 8 sts. Divide sts into 2, 2 and 4 on 3 needles. Join in round.
1st round: *yfwd. K1. Rep from * to end of round.
2nd and alt rounds: Knit.
3rd round: *yfwd. K3. yfwd. KB1. Rep from * to end of round.
5th round: *yfwd. K5. yfwd. KB1. Rep from * to end of round.
7th round: *yfwd. K7. yfwd. KB1. Rep from * to end of round.
9th round: *yfwd. Sl1. K1. psso. K2tog. yfwd. K1. Rep from * to end of round. 40 sts.
11th round: *K1. yfwd. K2tog. yfwd. K2. Rep from * to end of round.
13th round: *K2. yfwd. KB1. yfwd. K3. Rep from * to end of round.
15th round: *K3. yfwd. KB1. yfwd. K4. Rep from * to end of round.
17th round: *K4. yfwd. KB1. yfwd. K5. Rep from * to end of round.

19th round: *K5. yfwd. KB1. yfwd. K6. Rep from * to end of round.

21st round: *K6. yfwd. KB1. yfwd. K7. Rep from * to end of round.

23rd round: *K7. yfwd. KB1. yfwd. K8. Rep from * to end of round. 144 sts.

25th round: *Sl1. K1. psso. K5. yfwd. K3. yfwd. K5. K2tog. P1. Rep from * to end of round.

26th and alt rounds: *K17. P1. Rep from * to end of round.

27th round: *Sl1. K1. psso. K4. yfwd. K5. yfwd. K4. K2tog. P1. Rep from * to end of round.

29th round: *Sl1. K1. psso. K3. yfwd. K1. yfwd. Sl1. K1. psso. K1. K2tog. yfwd. K1. yfwd. K3. K2tog. P1. Rep from * to end of round.

31st round: *Sl1. K1. psso. K2. yfwd. K3. yfwd. Sl1. K2tog. psso. yfwd. K3. yfwd. K2. K2tog. P1. Rep from * to end of round.

33rd round: *Sl1. K1. psso. K1. yfwd. K11. yfwd. K1. K2tog. P1. Rep from * to end of round.

35th round: *Sl1. K1. psso. yfwd. K1. yfwd. (Sl1. K1. psso. K1. K2tog. yfwd. K1. yfwd) twice. K2tog. P1. Rep from * to end of round.

37th round: Sl1. *(yfwd. K3. yfwd. Sl1. K2tog. psso) twice. yfwd. K3. yfwd. K2tog. Slip the last st of right hand needle onto left hand needle. Slip the 2nd st on left hand needle over the first st. Slip this st back to right hand needle, thus having 1 st in place of 3 and closing the petal tip. Rep from * to end of round, closing the last petal with the st slipped at the beg of round.

38th round: Knit.

39th round: *yfwd. Sl1. K1. psso. K1. K2tog. yfwd. K1. Rep from * to end of round.

40th round: Knit.

41st round: *K1. (yfwd. Sl1. K2tog. psso. yfwd. K3) twice. yfwd. Sl1. K2tog. psso. yfwd. K2. Rep from * to end of round.

42nd round: Knit.

Make corners: Knit first 8 sts of round onto end of 3rd needle.

1st row: K1. (Sl1. K1. psso. K1. K2tog. yfwd. K1. yfwd) twice. Sl1. K1. psso. K1. K2tog. K1. **Turn. Working back and forth on these 17 sts proceed as follows:

2nd row: P17.

3rd row: K1. (Sl1. K2tog. psso. yfwd. K3. yfwd) twice. Sl1. K2tog. psso. K1.

4th row: P2tog. P11. P2tog.

5th row: K1. Sl1. K1. psso. K1. K2tog. yfwd. K1. yfwd. Sl1. K1. psso. K1. K2tog. K1.

6th row: P11.

7th row: K1. Sl1. K2tog. psso. yfwd. K3. yfwd. Sl1. K2tog. psso. K1.

8th row: P2tog. P5. P2tog.

9th row: K1. Sl1. K1. psso. K1. K2tog. K1.

10th row: P5.

11th row: K1. Sl1. K2tog. psso. K1.

12th row: K3tog. Fasten off leaving a long end.**

Slip next 17 sts onto a thread. Working on next 19 sts, join yarn and work from ** to ** as given for Corner.

FINISHING

Slip 17 sts of one Medallion onto a needle and 17 sts of another medallion onto another needle. Place the 2 needles tog, wrong side facing, and graft the 2 medallions tog. With ends of yarn left at corners, sew corner seam tog matching pat. Join rem Medallions tog to form a square 4 medallions by 4 medallions. With right side of work facing, join yarn to 17 sts left on length of yarn around outside edge and cast off knitways all sts.

Border: Cast on 24 sts.

1st row: K4. (yfwd. K2tog. K1) twice. P3. (K1. yfwd) twice. K1. P3. yrn. P2tog. K1. (yfwd) twice. K2.

2nd row: K2. (K1. P1) into "(yfwd) twice" K1. yrn. P2tog. K3. P5. K3. (yfwd. K2tog. K1) twice. K4.

3rd row: K4. (yfwd. K2tog. K1) twice. P3. K2. yfwd. K1. yfwd. K2. P3. yrn. P2tog. K5.

4th row: Cast off 2 sts. K3 (including st on needle after cast off). yrn. P2tog. K3. P7. K3. (yfwd. K2tog. K1) twice. K4.

5th row: K4. (yfwd. K2tog. K1) twice. P3. K3. yfwd. K1. yfwd. K3. P3. yrn. P2tog. K1. (yfwd) twice. K2.

6th row: K2. (K1. P1) into "(yfwd) twice" K1. yrn. P2tog. K3. P9. K3. (yfwd. K2tog. K1) twice. K4.

7th row: K4. (yfwd. K2tog. K1) twice. P3. Sl1. K1. psso. K5. K2tog. P3. yrn. P2tog. K5.

8th row: Cast off 2 sts. K3 (including st on needle after cast off). yrn. P2tog. K3. P7. K3. (yfwd. K2tog. K1) twice. K4.

9th row: K4. (yfwd. K2tog. K1) twice. P3. Sl1. K1. psso. K3. K2tog. P3. yrn. P2tog. K1. (yfwd) twice. K2.

10th row: K2. (K1. P1) into "(yfwd) twice" K1. yrn. P2tog. K3. P5. K3. (yfwd. K2tog. K1) twice. K4.

11th row: K4. (yfwd. K2tog. K1) twice. P3. Sl1. K1. psso. K1. K2tog. P3. yrn. P2tog. K5.

12th row: Cast off 2 sts. K3 (including st on needle after cast off). yrn. P2tog. K3. P3. K3. (yfwd. K2tog. K1) twice. K4. 24 sts. These 12 rows form pat.

Cont even in pat until border fits around entire shawl ending with 12th pat row, beg at center of one side edge, allowing sufficient length to gather at each corner and sewing in place as you work. Cast off. Sew ends of border tog. Roll shawl in a damp towel for several hours, then spread out flat, pin into shape and leave to dry. ▲

CUDDLY BEARS

1960s

PATONS

Beehive

as shown on page 16

SIZES

Chest measurement

2	22	ins	[56 cm]
4	24	"	[61 "]
6	26	"	[66 "]

Finished chest

2	26	ins	[66 cm]
4	28	"	[71 "]
6	29½	"	[75 "]

MATERIALS

Patons Decor (100 g)

Size	2	4	6	
Main Color (MC) 1602	2	2	3	balls
Contrast A (1714)	1	1	2	ball(s)
Contrast B (1662)	1	1	1	ball

Small amount of Contrast C (1633).
Sizes 3¾ mm (U.S. 5) and 4½ mm (U.S. 7)
knitting needles **or size needed to obtain tension.**
2 st holders. 5 (6-6) buttons

TENSION

20 sts and 26 rows = 4 ins [10 cm] with
larger needles in stocking st.

INSTRUCTIONS

*The instructions are written for smallest
size. If changes are necessary for larger sizes
the instructions will be written thus ( ).*

Note: When working from chart, wind
small balls of the colors to be used, one
for each separate area of color in the
design. Start new colors at appropriate
points. To change colors, twist the two
colors around each other where they
meet, on wrong side, to avoid a hole.

BACK

***With A and smaller needles, cast on
66 (**70**-74) sts.
1st row: (Right side). K2. *P2. K2. Rep
from * to end of row.
2nd row: P2. *K2. P2. Rep from * to end
of row.
Rep these 2 rows (K2. P2) ribbing for
2½ ins [6 cm] ending on a 2nd row.

Change to MC, larger needles and
work 4 (**10**-16) rows in stocking st
ending with right side facing for
next row.

Next row: (Right side). With MC, K11

(**13**-15). Work row 1 of Chart I across
next 23 sts reading row from **right** to
left. With MC, K5. Work row 1 of
Chart II across next 16 sts reading
row from **right** to left. With MC, K11
(**13**-15).
Charts I and II are shown on page 67.
Next row: With MC, P11 (**13**-15). Work
row 2 of Chart II across next 16 sts
reading row from **left** to right. With
MC, P5. Work row 2 of Chart I across
next 23 sts reading row from **left** to
right. With MC, P11 (**13**-15).
Charts I and II are now in position.
Cont working Charts I and II until
row 30 of both Charts is complete.

Raglan shaping: Keeping cont of
Charts I and II, cast off 2 (**3**-3) sts beg
next 2 rows.
1st row: With MC, K1. K2tog. K6 (**7**-9).
Work row 33 of Chart I across next
23 sts. With MC, K5. Work row 33 of
Chart II across next 16 sts. With MC,
K6 (**7**-9) Sl1. K1. psso. K1.
2nd row: With MC, P8 (**9**-11).
Work row 34 of Chart II across next
16 sts. With MC, P5. Work row 34 of
Chart I across next 23 sts. With MC,
P8 (**9**-11).
Charts I and II are complete.
3rd row: With MC, K1. K2tog. Knit to
last 3 sts. Sl1. K1. psso. K1.
4th row: Purl.
Rep last 2 rows to 24 (**26**-26) sts.

Next row: K1. K2tog. Knit to last 3 sts.
Sl1. K1. psso. K1.
Next row: P1. P2togtbl. Purl to last 3 sts.
P2tog. P1.
Rep last 2 rows to 16 (**18**-18) sts.
Cast off.

Note: Knit Front without buttonholes
first, thus knit Left Front for Girl or
Right Front for Boy.

LEFT FRONT

With A and smaller needles, cast on 36
(**40**-40) sts.
1st row: (Right side). K2. *P2. K2. Rep
from * to last 6 sts. K6 (front border).
2nd row: K6. *P2. K2. Rep from * to last

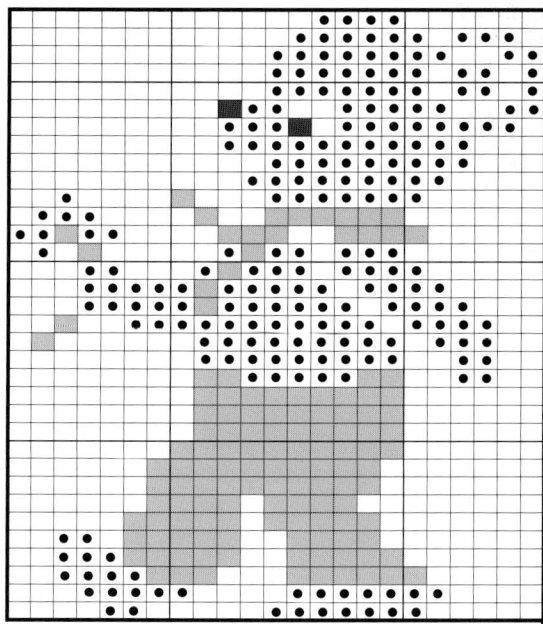

Chart I

Start Here

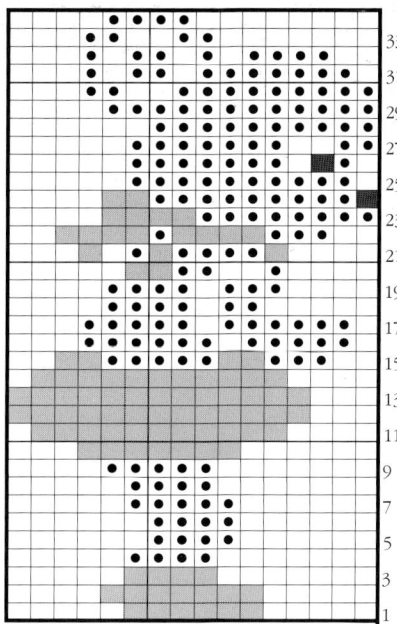

Chart II

Start Here

Work 32nd row of Chart III across next 19 sts. With MC, purl to end of row.

3rd row: With MC, K1. K2tog. K3 (**6**-8) Work 33rd row of Chart III across next 19 sts. With MC, knit to end of row.

4th row: With MC, K6. P3. Work 34th row of Chart III across next 19 sts. With MC, purl to end of row. Chart III is now complete.

Next row: With MC, K1. K2tog. Knit to end of row.

Next row: K6. Purl to end of row. Rep last 2 rows to 20 (**21**-22) sts. Ends with R.S.

Neck shaping: Next row: (Wrong side). Cast off 8 sts. Purl to end of row. Cont dec at armhole edge on next and every alt row, as before, **at the same time** dec 1 st at neck edge on every row to 7 (**8**-9) sts.

Keeping neck edge even, cont dec at armhole edge only on every alt row to 4 (**4**-6) sts, then every row to 2 sts.
Next row: P2tog. Fasten off.

Girl's Version only: On Left Front mark positions for buttons. Place marker for top button at center of sts left for neck on safety pin. Mark rem 4 (**5**-5) buttons evenly spaced, having bottom button 1 inch [2.5 cm] up from lower edge. Buttonholes are worked to correspond to buttonholes on Right Front as follows:
Next row: (Right side). K3. yfwd. K2tog. Knit to end of row.

RIGHT FRONT

With A and smaller needles, cast on 36 (**40**-40) sts.
1st row: (Right side). K8. *P2. K2. Rep from * to end of row.
2nd row: P2. *K2. P2. Rep from * to last 6 sts. K6.
Rep these 2 rows until work from beg

Key

☐ = MC

▨ = Contrast A

⊡ = Contrast B

▨ = Contrast C, duplicate st

Chart III

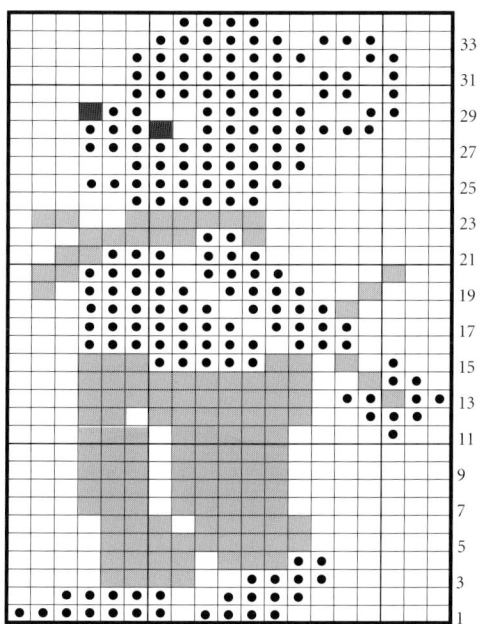

Start Here

2 sts. P2.
Rep these 2 rows until work from beg measures 2½ ins [6 cm], ending with right side facing for next row and inc 0 (**0**-2) sts evenly across last row. 36 (**40**-42) sts.

Change to MC, larger needles and keeping 6 front border sts in garter st (knit every row) work 4 (**10**-16) rows in stocking st ending with right side facing for next row.

Next row: (Right side). With MC, K8 (**12**-14). Work row 1 of Chart III across next 19 sts reading row from **right** to left. With MC, knit to end of row.
Next row: With MC, K6. P3. Work row 2 of Chart III across next 19 sts reading row from **left** to right. With MC, purl to end of row.
Chart III is now in position. Cont working Chart III until row 30 of Chart is complete.

Raglan shaping: 1st row: With MC, cast off 2 (**3**-3) sts. K6 (**9**-11) including st on needle after cast off. Work 31st row of Chart III across next 19 sts. With MC, knit to end of row.
2nd row: With MC, K6. P3.

measures 2½ ins [6 cm], ending with right side facing for next row and inc 0 (**0**-2) sts evenly across last row. 36 (**40**-42) sts.

Change to MC, larger needles and keeping 6 front border sts in garter st (knit every row) work 4 (**10**-16) rows even stocking st ending with right side facing for next row.

Next row: (Right side). With MC, K9. Work row 1 of Chart II across next 16 sts reading row from **right** to left. With MC, Knit to end of row.
Next row: With MC, P11 (**15**-17). Work row 2 of Chart II across next 19 sts reading row from **left** to right. With MC, purl to last 9 sts. P3. K6. Chart II is now in position.
Cont working Chart II until row 31 of Chart is complete, ending with **wrong** side facing for next row.

Raglan shaping: 1st row: Cast off 2 (**3**-3) sts. P9 (**12**-14). Work 32nd row of Chart II across next 16 sts. With MC, P3. K6.
2nd row: With MC, K9. Work 33rd row of Chart II across next 16 sts. With MC, K6 (**9**-11). Sl1. K1. psso. K1.
3rd row: With MC, P6 (**9**-11). Work 34th row of Chart II across next 16 sts. With MC, P3. K6. Chart II is now complete.

Next row: (Right side). With MC, knit to last 3 sts. Sl1. K1. psso. K1.
Next row: Purl to last 6 sts. K6.
Rep last 2 rows to 20 (**21**-22) sts.

Neck shaping: Next row: (Right side). Cast off 8 sts.
Knit to end of row.
Next row: Work 1 row even.
Cont dec at armhole edge on next and every alt row, as before, **at the same time** dec 1 st at neck edge on every row to 7 (**8**-9) sts.

Keeping neck edge even, cont dec at armhole edge only on every alt row to 4 (**4**-6) sts, then every row to 2 sts.
Next row: P2tog. Fasten off.

Boy's Version only: On Right Front mark positions for buttons. Place marker for top button at center of sts left for neck on safety pin. Mark rem 4 (**5**-5) buttons evenly spaced, having bottom button 1 inch [2.5 cm] up from lower edge. Buttonholes are worked to correspond to buttonholes on Left Front as follows:
Next row: (Right side). Knit to last 4 sts. yfwd. K2tog. K2.

SLEEVES

With A and smaller needles, cast on 34 sts. Work 2½ ins [6 cm] in ribbing as given for Back ending on a 2nd row

and inc 2 (**4**-6) sts evenly across last row. 36 (**38**-40) sts.

Change to MC and larger needles and proceed in stocking st inc 1 st each end of needle on 5th and every following 4th row to 50 (**54**-58) sts.

Cont even until work from beg measures 7½ (**9**-10½) ins [19 (**23**-26.5) cm] ending with right side facing for next row.

Raglan shaping: Cast off 2 (**3**-3) sts beg next 2 rows.
1st row: K1. K2tog. Knit to last 3 sts. Sl1. K1. psso. K1.
2nd row: Purl.
Rep last 2 rows to 8 sts.

Next row: K1. K2tog. K2. Sl1. K1. psso. K1.
Next row: P1. (P2tog) twice. P1. Cast off rem 4 sts.

Collar: With A and smaller needles, cast on 16 (**18**-18) sts.
Proceed in garter st (knit every row) for 11½ (**12**-12½) ins [29 (**30.5**-32) cm]. Cast off.

Finishing: Sew raglan seams. Sew side and sleeve seams. Sew Collar to neck edge placing each end 2 sts in from front edges.
With C, duplicate st nose and eyes as illustrated (See Helpful Hints). ♠

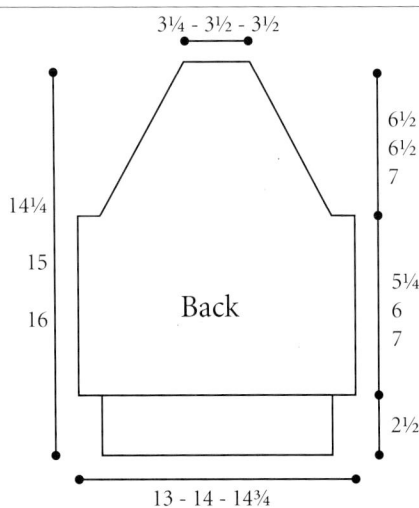

Back

3¼ - 3½ - 3½
6½
6½
7
14¼
15
16
5¼
6
7
2½
13 - 14 - 14¾

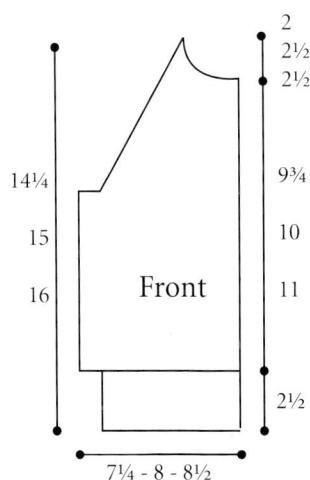

Front

2
2½
2½
14¼
15
16
9¾
10
11
2½
7¼ - 8 - 8½

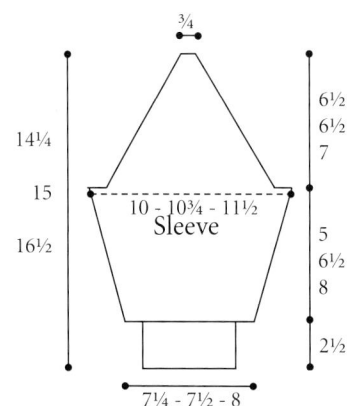

Sleeve

¾
6½
6½
7
14¼
15
16½
10 - 10¾ - 11½
5
6½
8
2½
7¼ - 7½ - 8

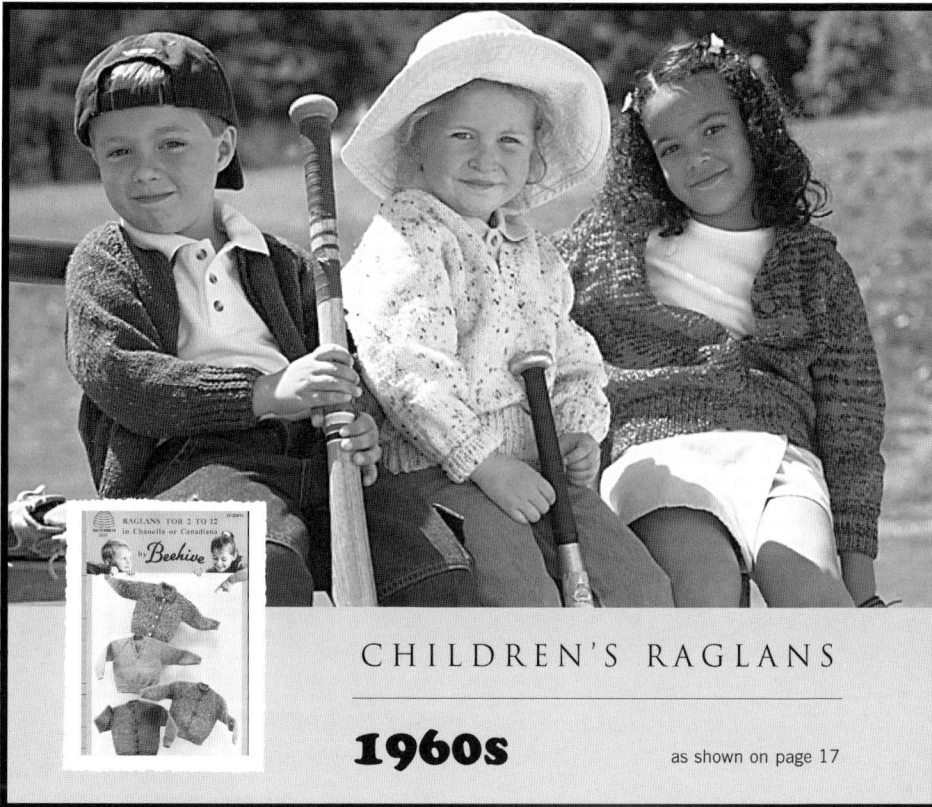

CHILDREN'S RAGLANS

1960s

as shown on page 17

as shown on page 17

SIZES

Chest measurement

2	22	ins	[56 cm]
4	24	"	[61 "]
6	26	"	[66 "]
8	28	"	[71 "]

Finished chest

2	26	ins	[66 cm]
4	28	"	[71 "]
6	30	"	[76 "]
8	31½	"	[80 "]

MATERIALS

Button Cardigan with Neckband or Collar

Patons Canadiana Colours (85 g)

Size	2	4	6	8	
7372	3	3	4	4	balls

V-neck Pullover

Patons Canadiana Tweeds (100 g)

Size	2	4	6	8	
6200	2	3	3	4	balls

Zippered Cardigan

Patons Canadiana Tweeds (100 g)

Size	2	4	6	8	
6196	2	3	3	4	balls

Sizes 3¾ mm (U.S. 5) and 4½ mm (U.S. 7) knitting needles **or size needed to obtain tension**. 5 (**6**-6-**6**) buttons for Buttoned Cardigan. Separating zipper for Zippered Cardigan

TENSION

20 sts and 26 rows = 4 ins [10 cm] with larger needles in stocking st.

INSTRUCTIONS

The instructions are written for smallest size. If changes are necessary for larger sizes the instructions will be written thus ( ).

Buttoned Cardigan with Ribbed Neckband Version

BACK

***With smaller needles, cast on 65 (**71**-75-**79**) sts.
1st row: (Right side). K1. *P1. K1. Rep from * to end of row.
2nd row: P1. *K1. P1. Rep from * to end of row.
Rep these 2 rows (K1. P1) ribbing for 2½ ins [6 cm] ending on a 2nd row.

Change to larger needles and proceed in stocking st until work from beg measures 7½ (**8½**-9¼-**10**) ins [19 (**21.5**-23.5-**25.5**) cm] ending with right side facing for next row.***

Raglan shaping: Cast off 2 (**3**-3-**3**) sts beg next 2 rows.
1st row: K1. K2tog. Knit to last 3 sts. Sl1. K1. psso. K1.
2nd row: Purl.
Rep last 2 rows to 25 (**27**-27-**29**) sts.

Next row: K1. K2tog. Knit to last 3 sts. Sl1. K1. psso. K1.
Next row: P1. P2togtbl. Purl to last 3 sts. P2tog. P1.
Rep last 2 rows to 17 (**19**-19-**21**) sts. Cast off.

Note: Knit Front without buttonholes first, thus knit Left Front for Girl or Right Front for Boy.

LEFT FRONT

With smaller needles, cast on 36 (**38**-40-**42**) sts.
1st row: (Right side). K2. *P1. K1. Rep from * to last 6 sts. K6 (front border).
2nd row: K6. *P1. K1. Rep from * to end of row.
Rep these 2 rows until work from beg measures 2½ ins [6 cm], ending with right side facing for next row and inc 0 (**0**-0-**1**) st in center of last row. 36 (**38**-40-**43**) sts.

Change to larger needles and keeping 6 front border sts in garter st (knit every row), cont even in stocking st until work from beg measures same length as Back to beg of raglan shaping ending with right side facing for next row.

Raglan shaping: Next row: Cast off 2 (**3**-3-**3**) sts. Knit to end of row.
Next row: K6. Purl to end of row.
Next row: K1. K2tog. Knit to end of row.
Rep last 2 rows to 20 (**21**-22-**24**) sts.

Neck shaping: Next row: (Wrong side). K6. P2. Leave these 8 sts on a safety pin. Purl to end of row.
Cont dec at armhole edge every alt row, as before, **at the same time** dec 1 st at neck edge on every row to 7 (**8**-9-**11**) sts.

Keeping neck edge even, cont dec at armhole edge only on every alt row to 4 (**4**-4-**6**) sts, then every row to 2 sts.
Next row: P2tog. Fasten off.

Girl's Version only: On Left Front mark positions for buttons. Place marker for top button at center of sts left for neck on safety pin. Mark rem 4 (**5**-5-**5**) buttons evenly spaced, having bottom button 1 inch [2.5 cm] up from lower edge. Buttonholes are worked to correspond to button markers on Right Front as follows:
Next row: (Right side). K3. yfwd. K2tog. Knit to end of row.

RIGHT FRONT

With smaller needles cast on 36 (**38**-40-**42**) sts.
1st row: (Right side). K7. *P1. K1. Rep from * to last st. K1.
2nd row: *K1. P1. Rep from * to last 6 sts. K6.
Rep these 2 rows until work from beg measures 2½ ins [6 cm] , ending with right side facing for next row and inc 0 (**0**-0-**1**) st in center of last row. 36 (**38**-40-**43**) sts.

Change to larger needles and keeping 6 front border sts in garter st, cont even in stocking st until work from beg measures same length as Back to beg of raglan shaping ending with **wrong** side facing for next row.

Raglan shaping: Next row: Cast off 2 (**3**-3-**3**) sts. Purl to end of row.
Next row: Knit to last 3 sts. Sl1. K1. psso. K1.
Next row: Purl to last 6 sts. K6.
Rep last 2 rows to 20 (**21**-22-**24**) sts ending with right side facing for next row.

Neck shaping: Next row: (Right side). K8. Leave these 8 sts on a safety pin. Knit to end of row.
Cont dec at armhole edge every alt row, as before, **at the same time** dec 1 st at neck edge on every row to 7 (**8**-9-**11**) sts.

Keeping neck edge even, cont dec at armhole edge every alt row to 4 (**4**-4-**6**) sts, then every row to 2 sts.
Next row: P2tog. Fasten off.

Boy's Version only: On Right Front mark positions for buttons. Place marker for top button at center of sts left for neck on safety pin. Mark rem 4 (**5**-5-**5**) buttons evenly spaced, having bottom button 1 inch [2.5 cm] up from lower edge. Buttonholes are worked to correspond to markers on Left Front as follows:
Next row: (Right side). Knit to last 4 sts. yfwd. K2tog. K2.

SLEEVES

With smaller needles, cast on 33 (**33**-35-**35**) sts. Work 2½ ins [6 cm] in ribbing as given for Back ending on a 2nd row and inc 3 (**5**-5-**7**) sts evenly

across last row. 36 (**38**-40-**42**) sts.

Change to larger needles and proceed in stocking st inc 1 st each end of needle on 5th and every following 4th row to 50 (**54**-58-**60**) sts.

Cont even until work from beg measures 7½ (**9**-10½-**11½**) ins [19 (**23**-26.5-**29**) cm] ending with right side facing for next row.

Raglan shaping: Cast off 2 (**3**-3-**3**) sts beg next 2 rows.
1st row: K1. K2tog. Knit to last 3 sts. Sl1. K1. psso. K1.
2nd row: Purl.
Rep last 2 rows to 8 sts.

Next row: K1. K2tog. K2. Sl1. K1. psso. K1.
Next row: P1. (P2tog) twice. P1. Cast off rem 4 sts.

FINISHING

Sew raglan seams. Sew side and sleeve seams.

Neckband: Girl's Version only: With right side of work facing and smaller needles, work across 8 sts from right front safety pin as follows: K3. yfwd. K2tog. K3. Pick up and knit 8 (**9**-10-**11**) sts up right front neck edge, 4 sts from right sleeve, 17 (**19**-19-**21**) sts across back neck edge, 4 sts across left sleeve and 8 (**9**-10-**11**) sts down left

---

Zippered Cardigan

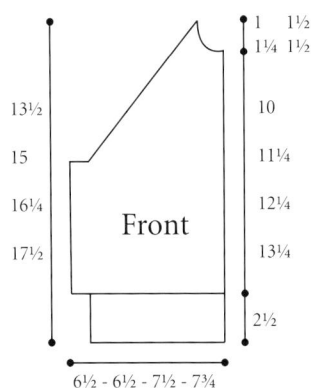

Front

13½
15
16¼
17½

1   1½
1¼ 1½
10
11¼
12¼
13¼

2½

6½ - 6½ - 7½ - 7¾

Buttoned Cardigan

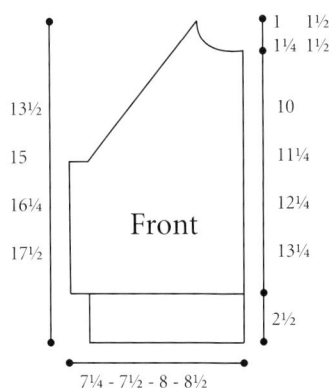

Front

13½
15
16¼
17½

1   1½
1¼ 1½
10
11¼
12¼
13¼

2½

7¼ - 7½ - 8 - 8½

V Neck Pullover

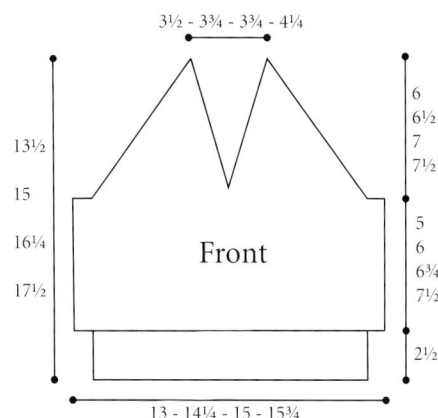

3½ - 3¾ - 3¾ - 4¼

Front

13½
15
16¼
17½

6
6½
7
7½

5
6
6¾
7½

2½

13 - 14¼ - 15 - 15¾

front neck edge. Knit across 8 sts from left front safety pin. 57 (**61**-**63**-**67**) sts.

Boy's Version only: With right side of work facing and smaller needles, knit across 8 sts from right front safety pin. Pick up and knit 8 (**9**-**10**-**11**) sts up right front neck edge, 4 sts across top of right sleeve, 17 (**19**-**19**-**21**) sts across back neck edge, 4 sts across top of left sleeve and 8 (**9**-**10**-**11**) sts down left front neck edge. Work across 8 sts from left front safety pin as follows: K4. yfwd. K2tog. K2. 57 (**61**-**63**-**67**) sts.

1st row: (Wrong side). K6. *P1. K1. Rep from * to last 7 sts. P1. K6.
2nd row: K6. *K1. P1. Rep from * to last 7 sts. K7.
Rep last 2 rows twice more, then 1st row once. Cast off in ribbing.

Sew on buttons to correspond to buttonholes.

Buttoned Cardigan with Collar Version

Work as given for Cardigan with Ribbed Neckband, casting off 8 sts at neck edge on fronts in place of leaving sts on a safety pin, and placing marker for top button ½ inch [1 cm] down from cast off sts at neck edge.

Collar: With smaller needles, cast on 16 (**16**-18-**18**) sts.
Proceed in garter st (knit every row) for 11½ (**12**-12½-**13**) ins [29 (**30.5**-32-**33**) cm]. Cast off. Placing each end 2 sts in from front edges, sew Collar to neck edge.

Zippered Cardigan Version

Back and Sleeves: Work as given for Buttoned Cardigan.

Right and Left Fronts: When casting on sts for each front, cast on 3 sts less so there will be 3 sts instead of 6 sts in garter st border at front edges. This

means that when you begin neck shaping you will dec to 17 (**18**-**19**-**21**) sts instead of 20 (**21**-**22**-**24**) sts and you will be leaving 5 sts on each safety pin at neck instead of 8 sts.

Sew raglan seams. Sew side and sleeve seams.

Neckband: With right side of work facing and smaller needles, knit across 5 sts from right front safety pin. Pick up and knit 8 (**9**-**10**-**11**) sts up right front neck edge, 4 sts from right sleeve, 17 (**19**-**19**-**21**) sts across back neck edge, 4 sts across left sleeve and 8 (**9**-**10**-**11**) sts down left front neck edge. Knit across 5 sts from left front safety pin. 51 (**55**-**57**-**61**) sts.

1st row: (Wrong side). K3. *P1. K1. Rep from * to last 4 sts. P1. K3.
2nd row: K3. *K1. P1. Rep from * to last 4 sts. K4.
Rep last 2 rows twice more, then 1st row once. Cast off in ribbing.

V Neck Pullover Version

Back and Sleeves: Work as given for Buttoned Cardigan.

Front: Work from *** to *** as given for Back of Buttoned Cardigan.

Raglan shaping: Next row: (Right side).

Cast off 2 (**3**-3-**3**) sts. Knit to end of row.
Next row: Cast off 2 (**3**-3-**3**) sts. P28 (**30**-32-**34**) including st on needle after cast off. K5 (center front). Purl to end of row.

Neck shaping: 1st row: K1. K2tog. K25 (**27**-29-**31**).
For Boy: K5.
For Girl: Cast on 5 sts.
Both Versions: Working over 32 (**34**-36-**38**) sts and leaving rem sts on a spare needle for right side, proceed as follows:
2nd row: K5 (garter st border). Purl to end of row.
3rd row: K1. K2tog. Knit to last 6 sts. K2tog. K4.

Keeping cont of garter st border, dec at armhole edge every alt row, at the same time, dec 1 st at neck edge inside border every following 6th (**6th**-6th-**4th**) row to 26 (**24**-30-**33**) sts.

Cont dec at armhole edge every alt row, at the same time, dec at neck edge every 8th (**8th**-8th-**6th**) row to 16 (**9**-10-**29**) sts.

Size 2 and 6 only: Keeping neck edge even, dec at armhole edge every row to 9 sts.

Size 8 only: Cont dec at armhole edge every alt row, at the same time, dec at

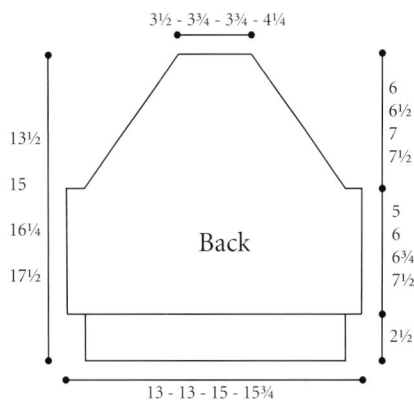

Back: 3½ - 3¾ - 3¾ - 4¼; 13½; 15; 16¼; 17½; 6, 6½, 7, 7½; 5, 6, 6¾, 7½; 2½; 13 - 13 - 15 - 15¾

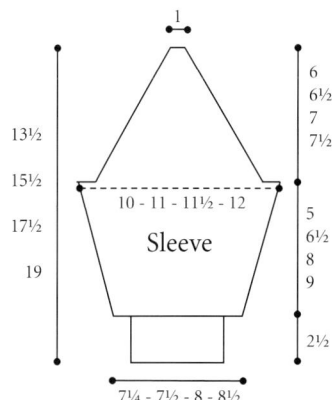

Sleeve: 1; 13½; 15½; 17½; 19; 10 - 11 - 11½ - 12; 6, 6½, 7, 7½; 5, 6½, 8, 9; 2½; 7¼ - 7½ - 8 - 8½

neck edge every 8th row to 9 sts.

All sizes: Keeping neck edge even, dec at armhole edge every row to 5 sts. Cont in garter st on these 5 sts for 2½ (**2½-2¾-2¾**) ins [6 (**6-7-7**) cm] for neckband. Cast off.

With right side of work facing join yarn to sts left of spare needle.
For Boy: 1st row: Cast on 5 sts.
For Girl: 1st row: K5. Knit to last 3 sts. Sl1. K1. psso. K1. 32 (**34-36-38**) sts.
Both Versions: 2nd row: Purl to last 5 sts. K5.
3rd row: K4. K2tog. Knit to last 3 sts. Sl1. K1. psso. K1.

Keeping cont of garter st border, dec at armhole edge every alt row, at the same time, dec 1 st at neck edge inside border every following 6th (**6th-6th-4th**) row to 26 (**24-30-33**) sts.

Cont dec at armhole edge every alt row, at the same time, dec at neck edge every 8th (**8th-8th-6th**) row to 16 (**9-10-29**) sts.

Size 2 and 6 only: Keeping neck edge even, dec at armhole edge every row to 9 sts.

Size 8 only: Cont dec at armhole edge every alt row, at the same time, dec at neck edge every 8th row to 9 sts.

All sizes: Keeping neck edge even, dec at armhole edge every row to 5 sts. Cont in garter st on these 5 sts for 2½ (**2½-2¾-2¾**) ins [6 (**6-7-7**) cm] for neckband. Cast off.

FINISHING

Sew raglan seams. Sew side and sleeve seams. Sew cast off edge of neckband tog. Place this seam at center back neck and sew in position. Sew the 5 cast on sts at center front in position to wrong side. ♠

LEAF AND LACE SET

1960s

PATONS
Beehive

as shown on page 17

MATERIALS

Patons Kroy 3 Ply (50 g)

Size	3 mos
383	3 balls

Sizes 3 mm (U.S. 2) and 3¼ mm (U.S. 3) knitting needles **or size needed to obtain tension.** 3 buttons. Medium size of crochet hook. 4 yds of ribbon.

TENSION

32 sts and 40 rows = 4 ins [10 cm] with larger needles in stocking st.

INSTRUCTIONS

The instructions are written for smallest size. If changes are necessary for larger sizes the instructions will be written thus ( ).

LACE PATTERN

1st row: K1. *P1. yfwd. Sl1. K1. psso. Rep from * to last 2 sts. P1. K1.
2nd row: K2. *P2. K1. Rep from * to last st. K1.
3rd row: K1. P1. *K2tog. yfwd. P1. Rep from * to last st. K1.
4th row: As 2nd row.
These 4 rows complete Lace pat.

JACKET

Beg at neck, with smaller needles, cast on 70 sts.
Work 5 rows garter st (knit every row), noting that first row is wrong side.

Proceed as follows:
1st row: (Right side). K5. P1. K3. *Inc 1 st in next st. K4. Rep from * to last 6 sts. P1. K1. Cast off 2 sts (buttonhole). K2. 81 sts.
2nd row: K2. Cast on 2 sts. K2. *P9. K1. Rep from * to last 5 sts. K5.

Proceed in Leaf pat as follows:
1st row: K5. *P1. K4. yfwd. K1. yfwd. K4. Rep from * to last 6 sts. P1. K5. 95 sts.
2nd row: K6. *P11. K1. Rep from * to last 5 sts. K5.
3rd row: K5. *P1. K5. yfwd. K1. yfwd. K5. Rep from * to last 6 sts. P1. K5. 109 sts.
4th row: K6. *P13. K1. Rep from * to last 5 sts. K5.
5th row: K5. *P1. K6. yfwd. K1. yfwd. K6. Rep from * to last 6 sts. P1. K5. 123 sts.
6th row: K6. *P15. K1. Rep from * to last 5 sts. K5.
7th row: K5. *P1. K7. yfwd. K1. yfwd. K7. Rep from * to last 6 sts. P1. K5. 137 sts.
8th row: K6. *P17. K1. Rep from * to last 5 sts. K5.
9th row: K5. *P1. K8. yfwd. K1. yfwd. K8. Rep from * to last 6 sts. P1. K5. 151 sts.

10th row: K6. *P19. K1. Rep from * to last 5 sts. K5.

11th row: K5. *P1. K9. yfwd. K1. yfwd. K9. Rep from * to last 6 sts. P1. K5. 165 sts.

12th row: K6. *P21. K1. Rep from * to last 5 sts. K5.

13th row: K5. P1. yfwd. Sl1. K1. psso. *K17. K2tog. yfwd. K1. yfwd. Sl1. K1. psso. Rep from * to last 25 sts. K17. K2tog. yfwd. P1. K5.

The lower half of 7 leaves are beginning to form and will be separated by garter st.

14th row: K7. *P19. K3. Rep from * to last 26 sts. P19. K7.

15th row: K5. P1. K1. *yfwd. Sl1. K1. psso. K15. K2tog. yfwd. K3. Rep from * to last 26 sts. yfwd. Sl1. K1. psso. K15. K2tog. yfwd. K1. P1. K5.

16th row: K8. *P17. K5. Rep from * to last 25 sts. P17. K8.

17th row: K5. P1. K2. *yfwd. Sl1. K1. psso. K13. K2tog. yfwd. K5. Rep from * to last 25 sts. yfwd. Sl1. K1. psso. K13. K2tog. yfwd. K2. P1. K1. Cast off 2 sts. K2.

18th row: K2. Cast on 2 sts. K5. *P15. K7. Rep from * to last 24 sts. P15. K9.

19th row: K5. P1. K3. *yfwd. Sl1. K1. psso. K11. K2tog. yfwd. K7. Rep from * to last 24 sts. yfwd. Sl1. K1. psso. K11. K2tog. yfwd. K3. P1. K5.

20th row: K10. *P13. K9. Rep from * to last 23 sts. P13. K10.

21st row: K5. P1. K4. *yfwd. Sl1. K1. psso. K9. K2tog. yfwd. K9. Rep from * to last 23 sts. yfwd. Sl1. K1. psso. K9. K2tog. yfwd. K4. P1. K5.

22nd row: K11. *P11. K11. Rep from * to end of row.

23rd row: K5. P1. K5. *yfwd. Sl1. K1. psso. K7. K2tog. yfwd. K11. Rep from * to last 22 sts. yfwd. Sl1. K1. psso. K7. K2tog. yfwd. K5. P1. K5.

24th row: K12. *P9. K13. Rep from * to last 21 sts. P9. K12.

25th row: K5. P1. K6. *yfwd. Sl1. K1. psso. K5. K2tog. yfwd. K13. Rep from * to last 21 sts. yfwd. Sl1. K1. psso. K5. K2tog. yfwd. K6. P1. K5.

26th row: K13. *P7. K15. Rep from * to last 20 sts. P7. K13.

27th row: K5. P1. K7. *yfwd. Sl1. K1. psso. K3. K2tog. yfwd. K15. Rep from * to last 20 sts. yfwd. Sl1. K1. psso. K3.

K2tog. yfwd. K7. P1. K5.

28th row: K14. *P5. K17. Rep from * to last 19 sts. P5. K14.

29th row: K5. P1. K8. *yfwd. Sl1. K1. psso. K1. K2tog. yfwd. K17. Rep from * to last 19 sts. yfwd. Sl1. K1. psso. K1. K2tog. yfwd. K8. P1. K5.

30th row: K15. *P3. K19. Rep from * to last 18 sts. P3. K15.

31st row: K5. P1. K9. *yfwd. Sl1. K2tog. psso. yfwd. K19. Rep from * to last 18 sts. yfwd. Sl1. K2tog. psso. yfwd. K9. P1. K5.

32nd row: K16. *P1. K21. Rep from * to last 17 sts. P1. K16.

33rd row: K5. P1. Knit to last 6 sts. P1. K5.

34th row: Knit.

35th row: K5. P1. K1. *Inc 1 st in next st. Rep from * to last 8 sts. K2. P1. K1. Cast off 2 sts. K2.

36th row: K2. Cast on 2 sts. Knit to end of row. 315 sts.

Change to larger needles and work 16 rows in Lace pat, thus ending with right side facing for next row.

With right side of work facing, slip first 51 sts for Left Front onto a thread. Slip next 60 sts for Left Sleeve onto a spare needle and place markers at each end of needle. Slip next 93 sts for Back onto a thread. Slip next 60 sts for Right Sleeve on a st holder and place markers at each end of st holder. Slip rem 51 sts for Right Front onto thread.

Sleeves: With larger needles and right side of work facing, join yarn to 60 sts of Left Sleeve on spare needle.
Work in Lace pat until Sleeve measures approx 4½ ins [11.5 cm] from marked row, ending with right side facing for next row.

Change to smaller needles and proceed as follows:
1st row: K2. *P2tog. K1. Rep from * to last 4 sts. P2tog. K2tog. 40 sts.
Work 9 rows in (K1. P1) ribbing. Cast off loosely in ribbing.

Slip 60 sts of Right Sleeve onto needle and work as given for Left Sleeve.

Make Body: Slip rem 51 sts for Left Front,

93 sts for Back and 51 sts for Right Front onto needle. With right side of work facing join yarn to Left Front. Change to larger needles proceed in Lace pat until work from marked row measures 5½ ins [14 cm] ending with right side facing for next row. Cast off.

Sew sleeve seams.
With right side of work facing, work 1 row sc around entire jacket, drawing neck edge in slightly if necessary. Sew buttons to correspond to buttonholes.

Bonnet: With smaller needles, cast on 27 sts.
1st row: K1. *P1. K2. yfwd. K1. yfwd. K2. Rep from * to last 2 sts. P1. K1.
2nd row: K2. *P7. K1. Rep from * to last st. K1.
3rd row: K1. *P1. K3. yfwd. K1. yfwd. K3. Rep from * to last 2 sts. P1. K1.
4th row: K2. *P9. K1. Rep from * to last st. K1.

Work Leaf pat as given for Jacket, noting that there will be 4 sts less at each end of row. That is 1st row and odd numbered rows will begin and end with K1 instead K5 and the 2nd and even numbered rows will begin with K2 instead K6 and end with K1 instead K5. End at 12th row of Leaf pat. 91 sts.
13th row: K1. P1. yfwd. Sl1. K1. psso. *K17. K2tog. yfwd. K1. yfwd. Sl1. K1. psso. Rep from * to last 21 sts. K17. K2tog. yfwd. P1. K1.
14th row: K3. *P19. K3. Rep from * to last 22 sts. P19. K3.
Leaf pat is now in position.
Cont working in Leaf pat until 32nd row of pat is complete.
Cont even in garter st until work from beg measures 5¼ ins [13 cm] ending with right side facing for next row.

Proceed as follows:
Next row: K1. *K2tog. K3. Rep from * to end of row. 73 sts.
Next row: (Eyelet row). K4. *yfwd. K2tog. K1. Rep from * to last 3 sts. K3.
Work 7 rows even in garter st. Cast off.
Gather cast on edge into circle and sew up back seam from top of crown for 3 ins [7.5 cm].

Thread ribbon through eyelets at face edge. Make ribbon rosettes and sew to bonnet as illustrated.

Booties: With smaller needles, cast on 36 sts.
Work 3 ins [7.5 cm] even in Lace pat, ending with right side facing for next row.

Shape Foot: K24. **Turn**. K12. **Turn**.
Work 23 rows garter st across center 12 sts.
Next row: Pick up and knit 12 sts along side of toe flap. Knit rem 12 sts.
Next row: K36. Pick up and knit 12 sts along other side of toe flap. Knit rem 12 sts. 60 sts.
Work 16 rows even in garter st.
Next row: K1. K2tog. Knit to center 4 sts. (K2tog) twice. Knit to last 3 sts. K2tog. K1.
Next row: Knit.
Rep last 2 rows twice more. Cast off **loosely**.
Sew back and sole seam.

Make Tassel: Wind yarn around 3 fingers 10 times. Break yarn leaving a long end and thread end through a needle. Slip needle through all loops and tie tightly. Remove cardboard and wind yarn tightly around loops ½ inch [1 cm] below fold. Fasten securely. Cut through rem loops and trim ends evenly.

Twisted cord: Cut 3 strands of yarn 28 ins [97 cm] long. With both strands together hold one end and with someone holding other end, twist strands to the right until they begin to curl. Fold the 2 ends together and tie in a knot so they will not unravel. The strands will now twist themselves together. Adjust length if desired. Thread through eyelet row at ankle. Sew tassels to each end of chain. ♠

R E I N D E E R
J A C K E T

1960s

PATONS
Beehive

as shown on page 18

SIZES

Chest measurement

10	34	ins	[86.5	cm	]
12	36	"	[91.5	"	]

Finished chest

10	39	ins	[99	cm	]
12	41	"	[104	"	]

MATERIALS

Patons Shetland Chunky (50 g)

Size	10	12	
Main Color MC (2279)	7	8	balls
Contrast A (2101)	5	5	balls
Contrast B (2096)	3	3	balls

Sizes 5½ mm (U.S. 9) and 6 mm (U.S. 10) knitting needles **or size needed to obtain tension**. 2 st holders. One separating zipper.

TENSION

15 sts and 20 rows = 4 ins [10 cm] with larger needles in stocking st.

INSTRUCTIONS

The instructions are written for smaller size. If changes are necessary for larger size the instructions will be written thus ( ).

Note: When working from Charts I and IV, carry yarn not in use loosely across wrong side of work but never over more than 5 sts. When it must pass over more than 5 sts, weave it over and under color in use on next st or at center point of sts it passes over. The colors are never twisted around one another.

When working from Charts II and III, wind small balls of the colors to be used, one for each separate area of color in the design. Start new colors at appropriate points. To change colors, twist the two colors around each other where they meet, on wrong side, to avoid a hole.

B A C K

With MC and smaller needles, cast on 73 (**77**) sts.
**1st row: (Right side). K1. * P1. K1. Rep from * to end of row.
2nd row: P1. *K1. P1. Rep from * to end of row.
Rep these 2 rows (K1. P1) ribbing 6 times more ending on a 2nd row (14 rows in all).

Change to larger needles and work

Chart I

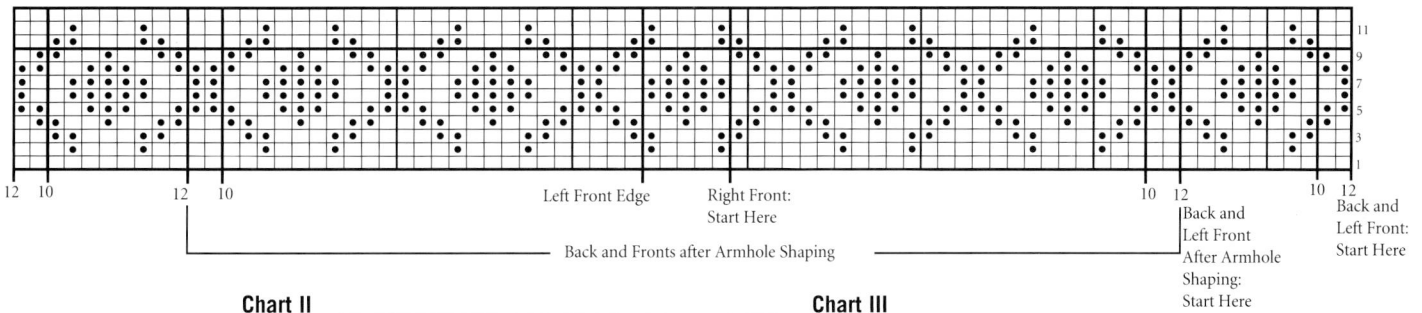

Left Front Edge

Right Front:
Start Here

Back and Fronts after Armhole Shaping

Back and
Left Front
After Armhole
Shaping:
Start Here

Back and
Left Front:
Start Here

Chart II

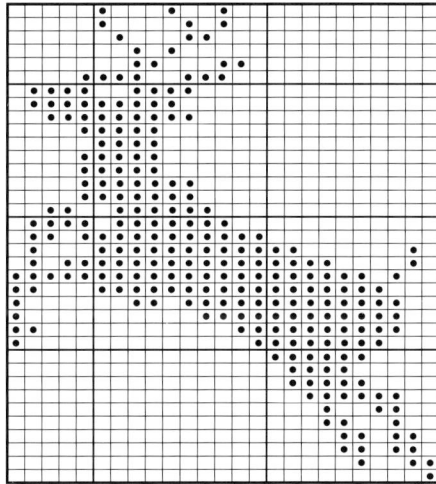

Start Here

Chart III

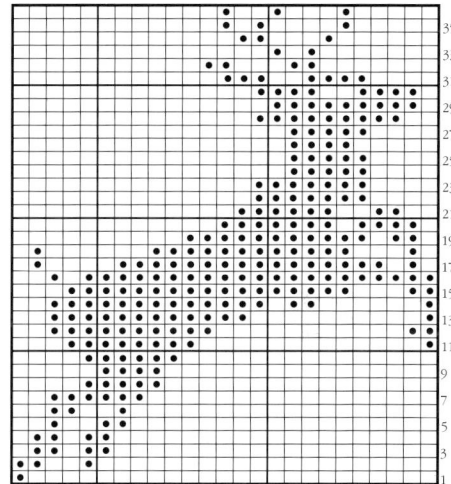

Start Here

Key

= MC

= Contrast A

= Contrast B

6 rows in stocking st, thus ending with right side facing for next row.

Work Chart I to end of chart reading **knit** rows from **right** to left and **purl** rows from **left** to right.**

With MC, work 10 rows stocking st, ending with right side facing for next row.
With A, work 2 rows stocking st.

Next row: (Right side). With A, K7 (**9**). Work row 1 of Chart II across next 25 sts reading row from **right** to left. With A, K9. Work row 1 of Chart III across next 25 sts reading row from **right** to left. With A, K7 (**9**).
Next row: With A, P7 (**9**). Work row 2 of Chart III across next 25 sts reading row from **left** to right. With A, P9. Work row 2 of Chart II across next 25 sts reading row from **left** to right.

With A, P7 (**9**).
Charts II and III are now in position. Cont working Charts II and III until row 34 of Charts is complete.

Armhole shaping: Keeping cont of Charts II and III, cast off 5 sts beg next 2 rows. Charts II and III are now complete.

With A, dec 1 st each end of needle on

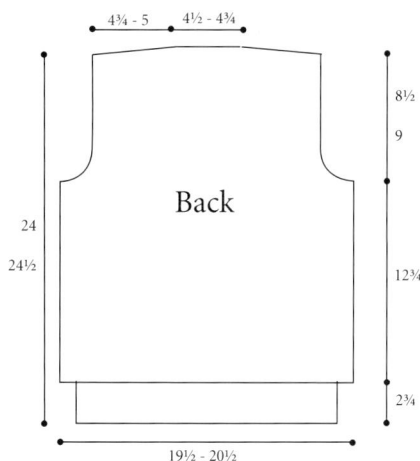

Back

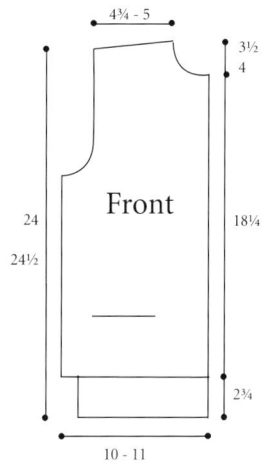

Front

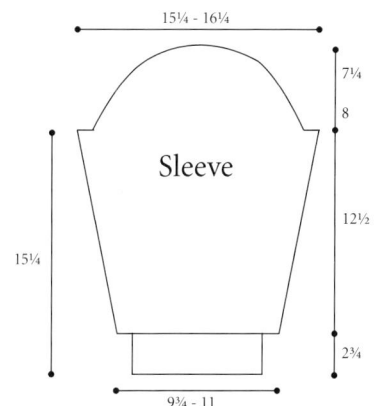

Sleeve

next 2 rows. 59 (**63**) sts.

With MC, working in stocking st, dec 1 st at each end of needle on next and every row to 53 (**57**) sts.
Work 9 rows even, ending with right side facing for next row.

Work Chart I to end of chart.

With MC, work 16 (**18**) rows even, ending with right side facing for next row.

Shoulder shaping:
Cast off 6 sts beg next 4 rows, then 6 (**7**) sts beg next 2 rows. Cast off rem 17 (**19**) sts.

P O C K E T S
(*make 2*)

With MC and larger needles, cast on 18 sts. Work 21 rows even in stocking st ending with a knit row. Slip these sts on a st holder.

L E F T
F R O N T
With MC and smaller needles, cast on 39 (**41**) sts.

Work from ** to ** as given for Back.
Next row: With MC, knit.
Next row: P13. K18. Purl to end of row. Rep last 2 rows twice more.
Next row: K8 (**10**). Cast off next 18 sts. Knit to end of row.

Chart VI

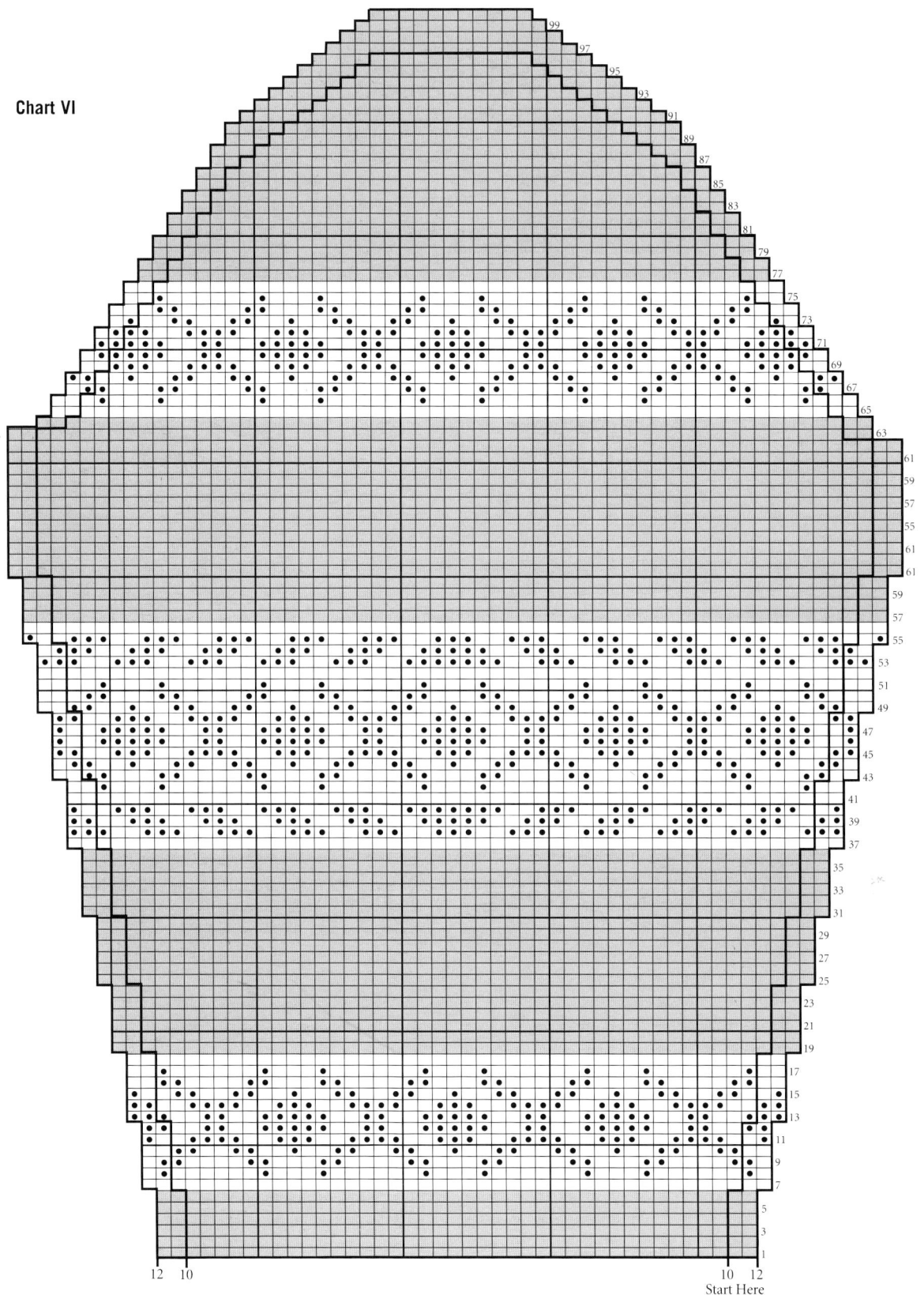

Next row: P13. Purl across 18 sts from pocket st holder. Purl to end of row. With MC, work 2 rows stocking st. With A, work 2 rows stocking st.

Next row: (Right side). With A, K7 (**9**). Work row 1 of Chart II across next

25 sts reading row from right to left. With A, K7.
Next row: With A, P7. Work row 2 of Chart II across next 25 sts reading row from **left** to right. With A, P7 (**9**). Chart II is now in position. Cont working Chart II until row 34 of chart is complete.

Armhole shaping: Next row: (Right side). Keeping cont of Chart II, cast off 5 sts beg next row (armhole edge). Work 1 row even. Chart II is now complete.

With A, dec 1 st at armhole edge on next 2 rows.

With MC, dec 1 st at armhole edge on next and every row to 29 (**31**) sts. Work 9 rows stocking st even, ending with right side facing for next row.

Work Chart I to end of chart.

Next row: (Right side). With MC, knit.

Neck shaping: Next row: With MC, cast off 6 sts (neck edge). Purl to end of row.
Dec 1 st at neck edge on next 5 (**6**) rows. 18 (**19**) sts.

With MC, cont even until Left Front measures same length as Back to beg of shoulder shaping, ending with right side facing for next row.

Shoulder shaping: Cast off 6 sts beg next and following alt row. Work 1 row even. Cast off rem 6 (**7**) sts.

RIGHT FRONT

With MC and smaller needles, cast on 39 (**41**) sts.
Work from ** to ** as given for Back.

Next row: With MC, knit.
Next row: P8 (**10**). K18. Purl to end of row.
Rep last 2 rows twice more.
Next row: K13. Cast off next 18 sts. Knit to end of row.
Next row: P8 (**10**). P18 from pocket st holder. Purl to end of row.
With MC, work 2 rows stocking st.
With A, work 2 rows stocking st.

Next row: (Right side). With A, K7. Work row 1 of Chart III across next 25 sts reading row from **right** to left. With A, K7 (**9**).

Next row: With A, P7 (**9**). Work row 2 of Chart III across next 25 sts reading row from **left** to right. With A, P7. Chart III is now in position. Cont working Chart III until row 35 of chart is complete.

Armhole shaping: Next row: (Wrong side). Keeping cont of Chart III, cast off 5 sts beg next row (armhole edge). Chart III is now complete.

With A, dec 1 st at armhole edge on next 2 rows.

With MC, dec 1 st at armhole edge on next and every row to 29 (**31**) sts. Work 9 rows even, ending with right side facing for next row.

Work Chart I to end of chart.

Neck shaping: Next row: (Right side). With MC, cast off 6 sts (neck edge). Knit to end of row.
Dec 1 st at neck edge on next 5 (**6**) rows. 18 (**19**) sts.

With MC, cont even until Right Front measures same length as Back to beg of shoulder shaping, ending with **wrong** side facing for next row.

Shoulder shaping: Cast off 6 sts beg next and following alt row. Work 1 row even. Cast off rem 6 (**7**) sts.

SLEEVES

With MC and smaller needles, cast on 37 (**41**) sts. Work 14 rows in (K1. P1) ribbing as given for Back ending on a 2nd row.

Change to larger needles and work Chart IV reading **knit** rows from **right** to left and **purl** rows from **left** to right noting side incs each end of needle on 7th and every following 6th row until there are 57 (**61**) sts.
Chart IV is shown on page 76.

Cont even until row 62 of Chart IV is complete.

Armhole shaping: Cast off 2 sts beg next 2 rows. Dec 1 st at each end of needle on next and every alt row to 31 sts, then every row to 11 sts. Cast off.

FINISHING

Collar: With MC and larger needles, cast on 7 sts.
1st row: K1. Inc 1 st in next st. K3. Inc 1 st in next st. K1.
2nd row: Knit.
3rd row: K1. Inc 1 st in next st. Knit to last 2 sts. Inc 1 st in next st. K1.
4th row: Knit.
5th to 8th rows: As 3rd and 4th rows twice more. 15 sts.
9th row: (Outside edge). K1. Inc 1 st in next st. Knit to end of row.
10th row: Knit.
Rep last 2 rows until there are 23 sts. Cont even in garter st (knit every row) until Collar from beg measures 13½ (**14½**) ins [34.5 (**37**) cm], ending at outside edge.

Proceed as follows:
1st row: K1. K2tog. Knit to end of row (neck edge).
2nd row: Knit.
3rd to 17th rows: As 1st and 2nd rows 7 times more. 15 sts.
17th row: K1. K2tog. Knit to last 3 sts. K2tog. K1.
18th row: Knit.
Rep last 2 rows until there are 7 sts ending with 17th row. Cast off.

Sew shoulder, side and sleeve seams. Sew in sleeves. Sew pockets in position on wrong side. Sew neck edge of Collar around neck, placing cast on and cast off ends along cast off sts of neck edge. Sew zipper in position under front border. ♠

HARMONY PULLOVERS

1960s

Beehive

as shown on page 19

as shown on page 19

SIZES

Crew Neck Version

Bust/chest measurement

Small	30–32 ins	[76–81	cm]
Medium	34–36 "	[86–91	"]
Large	38–40 "	[97–102	"]
Extra Large	42–44 "	[107–112	"]

Finished bust/chest

Small	40	ins [102	cm]
Medium	42	" [107	"]
Large	44	" [112	"]
Extra Large	46	" [117	"]

Collar Version

Bust measurement

Small	30–32 ins	[76–81	cm]
Medium	34–36 "	[86–91	"]

Finished bust

Small	38	ins [97	cm]
Medium	40	" [102	"]

MATERIALS

Patons Classic Merino Wool (100 g)

Crew Neck Version

Size	S	M	L	XL	
208	7	7	8	9	balls

Collar Version

Size	S	M	
204	6	7	balls

Sizes 4 mm (U.S. 6) and 5 mm (U.S. 8) knitting needles **or size needed to obtain tension**. 1 cable needle. 2 st holders.

TENSION

18 sts and 24 rows = 4 ins [10 cm] with larger needles in stocking st.

STITCH GLOSSARY

C4B = slip next 2 sts onto a cable needle and leave at back of work. K2, then K2 from cable needle.

C4F = slip next 2 sts onto a cable needle and leave at front of work. K2, then K2 from cable needle.

C6B = slip next 3 sts onto a cable needle and leave at back of work. K3, then K3 from cable needle.

C6F = slip next 3 sts onto a cable needle and leave at front of work. K3, then K3 from cable needle.

KB1 = knit into back of next st.

PB1 = purl into back of next st.

INSTRUCTIONS

The instructions are written for smallest size. If changes are necessary for larger sizes the instructions will be written thus ( ).

Panel Pat (worked over 30 sts).
1st row: KB1. P1. K4. P1. KB1. P1. K12. P1. KB1. P1. K4. P1. KB1.
2nd row: PB1. K1. P4. K1. PB1. K1. P12. K1. PB1. K1. P4. K1. PB1.
3rd row: KB1. P1. C4B. P1. KB1. P1. C6B. C6F. P1. KB1. P1. C4F. P1. KB1.
4th row: As 2nd row.
5th and 6th rows: As 1st and 2nd rows.
7th row: KB1. P1. C4B. P1. KB1. P1. K12. P1. KB1. P1. C4F. P1. KB1.
8th row: As 2nd row.
These 8 rows form panel pat.

Crew Neck Version

BACK

With smaller needles, cast on 103 (109**-113-**119**) sts.
1st row: (Right side). K1. *KB1. P1. Rep from * to last 2 sts. KB1. K1.
2nd row: K1. *PB1. K1. Rep from * to end of row.
Rep these 2 rows ribbing for 2½ ins [6 cm] ending on a 2nd row and inc 25 (**25**-27-**27**) sts evenly across last row. 128 (**134**-140-**146**) sts.

Change to larger needles and proceed in pat as follows:
1st row: (Right side). K1. (KB1. P2) 0 (**1**-2-**3**) time(s). *Work 1st row of panel pat. P2. Rep from * twice more. Work 1st row of panel pat. (P2. KB1) 0 (**1**-2-**3**) time(s). K1.
2nd row: K1. (PB1. K2) 0 (**1**-2-**3**) time(s). *Work 2nd row of panel pat. K2. Rep from * twice more. Work 2nd row of panel pat. (K2. PB1) 0 (**1**-2-**3**) time(s). K1.
Panel pat is now in position.

Cont working appropriate rows of panel pat until work from beg measures 15 (**15½**-16-**16½**) ins [38 (**39.5**-40.5-**42**) cm] ending with right side facing for next row.

Raglan shaping: Cast off 3 (**6**-3-**6**) sts beg next 2 rows.
1st row: K1. KB1. P2tog. Pat to last 4 sts. P2tog. KB1. K1.
2nd row: K1. PB1. K1. Pat to last 3 sts. K1. PB1. K1.
Rep last 2 rows to 64 (**64**-70-**70**) sts.**

1st row: K1. KB1. P2tog. Pat to last 4 sts. P2tog. KB1. K1.
2nd row: K1. PB1. K2tog. Pat to last 4 sts. K2tog. PB1. K1.
Rep last 2 rows twice more, then 1st row once more. 50 (**50**-56-**56**) sts.

Sizes S and M only: Next row: K1. PB1. K1. P1. (P2tog) 5 times. P1. K1. PB1. K1. (P2tog) twice. K1. PB1. K2tog. PB1. K1. (P2tog) twice. K1. PB1. K1. P1. (P2tog) 5 times. P1. K1. PB1. K1. 35 sts. Cast off.

Sizes L and XL only: Next row: K1. PB1. K2tog. PB1. K1. (P2tog. P1) 4 times. K1. PB1. K1. (P2tog) twice. K1. PB1. K2tog. PB1. K1. (P2tog) twice. K1. PB1. K1. (P2tog. P1) 4 times. K1. PB1. K2tog. PB1. K1. 41 sts. Cast off.

F R O N T

Work from ** to ** as given for Back.

Sizes S and M only: Next row: K1. PB1. K1. P4. K1. PB1. K1. P5. P2tog. P2. P2tog. P1. K1. PB1. K1. (P2tog) twice. K1. PB1. K2tog. PB1. K1. (P2tog)

twice. K1. PB1. K1. P1. P2tog. P2. P2tog. P5. K1. PB1. K1. P4. K1. PB1. K1. 55 sts.

Sizes L and XL only: Next row: K1. PB1. K2. PB1. K1. P4. K1. PB1. K1. P1. P2tog. (P2. P2tog) twice. P1. K1. PB1. K1. (P2tog) twice. K1. PB1. K2tog. PB1. K1. (P2tog) twice. K1. PB1. K1. P1. (P2tog. P2) twice. P2tog. P1. K1. PB1. K1. P4. K1. PB1. K2. PB1. K1. 59 sts.

Neck shaping: 1st row: (Right side). K1. KB1. P2tog. Pat across 8 sts. K2tog (neck edge). Cast off 27 (**27**-31-**31**) sts. K2tog (neck edge). Pat across 8 sts. P2tog. KB1. K1.
2nd row: K1. PB1. K2tog. Pat to end of row.
3rd row: K2tog. Pat to last 4 st. P2tog. KB1. K1.
Rep 2nd and 3rd rows once, then 2nd row once.
7th row: K1. P2tog. KB1. K1.
Keeping armhole edge even, dec 1 st at neck edge on next 2 rows. 2 sts.
Next row: K2tog. Fasten off.

With **wrong** side of work facing, join yarn to rem sts.
1st row: Pat to last 4 sts. K2tog. PB1. K1.
2nd row: K1. KB1. P2tog. Pat to last 2 sts. K2tog.
Rep 1st and 2nd rows once, then 1st row once.
6th row: K1. KB1. P2tog. K1.

Keeping armhole edge even, dec 1 st at neck edge on next 2 rows. 2 sts.
Next row: K2tog. Fasten off.

S L E E V E S

With smaller needles, cast on 43 (**43**-47-**47**) sts. Work 2½ ins [6 cm] in ribbing as given for Back ending on a 2nd row and inc 13 (**13**-15-**15**) sts evenly across last row. 56 (**56**-62-**62**) sts.

Change to larger needles and proceed in pat as follows:
1st row: (Right side). K1. (KB1. P2) 4 (**4**-5-**5**) times. Work 1st row of panel pat. (P2. KB1) 4 (**4**-5-**5**) times. K1.
2nd row: K1. (PB1. K2) 4 (**4**-5-**5**) times. Work 2nd row of panel pat. (K2. PB1) 4 (**4**-5-**5**) times. K1.
Panel pat is now in position.

Cont in pat, working appropriate rows of panel pat, inc 1 st each end of needle on next and every following 6th row to 80 (**80**-86-**86**) sts taking inc sts into (KB1. P2) pat.

Cont even in pat until work from beg measures 17 (**17½**-18-**18½**) ins [43 (**44.5**-45.5-**47**) cm] ending with right side facing for next row.

Raglan shaping: Cast off 3 (**6**-3-**6**) sts beg next 2 rows.

Sizes S and L only: 1st row: K1. KB1. P2tog. Pat to last 4 sts. P2tog. KB1. K1.
2nd row: K1. PB1. K1. Pat to last 3 sts. K1. PB1. K1.
Rep last 2 rows to 10 sts.

Sizes M and XL only: 1st row: K1. KB1. P2tog. Pat to last 4 sts. P2tog. KB1. K1.
2nd row: K1. PB1. K1. Pat to last 3 sts. K1. PB1. K1.
3rd row: K1. KB1. P1. Pat to last 3 sts. P1. KB1. K1.
4th row: As 2nd row.
Rep these 4 rows to (**62**-68) sts.
Rep 1st and 2nd rows only to 10 sts.

All sizes: Next row: K1. KB1. P2tog. Pat to last 4 sts. P2tog. KB1. K1.

Crew Neck Version

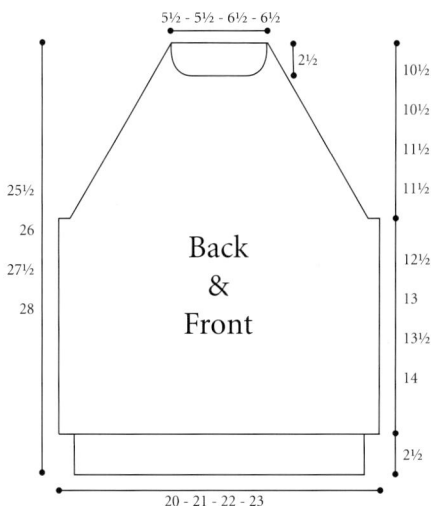

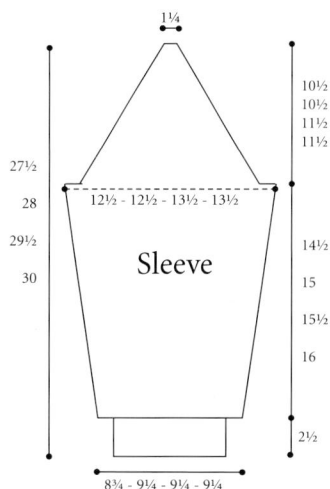

Back & Front
5½ - 5½ - 6½ - 6½
2½
10½
10½
11½
11½
25½
26
27½
28
12½
13
13½
14
2½
20 - 21 - 22 - 23

Sleeve
1¼
10½
10½
11½
11½
27½
28
29½
30
12½ - 12½ - 13½ - 13½
14½
15
15½
16
2½
8¾ - 9¼ - 9¼ - 9¼

Next row: K1. PB1. K1. P2tog. K1. PB1. K1. Cast off rem 7 sts.

FINISHING

Pin garment pieces to measurements and cover with a damp cloth leaving to dry. Sew raglan seams leaving left back raglan seam open.

Neckband: With right side of work facing and smaller needles, pick up and knit 7 sts across top of left sleeve, 9 sts down left front neck edge, 23 (**23**-27-**27**) sts from front, 9 sts up right front neck edge, 7 sts across top of right sleeve and 36 (**36**-42-**42**) across Back neck edge. 91 (**91**-101-**101**) sts.

Beg and ending on a 2nd row, work 3 ins [8 cm] in ribbing as given for Back. Cast off loosely in ribbing. Sew left back raglan and neckband seam. Fold neckband in half to wrong side and sew loosely in position. Sew side and sleeve seams.

Collar Version

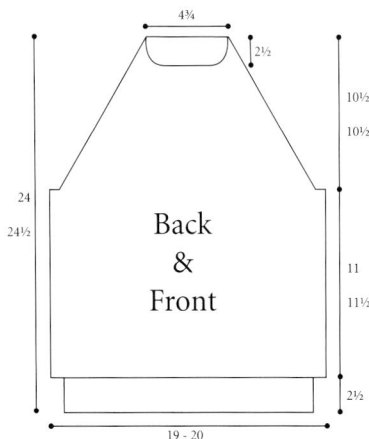

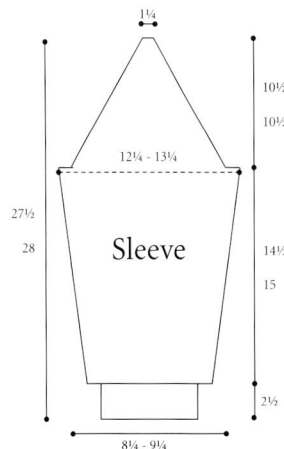

BACK

With smaller needles cast on 93 (99**) sts.
1st row: (Right side). K1. *KB1. P1. Rep from * to last 2 sts. KB1. K1.
2nd row: K1. *PB1. K1. Rep from * to end of row.
Rep these 2 rows ribbing for 2½ ins

[6 cm] ending on a 2nd row and inc 21 sts evenly across last row. 114 (**120**) sts.

Change to larger needles and proceed in pat as follows:
1st row: (Right side). K1. (KB1. P2) 3 (**4**) times. *Work 1st row of panel pat. P2. Rep from * twice more. KB1. (P2. KB1) 2 (**3**) times. K1.
2nd row: K1. (PB1. K2) 3 (**4**) times. *Work 2nd row of panel pat. K2. Rep from * twice more. Work 2nd row of panel pat. PB1. (K2. PB1) 2 (**3**) times. K1.
Panel pat is now in position.

Cont working appropriate row of panel pat until work from beg measures 13½ (**14**) ins [34.5 (**35.5**) cm] ending with right side facing for next row.

Raglan shaping: Cast off 3 (**6**) sts beg next 2 rows.
1st row: K1. KB1. P2tog. Pat to last 4 sts. P2tog. KB1. K1.
2nd row: K1. PB1. K1. Pat to last 3 sts. K1. PB1. K1.**
Rep last 2 rows to 44 sts.

Next row: K1. KB1. P2tog. Pat to last 4 sts. P2tog. KB1. K1.
Next row: K1. (PB1. K1) twice. (P2tog) twice. K1. PB1. K1. P1. (P2tog. P2) 3 times. P1. K1. PB1. K1. (P2tog) twice. (K1. PB1) twice. K1. 35 sts. Cast off.

FRONT

Work from ** to ** as given for Back.

Rep last 2 rows to 52 sts.
Next row: K1. KB1. P2tog. Pat to last 4 sts. P2tog. KB1. K1.
Next row: K1. PB1. K1. P3. K1. PB1. K2. PB1. K1. (P2tog) twice. K1. PB1. K1. P1. (P2tog. P2) twice. P2tog. P1. K1. PB1. K1. (P2tog) twice. K1. PB1. K2. PB1. K1. P3. K1. PB1. K1. 43 sts.

Neck shaping: 1st row: (Right side). K1. KB1. P2tog. Pat across 3 sts. K2tog (neck edge). Cast off 25 sts. K2tog (neck edge). Pat across 3 sts. P2tog. KB1. K1.
Work 1 row even across last 7 sts. Leave rem sts on a spare needle.
3rd row: K2tog. K1. P2tog. KB1. K1.
Work 1 row even.
5th row: K1. P2tog. KB1. K1.
Keeping armhole edge even, dec 1 st at neck edge on next 2 rows. 2 sts.
Next row: K2tog. Fasten off.

With **wrong** side of work facing, join yarn to rem 7 sts.
Work 1 row even.
3rd row: K1. KB1. P2tog. K1. K2tog.
Work 1 row even.
5th row: K1. KB1. P2tog. K1.
Keeping armhole edge even, dec 1 st at neck edge on next 2 rows. 2 sts.
Next row: K2tog. Fasten off.

SLEEVES

With smaller needles, cast on 39 (**43**) sts. Work 2½ ins [6 cm] in ribbing as given for Back ending on a 2nd row and inc 11 (**13**) sts evenly across last row. 50 (**56**) sts.

Change to larger needles and proceed in pat as follows:
1st row: (Right side). K1. (KB1. P2) 3 (**4**) times. Work 1st row of panel pat. (P2. KB1) 3 (**4**) times. K1.
2nd row: K1. (PB1. K2) 3 (**4**) times. Work 2nd row of panel pat. (K1. PB1) 3 (**4**) times. K1.
Panel pat is now in position.

Cont in pat, working appropriate rows of panel pat, inc 1 st each end of needle on next and every following 6th row until there are 74 (**80**) sts,

Collar Version

Back & Front

4¾
2½
10½
10½
24
24½
11
11½
2½
19 - 20

Sleeve

1¼
10½
10½
12¼ - 13¼
27½
28
14½
15
2½
8¼ - 9¼

taking inc sts into (KB1. P2) pat.

Cont even until work from beg measures 17 (**17½**) ins [43 (**44.5**) cm] ending with right side facing for next row.

Raglan shaping: Cast off 3 (**6**) sts beg next 2 rows.
1st row: K1. KB1. P2tog. Pat to last 4 sts. P2tog. KB1. K1.
2nd row: K1. PB1. K1. Pat to last 3 sts. K1. PB1. K1.
3rd row: K1. KB1. P1. Pat to last 3 sts. P1. KB1. K1.
4th row: As 2nd row.
Rep these 4 rows to 62 sts.
Rep 1st and 2nd rows to 10 sts.
Next row: K1. KB1. P2tog. Pat to last 4 sts. P2tog. KB1. K1.
Next row: K1. PB1. K1. P2tog. K1. PB1. K1. Cast off rem 7 sts.

FINISHING

Pin garment pieces to measurements and cover with a damp cloth leaving to dry. Sew raglan seams. Sew side and sleeve seams.

Collar: With larger needles cast on 101 sts. Work 6 ins [15 cm] in ribbing as given for Back ending with right side facing for next row.

Change to smaller needles and proceed as follows:
1st row: (Right side). K2tog. Rib 7. (K3tog. Rib 7) 9 times. K2tog. 81 sts. Place a marker at each end of last row.
2nd row: K1. *KB1. PB1. Rep from * to last 2 sts. KB1. K1.
3rd row: K1. *PB1. KB1. Rep from * to last 2 sts. PB1. K1.
Rep 2nd and 3rd rows 7 times more. Cast off in ribbing.

Sew side edges of neckband tog from cast off edge to marker, and placing this seam at center front, sew cast off edge evenly around neck edge. ⬥

HOCKEY JACKET

1960s

PATONS
Beehive

as shown on page 20

INSTRUCTIONS

The instructions are written for smallest

size. *If changes are necessary for larger sizes the instructions will be written thus ( ).*

Note: When working Fair Isle technique, carry yarn not in use loosely across wrong side of work but never over more than 5 sts. When it must pass over more than 5 sts, weave it over and under color in use on next st or at center point of sts it passes over. The colors are never twisted around one another.

When working color blocking technique, wind small balls of the colors to be used, one for each separate area of color in the design. Start new colors at appropriate points. To change colors, twist the two colors around each other where they meet, on wrong side, to avoid a hole.

BACK

With MC and smaller needles, cast on 59 (**65**) sts.
****1st row:** (Right side). K1. * P1. K1. Rep from * end of row.
2nd row: P1. *K1. P1. Rep from * to end of row.
Rep these 2 rows (K1. P1) ribbing 6 times more ending on a 2nd row (14 rows in all).**

Chart I

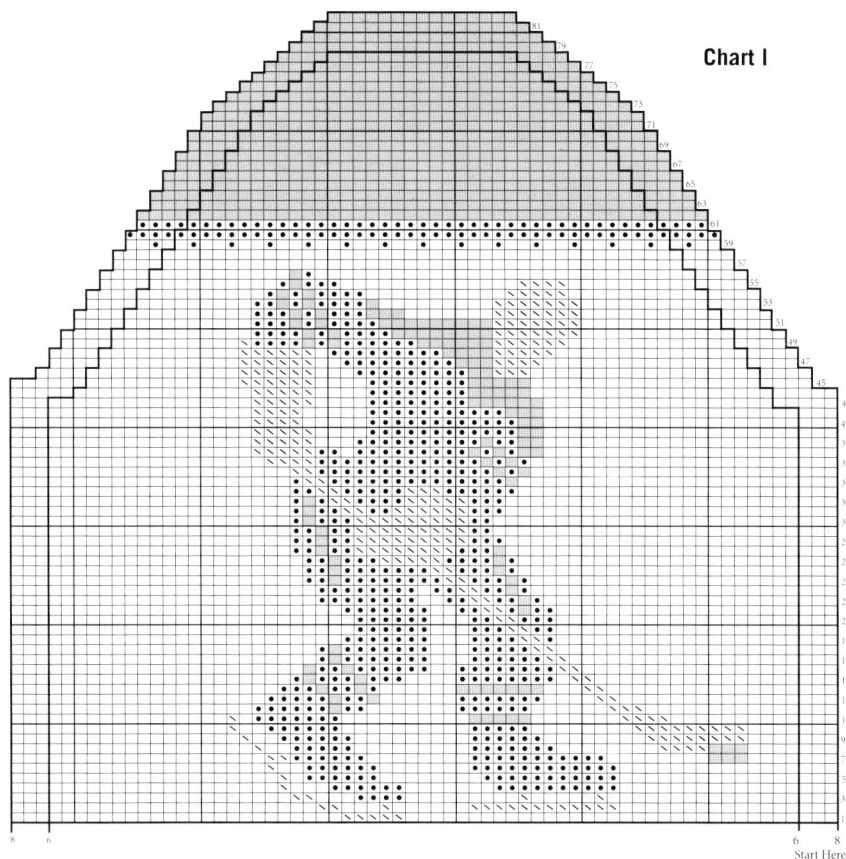

Start Here

Key

☐ = MC

▨ = Contrast A

⊡ = Contrast B

◩ = Contrast C

Next row: P7. Purl across 14 sts from pocket st holder. Purl to end of row. Work 2 rows stocking st, ending with right side facing for next row.

Work Chart II reading **knit** rows from **right** to left and **purl** rows from **left** to right until row 26 (**28**) of chart is complete.

Raglan shaping: Keeping cont of Chart II, cast off 2 sts beg next row. Work 1 row even in chart.

Dec 1 st at armhole edge on next and every alt row until row 49 (**53**) of Chart II is complete. 16 (**18**) sts.

Neck shaping: Next row: (Wrong side). Cast off 4 sts (neck edge). Work Chart II to end of row.

Cont working Chart II, dec 1 st at neck edge on next 3 rows **at the same time**, dec 1 st at raglan edge on next and

Change to larger needles and work 4 (**8**) rows in stocking st, thus ending with right side facing for next row.

Work Chart I reading **knit** rows from **right** to left and **purl** rows from **left** to right until row 42 (**44**) of chart is complete.

Raglan shaping: Keeping cont of Chart I, cast off 2 sts beg next 2 rows. Dec 1 st at each end of needle on next and every alt row 14 (**13**) times, then every row to 15 sts. Cast off (right side).

Pockets (make 2)
With MC and larger needles, cast on 14 sts.
Work 13 (**15**) rows even in stocking st ending with **wrong** side facing for next row.
Slip these sts on a st holder.

LEFT FRONT

With MC and smaller needles, cast on 29 (**32**) sts.
Work from ** to ** as given for Back.

Change to larger needles and work 12 (**16**) rows in stocking st, thus ending

with right side facing for next row.

Next row: Knit.
Next row: P7. K14. Purl to end of row. Rep last 2 rows once more.
Next row: K8 (**11**). Cast off next 14 sts. Knit to end of row.

Chart II

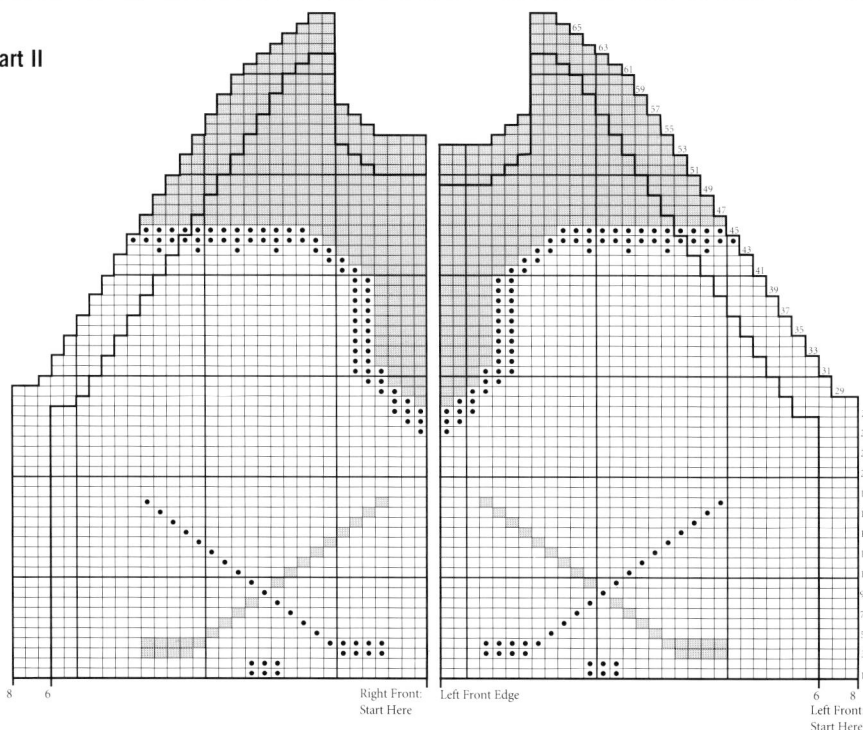

Right Front: Start Here   Left Front Edge   Left Front: Start Here

Chart III

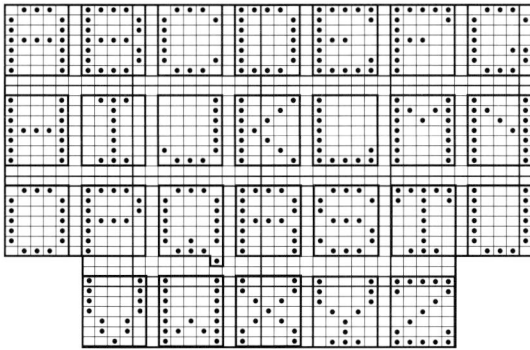

Next row: P8 (11). K14. Purl to end of row.
Rep last 2 rows once more.
Next row: K7. Cast off next 14 sts. Knit to end of row.
Next row: P8 (11). Purl across 14 sts from pocket st holder. Purl to end of row.
Work 2 rows stocking st ending with right side facing for next row.

Work Chart II until row 27 (**29**) of chart is complete.

Raglan shaping: Keeping cont of Chart II, cast off 2 sts beg next row. Dec 1 st at armhole on next and every alt row until row 50 (**54**) of Chart II is complete. 16 (**18**) sts.

Neck shaping: Next row: (Right side). Cast off 4 sts (neck edge). Work Chart II to last 2 sts. K2tog.

Cont working Chart II, dec 1 st at neck edge on next 3 rows at **the same time**, dec 1 st at raglan edge on next and every alt row to 3 (**7**) sts, then every row to 2 sts. K2tog. Fasten off.

Change to larger needles and work Chart IV reading **knit** rows from **right** to left and **purl** rows from **left** to right noting side incs each end of needle on 5th and following 4th row, then every following 6th row until there are 53 (**59**) sts.

Cont even in Chart IV until row 56 (**58**) of Chart is complete.

Raglan shaping: Cast off 2 sts beg next 2 rows. Dec 1 st each end of needle on next and every alt row to 23 (**29**) sts, then every row to 3 (**5**) sts. Cast off.

COLLAR

With A and larger needles, cast on 6 sts.

1st row: K1. Inc 1 st in next st. K2. Inc 1 st in next st. K1.
2nd row: Knit.
3rd row: K1. Inc 1 st in next st. Knit to last 2 sts. Inc 1 st in next st. K1.
4th row: Knit.
5th and 6th rows: As 3rd and 4th rows. 12 sts.
7th row: (Outside edge). K1. Inc 1 st in next st. Knit to end of row.
8th row: Knit.
Rep last 2 rows until there are 19 sts. Cont even in garter st (knit every row) until Collar from beg measures 13 (**13½**) ins [33 (**34.5**) cm], ending at outside edge.

Proceed as follows:
1st row: K1. K2tog. Knit to end of row (neck edge).
2nd row: Knit.
3rd to 14th rows: As 1st and 2nd rows 6 times more. 12 sts.
15th row: K1. K2tog. Knit to last 3 sts. K2tog. K1.
16th row: Knit.
Rep last 2 rows until there are 6 sts ending with 15th row. Cast off.

FINISHING

With B, work duplicate st embroidery of team name (or desired words) along center of each sleeve as illustrated.

every alt row to 3 (**7**) sts, then every row to 2 sts. K2tog. Fasten off.

RIGHT FRONT

With MC and smaller needles, cast on 29 (**32**) sts.
Work from ** to ** as given for Back.

Change to larger needles and work 12 (**16**) rows in stocking st, thus ending with right side facing for next row.

Next row: Knit.

Chart IV

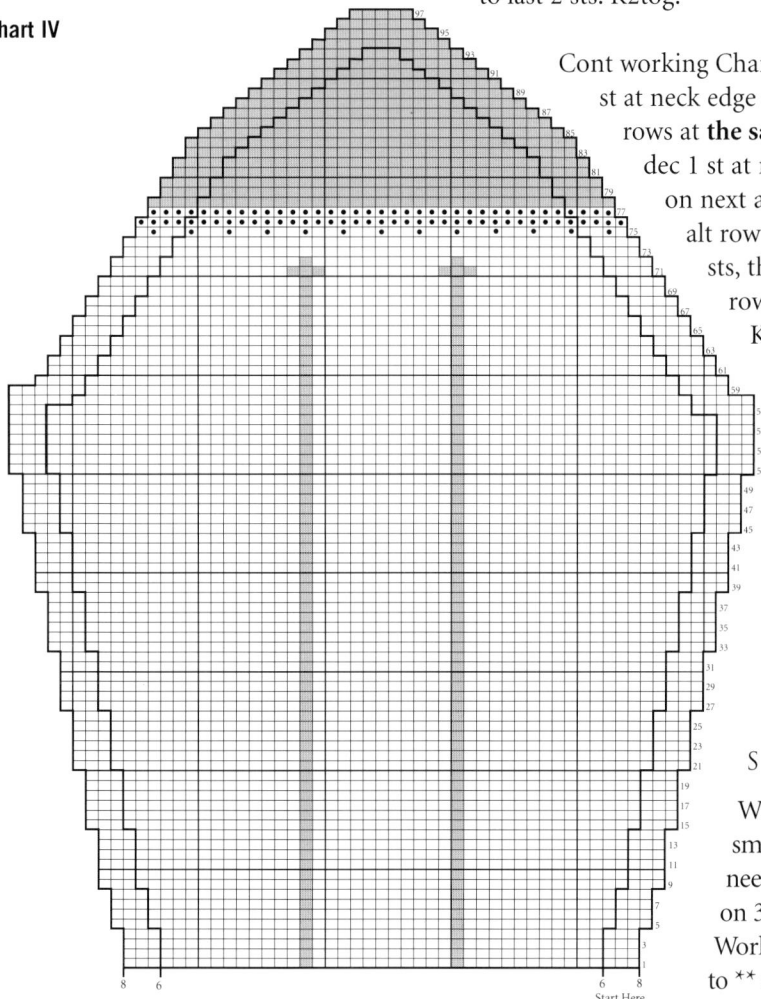
Start Here

SLEEVES

With MC and smaller needles, cast on 35 (**41**) sts. Work from ** to ** as given for Back.

Sew raglan seams. Sew side sleeve seams. Sew pockets in position on wrong side. Sew Collar to neck edge placing cast on and cast off ends along cast off sts at neck edge. Sew zipper in position under front border.

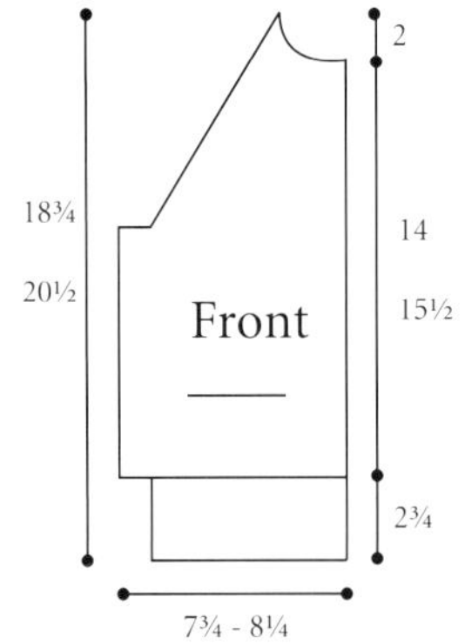

18¾
20½
Front
2
14
15½
2¾
7¾ - 8¼

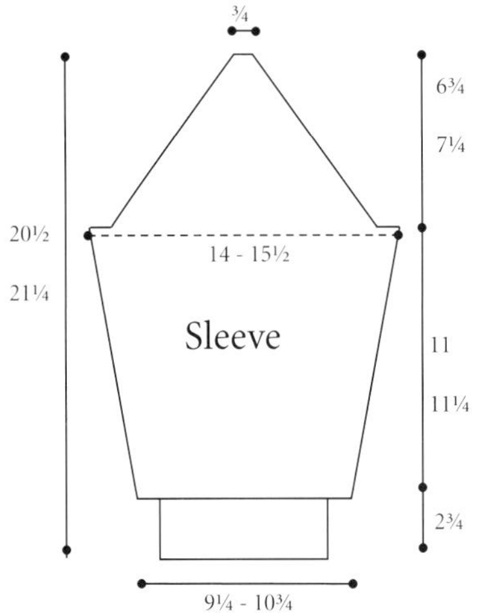

¾
6¾
7¼
20½
21¼
14 - 15½
Sleeve
11
11¼
2¾
9¼ - 10¾

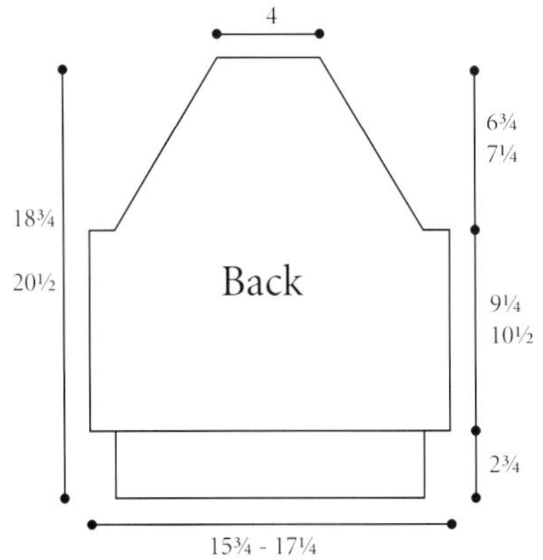

4
6¾
7¼
18¾
20½
Back
9¼
10½
2¾
15¾ - 17¼

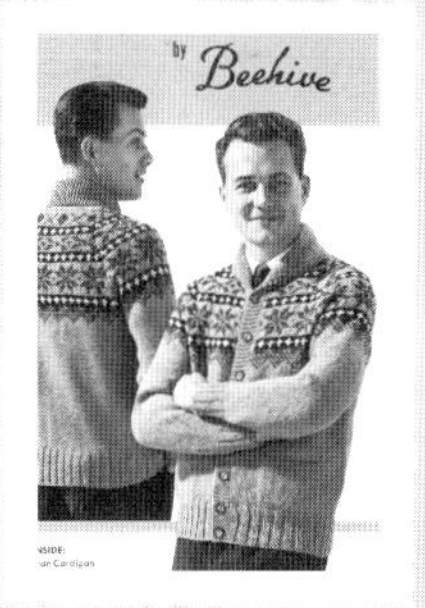

by Beehive

BALTIC CARDIGAN

1960s

PATONS Beehive

as shown on page 21

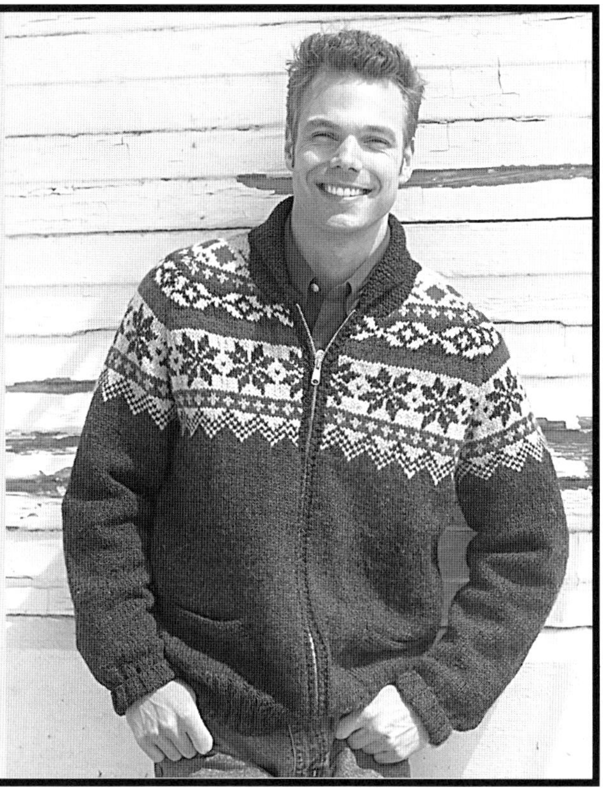

SIZES

Bust/chest measurement

Medium	36–38 ins	[91–97 cm]
Large	40–42 "	[102–107"]

Finished bust/chest

Medium	45½ ins	[115.5 cm]
Large	48 "	[122 "]

MATERIALS

Patons Classic Merino Wool (100 g)

Size	M	L	
Main Color (MC) (225)	5	6	**balls**
Contrast A (229)	1	1	**ball**
Contrast B (207)	1	1	**ball**
Contrast C (241)	1	1	**ball**
Contrast D (204)	1	1	**ball**

Sizes 4 mm (U.S. 6), 5 mm (U.S. 8) and 5½ mm (U.S. 9) knitting needles **or size needed to obtain tension**. 2 st holders. Separating zipper.

TENSION

18 sts and 24 rows = 4 ins [10 cm] with 5 mm needles in stocking st.

INSTRUCTIONS

The instructions are written for smaller size. If changes are necessary for larger size the instructions will be written thus ( ).

Note: When working from charts, carry yarn not in use loosely across wrong side of work but never over more than 5 sts. When it must pass over more than 5 sts, weave it over and under color in use on next st or at center point of sts it passes over. The colors are never twisted around one another.

BACK

With MC and 4 mm needles, cast on 102 (**106**) sts.

1st row: (Right side). K2. *P2. K2. Rep from * to end of row.

2nd row: P2. *K2. P2. Rep from * to end of row.

Rep these 2 rows (K2. P2) ribbing for 3 ins [8 cm] ending on a 2nd row and inc 1 (**3**) sts evenly across last row. 103 (**109**) sts.

Change to 5 mm needles and proceed in stocking st until work from beg measures 15½ (**16½**) ins [39.5 (**42**) cm] ending with right side facing for next row.

Change to 5½ mm needles and work Chart I in stocking st to end of chart reading **knit** rows from **right** to left and **purl** rows from **left** to right. Cast off rem 31 (**33**) sts.

Chart I is shown on page 85.

Pocket linings (Make 2)

With MC and 5 mm needles cast on 24 sts

and work 31 rows in stocking st, thus ending with a knit row. Leave these sts on a st holder.

LEFT FRONT

With MC and 4 mm needles, cast on 51 (55) sts.
1st row: (Right side). *K2. P2. Rep from * to last 3 sts. K3.
2nd row: K3. *K2. P2. Rep from * to end of row. These 2 rows form 3 st garter edge and (K2. P2) ribbing.
Rep these 2 rows for 3 ins [8 cm] ending on a 2nd row and inc 3 (2) sts evenly across last row. 54 (57) sts

Change to 5 mm needles and proceed in stocking st for 23 rows, thus ending with **wrong** side facing for next row.

Pocket Edging: 1st row: K3. P14 (15). K24. P13 (15).
2nd row: Knit.
Rep last 2 rows twice more, then 1st row once.
Next row: (Right side). K13 (15). Cast off next 24 sts. Knit to end of row.
Next row: K3. P14 (15). Purl across 24 sts from pocket lining. Purl to end of row. Cont in stocking st, keeping 3 st garter edge, until work from beg measures 15½ (16½) ins [39.5 (42) cm] ending with right side facing for next row.

Change to 5½ mm needles and work Chart II in stocking st to end of chart reading **knit** rows from **right** to left and **purl** rows from **left** to right and keeping 3 st garter edge, as before. 2 sts rem
Next row: Sl1. K1. psso. Fasten off.
Chart II is shown on page 86.

RIGHT FRONT

With MC and 4 mm needles, cast on 51 (55) sts.
1st row: (Right side). K3. *P2. K2. Rep from * to end of row.
2nd row: *P2. K2. Rep from * to last 3 sts. K3. These 2 rows form 3 st garter edge and (K2. P2) ribbing.
Rep these 2 rows for 3 ins [8 cm] ending on a 2nd row and inc 3 (2) sts evenly across last row. 54 (57) sts.

Change to 5 mm needles and proceed in stocking st for 23 rows, thus ending with **wrong** side facing for next row.

Pocket Edging: 1st row: P13 (15). K24. P14 (15). K3.
2nd row: Knit.
Rep last 2 rows twice more, then 1st row once.
Next row: (Right side). K17 (18). Cast off next 24 sts. Knit to end of row.
Next row: P13 (15). Purl across 24 sts from pocket lining. Purl to end of row.

Cont in stocking st, keeping 3 st garter edge, until work from beg measures 15½ (16½) ins [39.5 (42) cm] ending

with right side facing for next row. Change to 5½ mm needles and work Chart III in stocking st to end of chart reading **knit** rows from **right** to left and **purl** rows from **left** to right and keeping 3 st garter edge, as before. 2 sts rem
Next row: K2tog. Fasten off.
Chart III is shown on page 86.

SLEEVES

With MC and 4 mm needles, cast on 46 (50) sts. Work 3 ins [8 cm] in (K2. P2) ribbing as given for Back ending on a 2nd row and inc 1 st in center of last row. 47 (51) sts.

Change to 5 mm needles and proceed in stocking st inc 1 st each end of needle on 5th and following 6th rows until there are 71 (77) sts.

Cont even until work from beg measures 18 (19) ins [45.5 (48) cm] ending with right side facing for next row.

Change to 5½ mm needles and work Chart IV in stocking st to end of chart reading **knit** rows from **right** to left and **purl** rows from **left** to right. Cast off rem 5 sts.
Chart IV is shown on page 86.

COLLAR

With MC and 4 mm needles, cast on 6 sts.
1st row: (Right side). K1. Inc 1 st in next st. K2. Inc 1 st in next st. K1.

Key

☐ = MC

▨ = Contrast A

⊟ = Contrast B

⊡ = Contrast C

◺ = Contrast D

Chart I

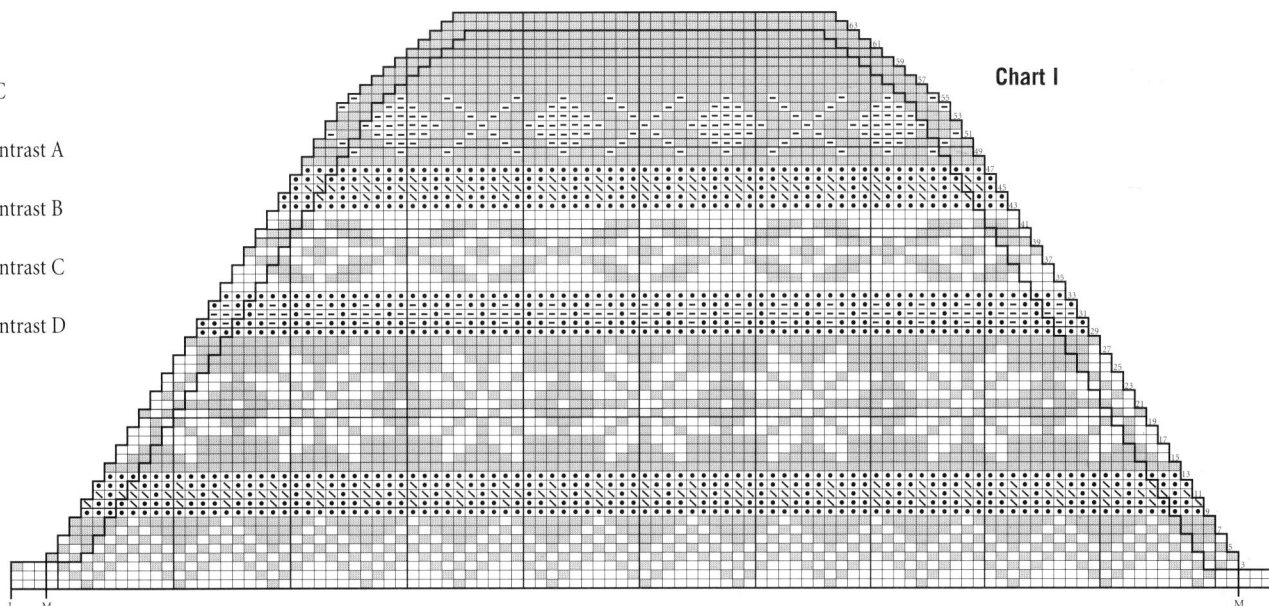

Start Here

Chart III

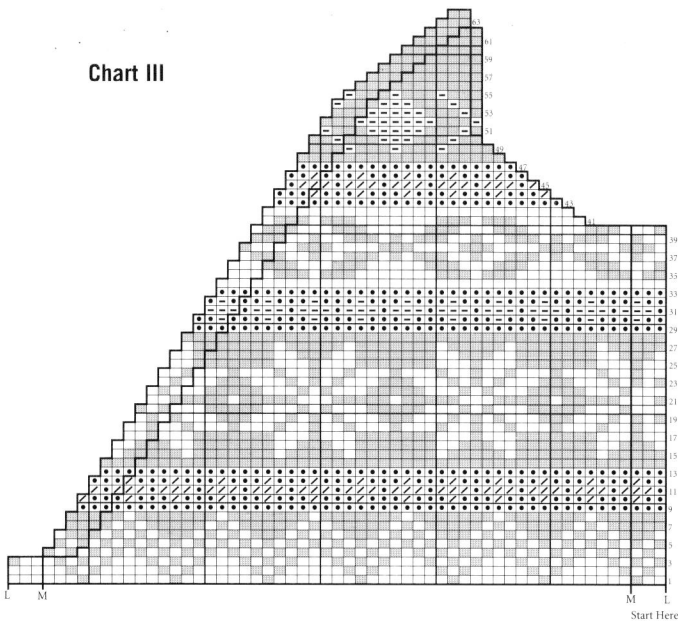

Chart II

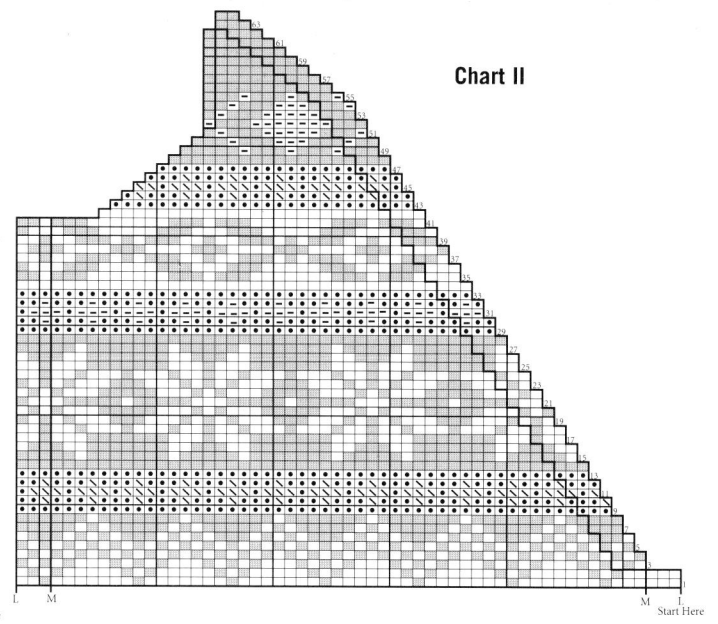

2nd row: Knit.
3rd row: K1. Inc 1 st in next st. Knit to last 2 sts. Inc 1 st in next st. K1.
4th row: Knit.
Rep last 2 rows 3 times more. 16 sts.
11th row: (Outside edge). K1. Inc 1 st in next st. Knit to end of row.
12th row: Knit.
Rep last 2 rows until there are 24 sts. Cont even in garter st (knit every row) until work from beg measures 14 ins [35.5 cm] ending with right side facing for next row.

Proceed as follows:
1st row: K1. K2tog. Knit to end of row (neck edge).
2nd row: Knit.

Rep last 2 rows until there are 16 sts, ending with a 2nd row.
Next row: K1. K2tog. Knit to last 3 sts. K2tog. K1.
Next row: Knit.
Rep last 2 rows until there are 6 sts. Cast off.

FINISHING

Pin garment pieces to measurements and cover with a damp cloth leaving to dry. Sew raglan seams. Sew side and sleeve seams. Sew pocket linings in position on wrong side. Placing cast on and cast off edges of Collar along the cast off edges of Fronts, sew neck edge of Collar to neck edge. Sew in zipper. ♠

Chart IV

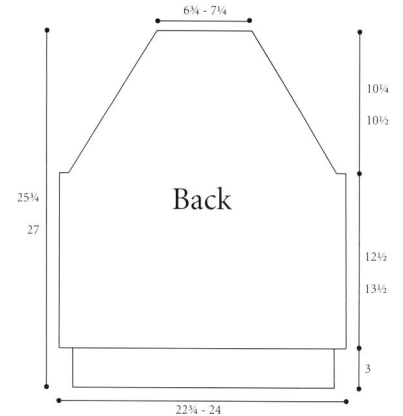

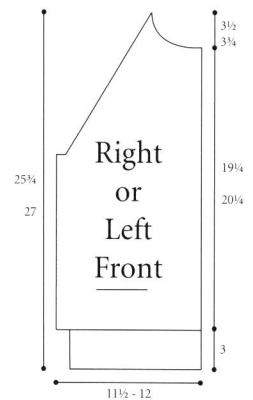

Back

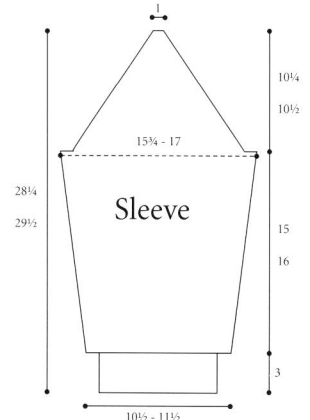

Right or Left Front

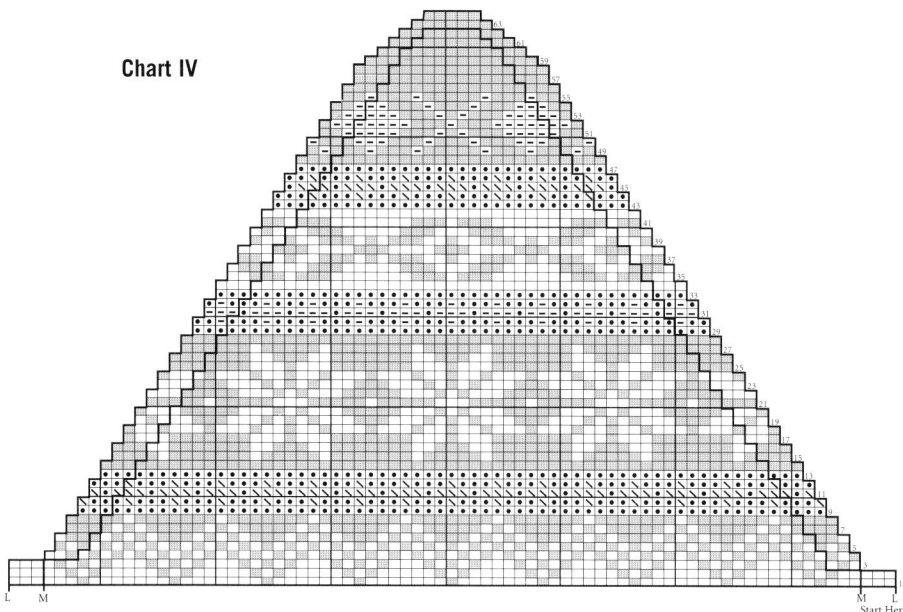

Sleeve

ARAN PONCHO

1970s

PATONS

as shown on page 22

MATERIALS

Patons Decor (100 g)

1602	9	**balls**

Sizes 8 mm (U.S. 11) knitting needles **or size needed to obtain tension**. 1 cable needle.

TENSION

12 sts and 16 rows = 4 ins [10 cm] with 2 strands of yarn tog in stocking st.

STITCH GLOSSARY

C2F = slip next st onto a cable needle and leave at front of work. P1, then K1 from cable needle.

C2B = slip next st onto a cable needle and leave at back of work. K1, then P1 from cable needle.

C4F = slip next 2 sts onto a cable needle and leave at front of work. K2, then K2 from cable needle.

Cr3F = slip next 2 sts onto a cable needle and leave at front of work. P1, then K2 from cable needle.

Cr3B = slip next st onto a cable needle and leave at back of work. K2, then P1 from cable needle.

KB1 = Knit into back of next st.

PB1 = Purl into back of next st.

INSTRUCTIONS

Panel Pat A (worked over 16 sts).
1st row: P5. Cr3B. Cr3F. P5.
2nd row: K5. P2. K2. P2. K5.
3rd row: P4. Cr3B. P2. Cr3F. P4.
4th row: K4. (P2. K4) twice.
5th row: P3. Cr3B. P4. Cr3F. P3.
6th row: K3. P2. K1. P4. K1. P2. K3.
7th row: P2. (Cr3B) twice. (Cr3F) twice. P2.
8th row: (K2. P2. K1. P2) twice. K2.
9th row: P1. (Cr3B) twice. P2. (Cr3F) twice. P1.
10th row: (K1. P2) twice. K4. (P2. K1) twice.
11th row: P1. K1. C2F. Cr3F. P2. Cr3B. C2B. K1. P1.
12th row: (K1. P1) twice. K1. P2. K2. P2. (K1. P1) twice. K1.
13th row: P1. K1. P1. C2F. Cr3F. Cr3B. C2B. P1. K1. P1.
14th row: K1. P1. K2. P1. K1. P4. K1. P1. K2. P1. K1.
15th row: P1. C2F. C2B. P1. C4F. P1. C2F. C2B. P1.
16th row: (K2. P2) twice. (P2. K2) twice.
These 16 rows complete Panel Pat A.

Panel Pat B (worked over 8 sts).
1st row: P2. K4. P2.
2nd row: K2. P4. K2.
3rd row: P2. C4F. P2.
4th row: K2. P4. K2.
These 4 rows complete Panel Pat B.

PONCHO PIECE (make 2 alike).

With 2 strands of yarn tog, cast on 80 sts.
1st row: (Right side). (K1. P1) 5 times. (Work 1st row of Panel Pat B. KB1. Work 1st row of Panel Pat A. KB1) twice. Work 1st row of Panel Pat B. (P1. K1) 5 times.
2nd row: (P1. K1) 5 times. (Work 2nd row of Panel Pat B. PB1. Work 2nd row of Panel Pat A. PB1) twice. Work 2nd row of Panel Pat B. (K1. P1) 5 times.
Panel pats are now in position.

Cont in pat until 9 complete Panel Pat A have been worked, thus ending with 16th row of Panel Pat A. Cast off in pat.

FINISHING

Sew cast on edge of first piece to side edge of 2nd piece. Sew cast on edge of 2nd piece to side edge of first piece to form head opening.

Fringe: Cut 14 ins [35.5 cm] lengths of yarn. Taking 6 strands tog, knot into fringe along lower edge of Poncho and trim ends evenly.
(See Helpful Hints) ♠

ARAN AFGHAN

1970s

PATONS

as shown on pages 22-23

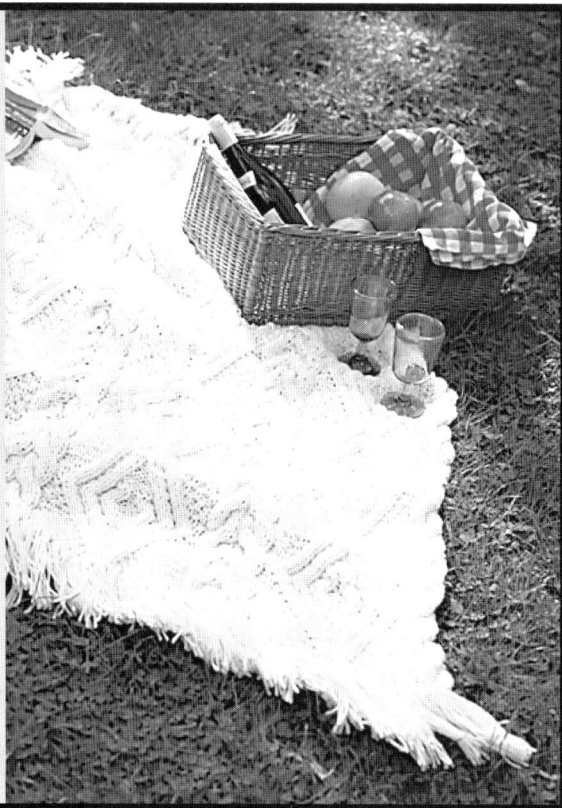

MEASUREMENT

Finished Size: Approx 29 ins across [73.5 cm]

MATERIALS

Patons Decor (100 g)

1602	17	**balls**

Size 9 mm (U.S. 13) knitting needles **or size needed to obtain tension**. One cable needle.

TENSION

12 sts and 15 rows = 4 ins [10 cm] in stocking st with 2 strands of yarn.

STITCH GLOSSARY

C6F = slip next 3 sts onto a cable needle and leave at front of work. K3, then K3 from cable needle.

C6B = slip next 3 sts onto a cable needle and leave at back of work. K3, then K3 from cable needle.

Cr3B = slip next st onto a cable needle and leave at back of work. K2, then P1 from cable needle.

Cr3F = slip next 2 sts onto a cable needle and leave at front of work. P1, then K2 from cable needle.

INSTRUCTIONS

Panel *(Make 4).*
With 2 strands of yarn, cast on 43 sts.
Foundation row: (Wrong side). K1. P6. (K1. P1) 5 times. K2. P2. K1. P2. K2. (P1. K1) 5 times. P6. K1.
Proceed in pat as follows:
1st row: P1. C6F. (P1. K1) 5 times. P1. Cr3B. P1. Cr3F. (P1. K1) 5 times. P1. C6B. P1.
2nd and alt rows: Knit all knit sts and purl all purl sts as they appear.
3rd row: P1. K6. P2. (K1. P1) 4 times. Cr3B. P3. Cr3F. (K1. P1) 4 times. P2. K6. P1.
5th row: P1. K6. P1. (K1. P1) 4 times. Cr3B. P5. Cr3F. P1. (K1. P1) 4 times. K6. P1.
7th row: P1. K6. P2. (K1. P1) 3 times. Cr3B. P1. (K2. P1) twice. Cr3F. (P1. K1) 3 times. P2. K6. P1.
9th row: P1. C6F. P1. (K1. P1) 3 times. (Cr3B. P1) twice. (Cr3F. P1) twice. (K1. P1) 3 times. C6B. P1.
11th row: P1. K6. P2. (K1. P1) twice. (Cr3B. P1) twice. P2. (Cr3F. P1) twice. (K1. P1) twice. P1. K6. P1.
13th row: P1. K6. P1. (K1. P1) twice. (Cr3B. P1) twice. P4. (Cr3F. P1) twice. (K1. P1) twice. K6. P1.
15th row: P1. K6. P2. K1. P1. (Cr3B. P1) twice. (K2. P1) twice. (Cr3F. P1) twice. K1. P2. K6. P1.
17th row: P1. C6F. P1. K1. P1. (Cr3B. P1) 3 times. (Cr3F. P1) 3 times. K1. P1. C6B. P1.
19th row: P1. K6. P2. (Cr3B. P1) 3 times. P2. (Cr3F. P1) 3 times. P1. K6. P1.
21st row: P1. K6. P1. K1. (Cr3F. P1) 3 times. P2. (Cr3B. P1) twice. Cr3B. K1. P1. K6. P1.
23rd row: P1. K6. P2. K1. (Cr3F. P1) 3 times. (Cr3B. P1) twice. Cr3B. K1. P2. K6. P1.
25th row: P1. C6F. (P1. K1) twice. (Cr3F. P1) twice. P6. Cr3B. P1. Cr3B. (K1. P1) twice. C6B. P1.
27th row: P1. K6. P1. (P1. K1) twice. (Cr3F. P1) twice. P4. Cr3B. P1. Cr3B. (K1. P1) twice. P1. K6. P1.
29th row: P1. K6. (P1. K1) 3 times. (Cr3F. P1) twice. P2. Cr3B. P1. Cr3B. (K1. P1) 3 times. K6. P1.
31st row: P1. K6. P2. (K1. P1) twice. K1. (Cr3F. P1) twice. Cr3B. P1. Cr3B. (K1. P1) 3 times. P1. K6. P1.
33rd row: P1. C6F. (P1. K1) 4 times. Cr3F. P7. Cr3B. (K1. P1) 4 times. C6B. P1.
35th row: P1. K6. P2. (K1. P1) 3 times. K1. Cr3F. P5. Cr3B. (K1. P1) 4 times. P1. K6. P1.
37th row: P1. K6. (P1. K1) 5 times. Cr3F. P3. Cr3B. (K1. P1) 5 times. K6. P1.
39th row: P1. K6. P2. (K1. P1) 4 times. K1. Cr3F. P1. Cr3B. (K1. P1) 5 times. P1. K6. P1.
40th row: As 2nd row.
These 40 rows form pat.

Work a further 160 rows of pat.
Next row: (Right side). P1. C6F. P1. (K1. P1) 5 times. K3. P1. K3. (P1. K1) 5 times. P1. C6B. P1.
Cast off in pat. Sew panels tog.

Make fringe: Cut 12 ins [30.5 cm] lengths of yarn and taking 6 strands tog, knot into fringe evenly across ends of Afghan. Trim fringe evenly. ♠

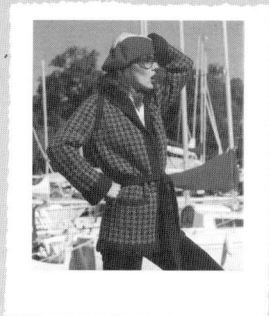

HOUNDSTOOTH JACKET

1970s

PATONS

as shown on page 23

SIZES

Bust measurement

Small	30–32 ins	[76–81	cm]
Medium	34–36 "	[86–91	cm]
Large	38–40 "	[97–102 "	]

Finished bust

Small	42	ins [107	cm]
Medium	44	" [112	"]
Large	46	" [117	"]

MATERIALS

Size	S	M	L	
Patons Shetland Ragg Chunky (100 g)				
Main Color (MC) (703)	7	8	8	**balls**
and **Patons Shetland Chunky** (50 g)				
Contrast A (2277)	7	8	9	**balls**

Sizes 5 mm (U.S. 8) and 6 mm (U.S. 10) knitting needles **or size needed to obtain tension**. 3 buttons. 2 st holders.

TENSION

16 sts and 18 rows = 4 ins [10 cm] with larger needles in chart pat.

INSTRUCTIONS

The instructions are written for smallest size. If changes are necessary for larger sizes the instructions will be written thus ( ).

Note: When working from chart, carry yarn not in use loosely across wrong side of work. The colors are never twisted around one another.

BACK

With MC and smaller needles, cast on 80 (**84**-88) sts.
Work 13 rows garter st (knit every row) noting that first row is wrong side and inc 4 sts evenly across last row. 84 (**88**-92) sts.

Change to larger needles and work Chart I in stocking st to end of chart reading **knit** rows from **right** to left and **purl** rows from **left** to right noting the 4 st rep will be worked 21 (22-23) times. Rows 1 to 4 of Chart I form pat.
Chart I is shown on page 90.

Cont in pat until work from beg measures 20½ ins [52 cm] ending with right side facing for next row.

Raglan shaping: Keeping cont of pat, cast off 2 sts beg next 2 rows.
1st row: With MC, K2. K2tog. Pat to last 4 sts. With MC, Sl1. K1. psso. K2.

2nd row: With MC, P4. Pat to last 4 sts. With MC, P4.
Rep last 2 rows until there are 50 (**48**-50) sts, ending with right side facing for next row.
1st row: With MC, K2. K2tog. Pat to last 4 sts. With MC, Sl1. K1. psso. K2.
2nd row: With MC, P2. P2togtbl. Pat to last 4 sts. With MC, P2tog. P2.
Rep last 2 rows until there are 26 (**28**-30) sts. Cast off.

Pocket Linings *(Make 2).*
With MC and larger needles, cast on 21 sts and work 4 ins [10 cm] in stocking st, ending with right side facing for next row. Leave these sts on a st holder.

LEFT FRONT

With MC and smaller needles, cast on 42 (46**-50) sts and work 13 rows garter st noting that first row is **wrong** side and inc 2 sts evenly across last row. 44 (**48**-52) sts.

Change to larger needles and work Chart I in stocking st to end of chart reading **knit** rows from **right** to left and **purl** rows from **left** to right noting the 4 st rep will be worked 11 (**12**-13) times. Rows 1 to 4 of Chart I form pat.

Cont in pat until work from beg measures 8½ ins [21.5 cm] ending with right side facing for next row.**

Pocket placement: Next row: Pat across 12 sts . Slip next 21 sts onto a st holder. Pat across 21 sts from pocket lining. Pat to end of row.

Cont even in pat until work from beg measures 20½ ins [52 cm] ending with right side facing for next row.

Raglan and neck shaping: Keeping cont of pat, cast off 2 sts beg next row.
Work 1 row even in pat.
1st row: With MC, K2. K2tog. Pat to last 2 sts. Work 2tog (neck edge).
2nd row: Pat to last 4 sts. With MC, P4.
Rep last 2 rows until there are 28 (**22**-16) sts, ending with a 2nd row.

Chart I

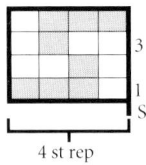

Key

= MC
= Contrast A

4 st rep
Start Here

1st row: With MC, K2. K2tog. Pat to end of row.
2nd row: Pat to last 4 sts. With MC, P4.
3rd row: With MC, K2. K2tog. Pat to last 2 sts. Work 2tog.
4th row: As 2nd row.
Rep last 4 rows 3 (**2**-0) times more.
16 (**13**-13) sts.

1st row: With MC, K2. K2tog. Pat to end of row.
2nd row: Pat to last 4 sts. With MC, P2tog. P2.
3rd row: With MC, K2. K2tog. Pat to last 2 sts. Work 2tog.
4th row: As 2nd row.
Rep last 4 rows 1 (**0**-0) time more.
6 (**8**-8) sts.

1st row: With MC, K2. K2tog. Pat to end of row.
2nd row: Pat to last 4 sts. With MC, P2tog. P2.

Rep last 2 rows 1 (**2**-2) time(s) more.
2 sts.
Next row: K2tog. Fasten off.

RIGHT FRONT

Work from ** to ** as given for Left Front.

Pocket placement: Next row: Pat across 11 (**15**-19) sts . Slip next 21 sts onto a st holder. Pat across 21 sts from pocket lining. Pat to end of row.

Cont even in pat until work from beg measures 20½ ins [52 cm] ending with **wrong** side facing for next row.

Raglan and neck shaping: Keeping cont of pat, cast off 2 sts beg next row.
1st row: Work 2tog (neck edge). Pat to last 4 sts. With MC, Sl1. K1. psso. K2.
2nd row: With MC, P4. Pat to end of row.
Rep last 2 rows until there are 28 (**22**-16) sts, ending with a 2nd row.

1st row: Pat to last 4 sts. With MC, Sl1. K1. psso. K2.
2nd row: With MC, P4. Pat to end of row.
3rd row: Work 2tog. Pat to last 4 sts. With MC, Sl1. K1. psso. K2.

4th row: As 2nd row.
Rep last 4 rows 3 (**2**-0) times more.
16 (**13**-13) sts.

1st row: Pat to last 4 sts. With MC, Sl1. K1. psso. K2.
2nd row: With MC, P2. P2togtbl. Pat to end of row.
3rd row: Work 2tog. Pat to last 4 sts. With MC, Sl1. K1. psso. K2.
4th row: As 2nd row.
Rep last 4 rows 1 (**0**-0) time more.
6 (**8**-8) sts.

1st row: Pat to last 4 sts. With MC, Sl1. K1. psso. K2.
2nd row: With MC, P2. P2togtb. Pat to end of row.
Rep last 2 rows 1 (**2**-2) time(s) more.
2 sts.
Next row: K2tog. Fasten off.

SLEEVES

With MC and smaller needles cast on 48 (**48**-52) sts and work 3½ ins [9.5 cm] in garter st, noting that first row is **wrong** side and inc 4 sts evenly across last row. 52 (**52**-56) sts. Place a marker at each end of last row.
Change to larger needles and work Chart I in stocking st to end of chart

---

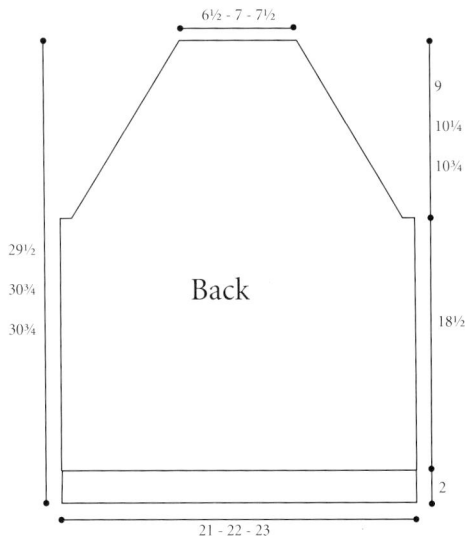

Back

6½ - 7 - 7½

9
10¼
10¾

29½
30¾
30¾

18½

2

21 - 22 - 23

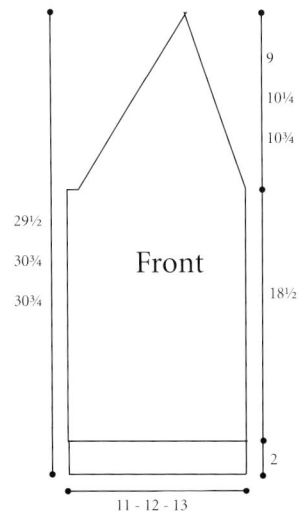

Front

9
10¼
10¾

29½
30¾
30¾

18½

2

11 - 12 - 13

reading **knit** rows from **right** to left and **purl** rows from **left** to right noting the 4 st rep will be worked 13 (**13**-14) times.
Rows 1 to 4 of Chart I form pat.

Keeping cont of pat, inc 1 st each end of needle on next and following 6th rows until there are 72 (**74**-76) sts, taking inc sts into pat.

Cont even in pat until work from markers measures 17 (**17½**-18) ins [43 (**44.5**-45.5) cm] ending with right side facing for next row.

Raglan shaping: Keeping cont of pat, cast off 2 sts beg next 2 rows.
1st row: With MC, K2. K2tog. Pat to last 4 sts. With MC, Sl1. K1. psso. K2.
2nd row: With MC, P4. Pat to last 4 sts. With MC, P4.
Rep last 2 rows until there are 48 (**44**-44) sts, ending on a 2nd row.
1st row: With MC, K2. K2tog. Pat to last 4 sts. With MC, Sl1. K1. psso. K2.
2nd row: With MC, P2. P2togtbl. Pat to last 4 sts. With MC, P2tog. P2.
Rep last 2 rows until there are 4 sts. Cast off.

FINISHING

Pocket Edging: With right side of work

facing, smaller needles and MC, knit across 21 sts on pocket st holder. Work a further 4 rows garter st. Cast off knitways (wrong side).

Sew raglan seams. Sew side and sleeve seams, reversing seams at markers on sleeves for cuff turnback. Sew pocket linings in position on wrong side and pocket edgings in position on right side.

Right Front Band and Collar: With MC and smaller needles, cast on 10 sts. Proceed in garter st until band, when slightly stretched, measures length to fit up Right Front edge to first neck dec, sewing in place as you work and noting that first row is **wrong** side.
Next row: (Right side). K1. Inc 1 st in next st. Knit to end of row.
Next row: Knit.
Rep last 2 rows until there are 28 sts. Cont even in garter st until band, when slightly stretched, measures length to fit to center back neck edge. Cast off.

Left Front Band and Collar: With MC and smaller needles, cast on 10 sts. Proceed in garter st until band, when slightly stretched, measures length to fit up Left Front edge to first neck dec,

sewing in place as you work and noting that first row is **wrong** side.
Next row: (Right side). Knit to last 2 sts. Inc 1 st in next st. K1.
Next row: Knit.
Rep last 2 rows until there are 28 sts. Cont even in garter st until band, when slightly stretched, measures length to fit to center back neck edge. Cast off. Sew center back Collar seam.

Optional:
Belt: With MC and smaller needles, cast on 7 sts and proceed in garter st until Belt, when slightly stretched, measures 54 (**58**-60) ins [137 (**147.5**-152) cm]. Cast off.

Belt Loops: Make 2 twisted cords and sew in position at side seams.

Make twisted cord: Cut 2 strands of MC 10 ins [25 cm] long. With both strands tog hold one end and with someone holding other end, twist strands to the right until they begin to curl. Fold the 2 ends tog and tie in a knot so they will not unravel. The strands will now twist themselves tog.

Note: To work buttonholes in Right Front Band, follow instructions below:

Work **Left Front Band and Collar** first.

On this band mark positions for 3 buttons evenly spaced having top button at first front dec and bottom button 10 ins [25 cm] above lower edge.

Right Front Band and Collar: With MC and smaller needles cast on 10 sts. Proceed in garter st working buttonholes to correspond to button markers as follows:
Next row: (Right side). K4. Cast off 2 sts. K4
Next row: Knit, casting on 2 sts over cast off sts. ♠

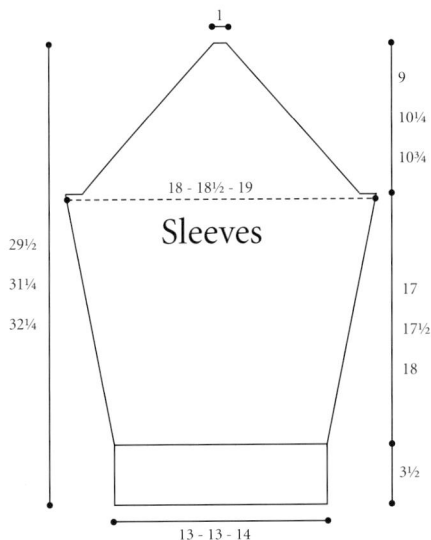

Sleeves

18 - 18½ - 19

1

9
10¼
10¾

29½
31¼
32¼

17
17½
18

3½

13 - 13 - 14

PARTY PRETTY

1970s

PATONS

as shown on page 24

SIZE

Bust measurement

2	22	ins	[56	cm]
4	24	"	[61	"	]
6	26	"	[66	"	]

Finished bust

2	23½	ins	[59.5	cm]
4	27	"	[68.5	"	]
6	28½	"	[72.5	"	]

MATERIALS

Patons Cotton DK (50 g)

	2	4	6	
6306	4	6	7	balls

Size 3.25 mm (U.S. D) crochet hook **or size needed to obtain tension**. 4 buttons.

TENSION

20 sts and 13 rows = 4 ins [10 cm] in Bodice pat.

INSTRUCTIONS

The instructions are written for smallest size. If changes are necessary for larger sizes the instructions will be written thus ( ).

FRONT BODICE

**Ch 60 (68-72).

1st row: (Foundation row). (Right side). 1 sc in 2nd ch from hook. 1 sc in each ch to end of row. Ch 3. Turn. 59 (67-71) sts.

2nd row: Miss first 2 sc. *1hdc in next sc. Ch 1. Miss next sc. Rep from * to last sc. 1 hdc in last sc. Ch 2. Turn.

3rd row: Miss first hdc. *1 hdc in next ch 1 sp. 1 hdc in next hdc. Rep from * to turning ch. 1 hdc in each of next 2 ch of turning ch. Ch 3. Turn.

4th row: Miss first 2 hdc. *1 hdc in next hdc. Ch 1. Miss next hdc. Rep from * ending with 1 hdc in top of turning ch. Ch 2. Turn.

Rep 3rd and 4th rows to form pat.
Rep last 2 rows 2 (2-3) times more, then 3rd row once omitting turning ch at end of last row.

Shape armholes: 1st row: (Right side). 1 ss in each of first 4 sts. Ch 3. Pat to last 4 sts. **Turn.**

2nd row: Ch 2. Work even in pat omitting turning ch at end of row.

3rd row: 1 ss in each of first 2 sts. Ch 3. Pat to last 2 sts. **Turn.**

Rep last 2 rows 2 (3-3) times more. 39 (43-47) sts.**

Shape neck: 1st row: Pat across 13 (15-15) sts (neck edge). **Turn.**

2nd row: 1 ss in each of first 2 sts. Ch 3. Pat to end of row. Ch 2. **Turn.**

3rd row: Pat across 11 (13-13) sts. **Turn.**

4th row: As 2nd row.

5th row: Pat across 9 (11-11) sts. Ch 3. **Turn.**

Work 4 rows even in pat omitting turning ch at end of last row.
Fasten off.

With right side of work facing, miss center 13 (13-17) sts. Join yarn to next st. Ch 2. Pat to end of row. Ch 3. **Turn.**

Next row: Pat across 11 (11-13) sts. **Turn.**

Next row: 1 ss in each of first 2 sts. Ch 2. Pat to end of row. Ch 3. **Turn.**

Next row: Pat across 9 (9-11) sts. **Turn.**

Work 5 rows even in pat omitting turning ch at end of last row.
Fasten off.

BACK BODICE

Work from ** to ** as given for Front Bodice.
Cont even in pat until Back measures 2 rows less than Front to shoulders. Fasten off. Sew side seams.

SKIRT

With right side of work facing, join yarn at side seams with ss and work into ch at lower edge of Front and Back Bodice as follows:

1st round: Ch 4. [(1 dc. Ch 1) twice. 1 dc] in first ch. *Miss next 3 ch. [(*1 dc. Ch 1*) 3 times. 1 dc – shell made] in next ch. Rep from * around. Join in round with ss in top of ch 4. 29 (33-35) shells.

2nd round: Ss to center of first shell. Ch 4. [(1 dc. Ch 1) twice. 1 dc] in same sp as last ss. *Shell in center of next shell. Rep from * around. Join with ss in top of ch 4.

Rep last round until work from top to

shoulders at Back measures
15½ (**17**-18½) ins [39.5 (**43**-47) cm].

Next round: *Ch 1. Shell in center of
next shell. Ch 1. 1 sc in sp between
last shell and next shell. Rep from *
around. Ss in ch 1. Fasten off.

FINISHING

Front Neck Edging: 1st row: With **wrong**
side of work facing, join yarn to top
right corner of neck. Work 1 row
of sc across Front Neck edge to next
shoulder. Ch 1. Turn.
2nd row: Work 1 sc in each sc across.
Fasten off.

Back Neck Edging: 1st row: With **wrong**
side of work facing, join yarn to top
right corner of neck. Work 1 row
of sc across Front Neck edge to next
shoulder. Ch 1. Turn.
2nd row: Work 1 sc in each sc across.
Fasten off.

Armhole Edging: 1st round: 1st row: With
wrong side of work facing, join yarn
to top right corner of armhole. Work
1 row of sc across Front Neck edge to
next shoulder. Ch 1. Turn.
2nd round: Work 1 sc in each sc across.
Fasten off.

Sew 2 buttons to back shoulders
using eyelet pattern of Front Bodice
shoulders to make buttonholes.

Optional:
Thread ribbon through first row of
Back and Front eyelets and tie into
bow at center front as illustrated. ◆

CROCHETED BEAUTY

1970s

PATONS

as shown on page 24

SIZE

Bust measurement

Small	30–32 ins	[76-81	cm]
Medium	34–36 "	[86-91	"]
Large	38–40 "	[97-102 "	]

Finished bust

Small	39 ins	[99	cm]
Medium	41 "	[104	"]
Large	43½ "	[110.5	"]

MATERIALS

Patons Cotton DK (50 g)

	S	M	L
6303	8	9	10 **balls**

Size 2.50 mm (U.S. 0) crochet hook **or size
needed to obtain tension**.

TENSION

4 pat reps and 11 rows = 4½ ins [11.5 cm].

INSTRUCTIONS

*The instructions are written for smallest
size. If changes are necessary for larger sizes
the instructions will be written thus ( ).*

BACK

Ch 107 (**113**-119).
1st row: (Foundation row). (Right side).
2 tr in 5th ch from hook. *Miss next 2
ch. 1 sc in next ch. Miss next 2 ch. *5 tr
in next ch* - Shell made. Rep from * to
last 6 ch. Miss next 2 ch. 1 sc in next
ch. Miss next 2 ch. 3 tr in last ch. Ch 4.
Turn. 103 (**109**-115) sts.
2nd row: Miss first 3 tr. *1 tr in next sc.
Ch 2. Miss next 2 tr. 1 sc in next tr.
Ch 2. Miss next 2 tr. Rep from * to last
6 sts. 1 tr in next sc. Ch 2. Miss next
2 tr. 1 sc in top of ch 4. Ch 4. Turn.
3rd row: 2 tr in first sc. *1 sc in next tr.
Shell in next sc. Rep from * to last tr.
1 sc in last tr. 3 tr in first ch of ch 4.
Ch 4. Turn.

Last 2 rows form pat.

Cont even in pat until work from
beg measures 14 (**14½**-14½) ins
[35.5 (**37**-37) cm], thus ending on
a 2nd row and omitting turning ch
at end of last row.

Shape armholes: 1st row: (Right side).
1 ss in first sc. 1 ss in each of next 2 ch.
Ch 1. 1 sc in next tr. Pat to last tr. 1 sc
in last tr. **Turn.**
2nd row: 1 ss in each of next 2 tr. Ch 1.

Knitting true to fashion.

1 sc in next tr. Pat to last Shell. 1 sc in third tr of last Shell. **Turn**.
Rep last 2 rows once more.
79 (**85**-91) sts.

Cont even in pat until work from beg measures 19 (**19½**-20) ins [48 (**49.5**-51) cm], thus ending on a 2nd row.

Shape neck: 1st row: Ch 4. 2 tr in first sc. *1 sc in next tr. Shell in next sc. Rep from * 3 times more. 1 sc in next tr. **Turn**.
2nd row: 1 ss in first sc. 1 ss in each of next 2 tr. Ch 1. 1 sc in next tr. Pat to end of row. Ch 4. **Turn**.
3rd row: 2 tr in first sc. *1 sc in next tr. Shell in next sc. Rep from * twice more. 1 sc in next tr. **Turn**. 19 sts.

4th row: As 2nd row.
Work 6 rows even in pat omitting turning ch at end of last row.
Fasten off.

With right side of work facing, miss center 23 (**29**-35) sts. Join yarn to next tr. Ch 1. 1 sc in same tr. Pat to end of row. Ch 4. Turn.
Next row: Miss first 3 tr. *1 tr in next sc. Ch 2. Miss next 2 tr. 1 sc in next tr. Ch 2. Miss next 2 tr. Rep from * twice more. 1 tr in next sc. Ch 2. Miss next 2 tr. 1 sc in next tr. **Turn**.
Next row: 1 ss in first sc. 1 ss in each of next 2 ch. Ch 1. 1 sc in first tr. Pat to end of row. Ch 4. **Turn**.
Next row: Miss first 3 tr. *1 tr in next sc. Ch 2. Miss next 2 tr. 1 sc in next tr.

Ch 2. Miss next 2 tr. Rep from * once more. 1 tr in next sc. Ch 2. Miss next 2 tr. 1 sc in next tr. **Turn**. 19 sts.
Work 6 rows even in pat omitting turning ch at end of last row.
Fasten off.

FRONT

Work as given for Back.

FINISHING

Sew side and shoulder seams.

Neck edging: 1st round: With right side of work facing, join yarn at left shoulder. Work 108 (**120**-132) sc evenly around neck. Join in round with ss in first sc. Ch 1.
2nd round: 1 sc in first sc. *Miss next 2 sc. Shell in next sc. Miss next 2 sc. 1 sc in next sc. Rep from * to last 5 sc. Miss next 2 sc. Shell in next sc. Miss next 2 sc. Join with ss in first sc. Fasten off.

Armhole edging: 1st round: With right side of work facing, join yarn at underarm seam. Work 72 (**72**-78) sc evenly around armhole. Join in round with ss in first sc. Ch 1.
2nd round: Work as given for 2nd round for Neck edging. Fasten off. ♠

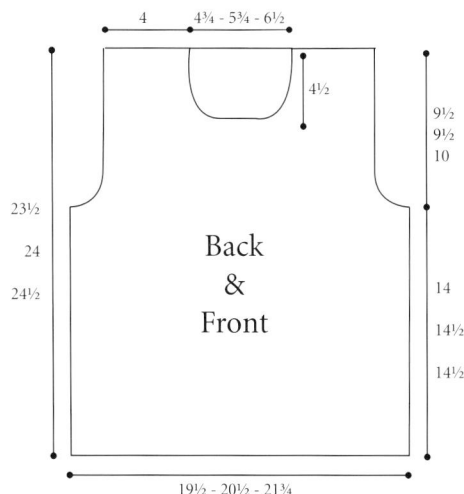

Back & Front diagram

4   4¾ - 5¾ - 6½

4½

9½
9½
10

23½
24
24½

14
14½
14½

Back
&
Front

19½ - 20½ - 21¾

For best results, be sure to use the yarn recommended in the pattern, and purchase enough of one dye lot to complete your project. It is a good idea to retain ball bands in case of inquiry.

Before you begin, check your tension by making a test swatch and adjusting needle/hook sizes, if necessary, to obtain the tension quoted in the pattern. Inaccurate tension results in a garment/afghan too large or too small. Even a variation of half a stitch makes an obvious difference in the finished size. Loose tension can result in the garment or afghan losing its shape during wear or laundering.

Before beginning, read the instructions and underline all figures applying to your size. Sizes should be chosen from actual bust or chest measurements and not ready-to-wear sizes.

Note: Never put an iron directly on yarns containing synthetic fibres. If pressing is required before assembly, lay each piece right side down on a clean, flat surface and pin to size using rust proof pins. Cover with a damp cloth and leave to dry.

Patons Wools are very resilient. Garment pieces should be steamed into shape before assembly. Pin each piece into shape onto a flat surface, following the dimensions on the schematic diagrams with each pattern. Cover with a damp cloth and press lightly using a steam iron. When dry, unpin and proceed with the Finishing Instructions given in the pattern. If you wish, you may also lightly steam

the seams after assembly.

WASHING INSTRUCTIONS

Patons Classic Merino Wool and **Patons Rustic Wool:** Hand wash. Dry Flat.

Patons Canadiana, Patons Canadiana Tweeds, Patons Canadiana Colours, Patons Kroy 3 & 4 Ply, Patons Beehive Baby, Patons Astra, Patons Look at Me! and **Patons Decor**: Machine wash. Machine dry.

Patons Shetland Chunky and **Patons Shetland Ragg Chunky**: Machine wash. Dry flat.

HAND WASHING

Note the measurements of the garment/afghan before washing. Thoroughly dissolve soap or mild detergent in lukewarm water. Place the garment/afghan in the suds and

squeeze gently. Do not rub or leave to soak. Support the garment/afghan with your hands as you remove it from the water. Rinse twice in clean, lukewarm water. Remove excess moisture by rolling in a thick towel.

Drying Flat
Do not wring, twist or hang to dry. Lay garment/afghan on a flat surface away from lights, sunlight and excessive heat. While still damp, gently push garment/afghan back to its original measurements.

MACHINE WASHING

Do up buttons and turn the item inside out. Wash the item, preferably on its own, with a gentle cycle, using lukewarm water and detergent. Softener may be added to the final rinse. Do not use bleach.

Machine Drying
Tumble dry at low setting. Do not overheat.

French Knot

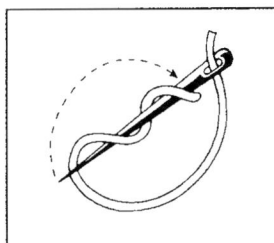
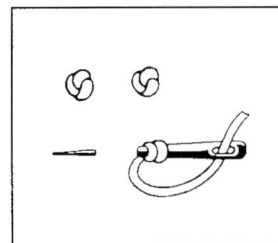

duplicate stitch 1

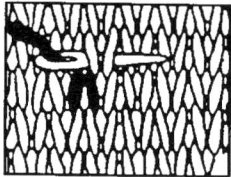
duplicate stitch 2

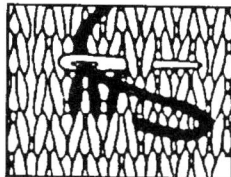
duplicate stitch 3

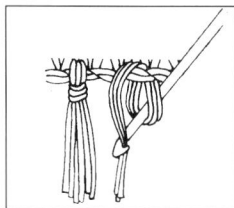
Fringe Knot

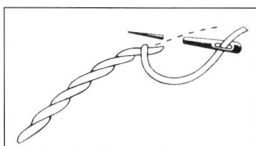
Stem Stitch

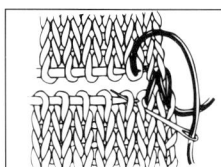
Grafting

PATONS COTTON DK

For best results, projects made from 100% Cotton require a little extra pampering.

The standard washing instructions, "hand wash, dry flat" are appropriate any time after the first washing.

The very first time you wash the piece, however, a slightly different procedure is advised. This is because some strong shades may contain excess dye which comes off in the first washing. Special care is required to ensure that this dye does not transfer to other shades in the garment/afghan, or to other items in the wash.

The first time you wash your garment or afghan:

1. Hand wash separately using luke-warm water and a mild soap. Do not use a detergent.

2. Rinse thoroughly until all soap and excess dye are removed, and water runs clear. Do not leave the garment/afghan to soak.

3. If the item contains more than one color, remove excess moisture using the spin cycle in your washing machine.

4. Dry the item briefly in a tumble dryer on delicate cycle, using cool or very low heat. For extra protection you may wish to put the piece inside a pillow slip or laundry bag. Complete drying on a flat surface away from direct sunlight, blocking garment/afghan into original finished measurements as necessary.

Subsequent laundering can be "hand wash, dry flat".

ABBREVIATIONS

mm	=	millimetre(s)
cm	=	centimetre(s)
in(s)	=	inch(es)
g	=	gram(s)
beg	=	beginning
alt	=	alternate
st(s)	=	stitch(es)
inc	=	increase
dec	=	decrease
0	=	no sts, times or rows
K	=	knit
P	=	purl
tbl	=	through back of loop(st)
tog	=	together
cont	=	continue(ity)
rep	=	repeat
sl	=	slip
pat	=	pattern
psso	=	pass slipped st over
Sl1K	=	slip next st knitways
tbl	=	through back loop
sc	=	single crochet
dc	=	double crochet
hdc	=	half double crochet
ch	=	chain
ss	=	slip st
sp	=	space
tr	=	treble crochet
yrn	=	yarn over needle

* = The star symbol is a repeat sign and means that you follow the printed instructions from the first * until you reach the second *. You will then repeat from * to * the given number of times which does not include the first time. The ** and *** are used in the same way.

( ) = The figures inside the brackets mean the instructions for the various sizes for which the pattern has been written. Brackets can also mean that the enclosed instructions are to be worked the number of times stated after the brackets.

U.S. KNITTERS PLEASE NOTE:

Canadian and American terminologies differ slightly. Equivalents are shown below.

Canadian	U.S.
yfwd	yarn over (yo)
yrn	yarn over (yo)
tension	gauge
cast off	bind off